Firefox® For Dummies®

General Keyboard Shortcuts

Action	Windows Shortcut	Mac Shortcut
Go Back	Backspace	
Go Forward	Shift+Backspace	
Go to Home Page	Alt+Home	
Reload Page	Ctrl+R	⌘+R
Stop	Esc	Escape
Select the Location Bar	Ctrl+L	⌘+L
Select the Search Box	Ctrl+K	⌘+K
Open New Tab	Ctrl+T	⌘+T
Open New Window	Ctrl+N	⌘+N
Close Tab/Window	Ctrl+W	⌘+W
Open the Find Bar	Ctrl+F	⌘+F
Open Bookmarks	Ctrl+B	⌘+B
Open Browsing History	Ctrl+H	⌘+H
Compose New E-mail	Ctrl+M	⌘+M
Bookmark This Page	Ctrl+D	⌘+D
Clear Private Data	Ctrl+Shift+Delete	⌘+Shift+Delete
Enlarge Web Site Text	Ctrl++	⌘++
Shrink Web Site Text	Ctrl+-	⌘+-

Tabbed Browsing Keyboard Shortcuts

Action	Windows Shortcut	Mac Shortcut
Open Address in New Tab	Alt+Enter	Option+Return
Open Focused Link in New Tab	Ctrl+Enter	⌘+Return
Open New Tab	Ctrl+T	⌘+T
Select Next Tab	Ctrl+Tab	⌘+Tab
Select Previous Tab	Ctrl+Shift+Tab	⌘+Shift+Tab
Select a Specific Tab	Ctrl+[1-9] *	⌘+[1-9] *
Close the Selected Tab	Ctrl+W	⌘+W

* The numbers correspond to the tab. The first tab is 1, the second is 2, and so on.

Copyright © 2006 Wiley Publishing, Inc. All rights reserved. Item 4899-4. For more information about Wiley Publishing, call 1-800-762-2974.

For Dummies: Bestselling Book Series for Beginners

Firefox® For Dummies®

Cheat Sheet

Useful Mouse Shortcuts

- **Middle-click (if your mouse has a middle button or scroll wheel) links to open them in new tabs.** For example, you can middle-click the Back, Forward, and Home buttons, your bookmarks, or links on a page. You can also middle-click a bookmarks folder to open *all* its Web sites in tabs.

- **Hold Shift while scrolling with your mouse's scroll wheel to navigate through recent browsing history.** You can also hold Ctrl (⌘ on a Mac) to change the text size on a page, or Alt (Option on a Mac) to scroll just one line at a time.

- **Drag a link onto the Bookmarks Toolbar to bookmark it instantly.**

- **Drag a link onto the tab bar to open it in a new tab.**

- **Drag a link onto the Home button to set it as your new home page.**

- **Drag and drop text to the Search Box (to the right of the Location Bar) to search for it.**

Little-Known Tips

- Click the Activity Indicator in the upper-right corner to go directly to Firefox Central, which offers a wealth of Firefox resources.

- You can drag and drop a tab to a new location on the tab bar.

- Select a word, right-click it, and choose Search the Web to search for the selection.

- The Search Box offers plenty beyond Google. Click the G icon to see a list of additional search engines you can use.

- To make more room for the page you're viewing, choose View⇨Full Screen (or press F11) to temporarily hide toolbars and other clutter. To exit Full Screen and get your toolbars back, simply choose the Full Screen option again.

Firefox Search Keywords

Type these keywords into the Location Bar, followed by a search phrase (for example, **google New York**), and then press Enter.

Keyword	Action	Example
google	Searches for a word or phrase on Google	google New York
dict	Retrieves the definition of a word on Answers.com	dict facetious
wp	Searches for a word or phrase on Wikipedia, a community-edited encyclopedia	wp war of 1812
quote	Retrieves trading information for a stock ticker on Google's stock quote service	quote GOOG

Online Resources

Name	Address	Description
Mozilla Update	http://update.mozilla.org	Hundreds of Firefox themes and extensions organized by category and rated by other people from the Firefox community.
Firefox Central	www.mozilla.org/products/firefox/central	Your one-stop shop to all things Firefox, including frequently asked questions, new search engines, online support, and yes, even the Mozilla Store.
Get Firefox	www.getfirefox.com	The place to send your friends when you tell them to "get Firefox!" This is also the first place to offer new versions of Firefox (including betas), so visit frequently!

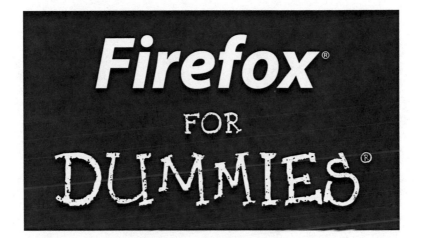

by Blake Ross

WILEY

Wiley Publishing, Inc.

Firefox® For Dummies®

Published by
Wiley Publishing, Inc.
111 River Street
Hoboken, NJ 07030-5774
www.wiley.com

Copyright © 2006 by Wiley Publishing, Inc., Indianapolis, Indiana

Published by Wiley Publishing, Inc., Indianapolis, Indiana

Published simultaneously in Canada

For general information on our other products and services, please contact our Customer Care Department within the U.S. at 800-762-2974, outside the U.S. at 317-572-3993, or fax 317-572-4002.

For technical support, please visit www.wiley.com/techsupport.

Wiley also publishes its books in a variety of electronic formats. Some content that appears in print may not be available in electronic books.

Library of Congress Control Number: 2005933668

ISBN-13: 978-0-471-74899-1
ISBN-10: 0-471-74899-4

10 9 8 7 6 5 4 3 2 1

1O/RW/RS/QV/IN

WILEY

About the Author

Blake Ross discovered computers when he was 4 and hasn't had time to eat since then. He began working at Netscape at 14 and cofounded the Firefox project two years later to make the Web easy to use for plain old human beings. He also cofounded the SpreadFirefox.com community evangelism project, which has changed the face of software marketing and distribution. Blake was featured on the cover of *Wired Magazine* in early 2005, and he has since been featured in dozens of international publications and television shows to promote computing simplicity. He is on leave from Stanford University, where he is an undergraduate.

Blake is currently working on a new project with some of the original Firefox team. If you enjoy Firefox, you'll enjoy what's coming next, so sign up at www.blakeross.com to hear when it launches.

Dedication

For my family, who taught me everything I know. Except the computer stuff.

Author's Acknowledgments

Many thanks to my family and friends for sticking by me and putting up with my crazy hours (the sun is rising as I write this).

Thanks to Mark Enochs and Steve Hayes at Wiley for reminding me to actually, you know, finish this book, and for putting up with the idiosyncrasies of a first-time *For Dummies* author. Likewise, this wouldn't have happened without Virginia Sanders and James Russell, who rigorously reviewed the book and fixed every sentence-ending preposition you can think of. (Almost.)

Many thanks to Jatin Billimoria for helping to plan and write the book when my time was sparse.

Thanks to the MozillaZine community for their generous contributions to the book.

And finally, thanks to everyone at Mozilla who helped take Firefox to the top: Mitchell Baker, Chris Beard, Asa Dotzler, Rafael Ebron, Brendan Eich, Ben Goodger, Joe Hewitt, Chris Hofmann, Dave Hyatt, Dave Hyatt's closet, Paul Kim, John Lilly, Scott MacGregor, Marcia Knous, Gervase Markham, Stuart Parmenter, Jesse Ruderman, Brian Ryner, Mike Shaver, Boris Zbarsky, and everyone else. On to the next 100 million!

Publisher's Acknowledgments

We're proud of this book; please send us your comments through our online registration form located at www.dummies.com/register/.

Some of the people who helped bring this book to market include the following:

Acquisitions, Editorial, and Media Development

Project Editor: Mark Enochs

Senior Acquisitions Editor: Steven Hayes

Copy Editor: Virginia Sanders

Technical Editor: James "Kovu" Russell

Editorial Manager: Leah Cameron

Editorial Assistant: Amanda Foxworth

Cartoons: Rich Tennant (www.the5thwave.com)

Composition Services

Project Coordinator: Adrienne Martinez

Layout and Graphics: Carl Byers, Andrea Dahl, Lauren Goddard, Denny Hager, Barbara Moore, Lynsey Osborn, Heather Ryan

Proofreaders: Leeann Harney, TECHBOOKS Production Services

Indexer: TECHBOOKS Production Services

Publishing and Editorial for Technology Dummies

    Richard Swadley, Vice President and Executive Group Publisher

    Andy Cummings, Vice President and Publisher

    Mary Bednarek, Executive Acquisitions Director

    Mary C. Corder, Editorial Director

Publishing for Consumer Dummies

    Diane Graves Steele, Vice President and Publisher

    Joyce Pepple, Acquisitions Director

Composition Services

    Gerry Fahey, Vice President of Production Services

    Debbie Stailey, Director of Composition Services

Contents at a Glance

Table of Contents

Introduction

*I*f you're the kind of person who walks away from the computer thinking, "That was pleasant! Let me bake some cookies for those kids at MIT," neither Firefox nor this book is for you.

Firefox was created for people who hate computers; who are fed up with popup ads and an Internet that takes regular coffee breaks; and who are baffled by software that seems to have a mind of its own. In short, Firefox was created for *people* — not programmers.

The reason a mild-mannered author can make such a bold claim is that underneath this cool exterior, I'm not only an author — I'm also a founder! I helped start Firefox — not to make money (it's free), or sell a company (it's non-profit), but for the express purpose of making your life easier. The other developers and I want every Firefox experience to feel like your first foray onto the Net. We want to take you back to a time when the Web was new and exciting, when spam was lunch meat and advertisements were found only in books, on television, throughout public transportation systems, on people . . . you get the idea.

But we wouldn't turn down cookies.

About This Book

If Firefox is your time machine, *Firefox For Dummies* is your H.G. Wells. The goal of this book is not just to show you Firefox itself, but to help you have a more enjoyable and productive online experience with Firefox. Remember your high school science fair? We're not here to blow up celery. We're here to blow up celery *to test the effects of explosives on vegetables.* It's a very strong practical focus, and one I strive to maintain throughout the book.

Along the way, I offer a behind-the-scenes look at Firefox development through sidebars that don't distract from the main content. Some of these sidebars offer insight into why we made certain product designs. Others are lighthearted anecdotes of the growing pains that occurred as Firefox evolved from a tiny hobbyist project to an international success. (Note: This book is written for Firefox 1.5.)

One great thing about developer-authors is that if *anything* goes wrong with your Firefox experience, whether the error lies in this book or in the software, it's my fault. You don't have to spend any time figuring out who deserves an earful. It's me, all me. See? Firefox is making your life easier already!

How This Book Is Organized

Like most *For Dummies* books, this book is organized into parts, which are divided into chapters.

When we began work on Firefox, we identified four key issues to focus on:

- Painless transition from other browsers
- A simplified browsing experience
- Online security and privacy
- Personal customization

Likewise, the first four parts of this book focus on those areas, and the fifth part encompasses additional reference material and little-known tips and tricks.

Part I: Getting Fired Up

This part introduces you to the fundamental concepts of the World Wide Web, explains Firefox's role in the system, and helps you begin using it. If you currently use another Web browser, such as Microsoft Internet Explorer or Apple Safari, this part can also help you make a smooth transition to Firefox by explaining terminology differences and showing you how to import your information, such as browsing history and bookmarks.

Part II: Ready, Aim, Firefox

After you've gotten your feet wet, this part helps you dive into the core activities you'll do online everyday — finding and downloading information, bookmarking and revisiting your favorite sites, and printing. This is also your first glimpse of Firefox's innovative tabbed browsing system, which will forever change the way you surf the Web.

Part III: Outfoxing Hackers

This part explains some basic principles of online safety, outlines how Firefox protects you, and suggests additional steps you can take to protect yourself. It also offers a comprehensive look at the kinds of information Firefox records during your online travels — such as saved passwords and Web site history — and shows you how to clear this information.

Part IV: Dressing Up the Fox

This is the really fun part — the one that shows you how to customize your online experience, both how it looks (with themes) and how it feels (with preferences). If you want your browser to have a particular theme, this is the chapter to visit. As if that weren't enough, this part also introduces you to Firefox's powerful extensions system, which allows you to extend Firefox beyond its typical capabilities by installing tiny plug-ins with one click.

Part V: The Part of Tens

The usual cap on most *For Dummies* books, this part offers the poor geek's version of David Letterman's top ten lists, including the top ten ways Firefox makes your life easier and the ten things you don't know about Firefox but should.

Icons Used in This Book

Tips are helpful Firefox shortcuts that you might not discover on your own. You don't have to follow any tips to get the job done, but they'll often save you time.

These icons point out the kind of nuts-and-bolts information that make the geek in me smile, but might be of little interest to you. However, feel free to check them out if your inner geek wants some extra information.

Warnings are in place to prevent you from losing data, revealing your passwords to nosy onlookers, or otherwise doing something most people would consider undesirable and unintended. You should always read and make sure you understand warnings before continuing.

File these rare tidbits of information away in your brain for later reference. They're sure to come in handy.

Conventions

Most of this book is written in the English language, which appears to be just fine with you. However, I discuss keyboard shortcuts so frequently that it helps to refer to them in shorthand. As the name suggests, a *keyboard shortcut* is a quick way to access a program command from the keyboard, and you execute them by pressing two or three keys simultaneously — special keys, such as Control (Ctrl), and a letter, such as C. (This is a common shortcut to copy text.) Rather than spelling out shortcuts each time, I abbreviate them as *key+letter* (for example, Ctrl+C).

When I suggest or mention keywords that can be entered on-screen as search terms, I put them *in italic*. When you have to choose commands from menus, I write File⇨Exit when you should choose the Exit command from the File menu.

Feedback

Firefox — and, by extension, this book — exists because hundreds of people just like you asked for a better Internet experience. Your feedback motivates us to keep working toward that goal. I encourage you to send comments, suggestions, or rants about this book or Firefox itself to me at:
blake@firefox.com.
I read and respond to all mail.

Part I
Getting Fired Up

The 5th Wave   By Rich Tennant

SOMEWHERE IN THE CITY, SASQUATCH, BIGFOOT AND ELVIS SPEND ANOTHER WARY NIGHT.

"Look—all I'm saying is every time they come out with a new browser with an improved search function, it's just a matter of time."

In this part . . .

Adapting to new software can be painful, but Firefox makes it easy to transition away from your current browser. The developers of Firefox have purposely mimicked certain design elements and keyboard short-cuts of Internet Explorer and other browsers, and Firefox can import your settings, bookmarks, browsing history, and saved passwords.

This part opens with a brief overview of why Firefox is worth switching to and then walks you through the brief transition process. The chapters in this part help you on your way to a better browsing experience.

Chapter 1

Why You Should Fire
Your Old Browser

* *

In This Chapter

▶ Discovering what a browser is

▶ Finding out why you should switch to Firefox

▶ Looking at a little bit of history

* *

There's just one Internet, but there isn't one Internet experience. How safely, easily, and quickly you browse the Web is a function of the browser you're using. Firefox is the only one designed to meet the demands of a wired world, so if you're not using it, you're stuck in rush hour traffic — while 100 million others whiz by you in the carpool lane. But before I tell you why to change lanes, I tell you what a browser is.

What Is a Browser, Anyway?

Many people confuse a *Web browser* with a *search engine,* such as Google. It's a reasonable mistake because most daily browsing begins with a search. However, whereas a search engine finds Web sites, a browser displays them. Think of the browser as your window to the Web. It doesn't have specific knowledge about the scenery (like a search engine), but you need to look through it to see what's out there.

In addition to displaying Web sites, the browser provides tools to help you navigate among them. I talk about basic commands like Back and Forward in Chapter 2, but most browsers also include features like Bookmarks, which help you keep track of your favorite pages. Successful browsers hide the complex underpinnings of the Web and make surfing safe, pleasurable, and easy. Check out Figure 1-1.

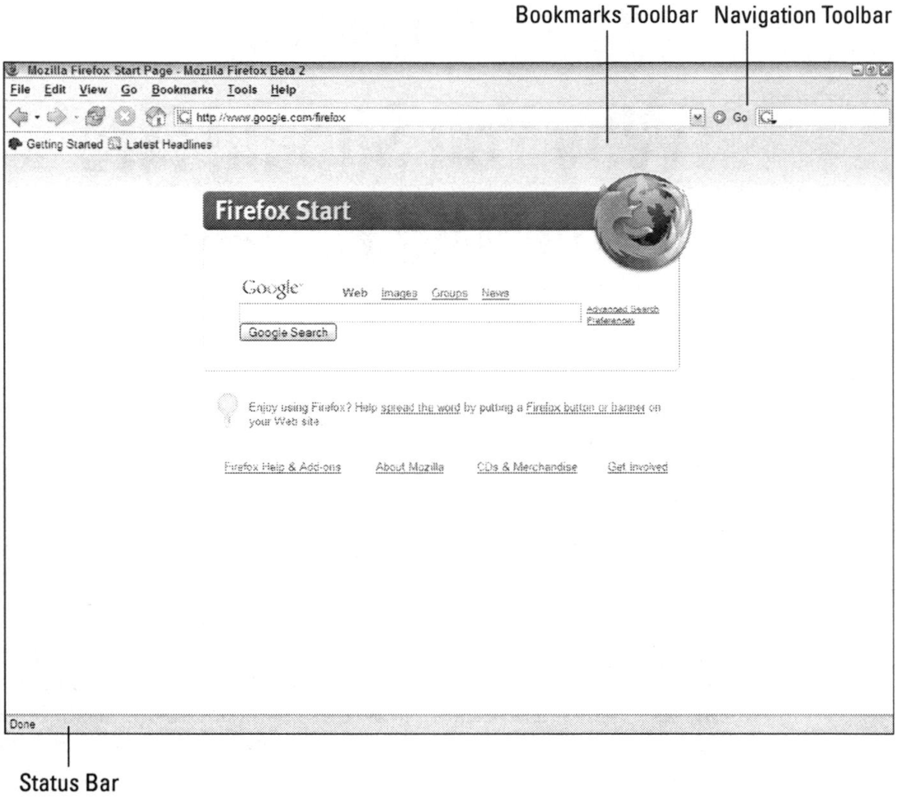

Bookmarks Toolbar   Navigation Toolbar

Figure 1-1:
Firefox
includes just
the features
you need,
making the
Web the
center of
attention.

Status Bar

Why Use Firefox?

On the day the other developers and I started work on Firefox, before we had any users, and back when a *firefox* was just a red panda (it's true!), we wrote down our goals in a one-page "vision" document. It began:

> **"Why Create Firefox?** We want to have fun and build an excellent, user-friendly browser without all the constraints (features, compatibility, marketing, month long discussions, etc.) that afflict the current browser development."

The document went on to outline the requirements Firefox had to meet, as I discuss in the following sections.

Giving birth to a Firefox (or, how I spent my high school years)

For a browser so focused on delivering simplicity, Firefox boasts an absurdly complicated past that dates back to the beginning of the mainstream Web itself. The story begins with a little company called Netscape, which made the first consumer-oriented, visual Web browser. Netscape almost single-handedly sparked the online revolution, and from 1995 through 1997, it dominated the browser industry. As the millennium drew to a close, however, Netscape faced increasingly fierce competition from Microsoft, which undercut Netscape by making its browser free. With billions in the bank, Microsoft could afford to throw thousands of engineers at its fledgling — Internet Explorer — and lose money for years.

Two milestones radically — but, in hindsight, futilely — changed Netscape's direction around this time. First, the online service juggernaut America Online (AOL) purchased Netscape for $4.2 billion. Second, Netscape tried to level the playing field against Microsoft by making the historic decision to release its browser code through a development model called *open source*. Most software companies jealously guard their source code because any competitor who obtains it can easily copy the product. However, desperate times called for desperate measures. Netscape was banking on a global community of volunteer developers to emerge and help build its next-generation browser. Volunteers, in turn, would get a chance to influence and develop an Internet browser still used by millions. Leveraging free talent was Netscape's only shot against the world's richest software company.

Although it ultimately failed to keep the company afloat in the browser wars, Netscape's decision to open source the code lead to a vibrant community of volunteers known as Mozilla that persevered long after Netscape bowed out. Self-governing, passionate about the Web, and funded largely on donations, the Mozilla community quickly garnered respect in the development community. The great thing about open source is that anyone can join, regardless of experience, age or other constraints typically imposed on candidates in the professional world. I joined the community during high school at age 14, and soon afterward, my efforts landed me a series of internships at (rapidly sinking) Netscape.

Working in the Mozilla community and later interning at Netscape were wonderful experiences, and I probably couldn't have asked for a better job. However, there was an itch that couldn't be scratched in either role: the obsessive desire to create a simple, lightweight browser that didn't encumber non-technical people with meaningless jargon and endless options. It was difficult to achieve this in Mozilla because the volunteer developers were more interested in creating a browser that catered to themselves (with all of the associated power-user features). It was also difficult to achieve this at Netscape because the company — now hanging on by a thread — resorted to monetizing its flagship browser at the cost of a simple user experience. Meanwhile, having won the browser wars, Microsoft all but abandoned the browser market entirely. Intrigued by such a wide-open opportunity, I found a small group of others within Mozilla and Netscape who shared my itch, and in 2002, we scratched it. Firefox was born.

Firefox solves your Internet headaches

It's little wonder that computers are so difficult to use: The developers who make them have a much higher tolerance for pain. Something that's "hard" for an average user is easy for them, and when the user is screaming "I swear I'll throw this computer out the window!" the developer is just getting warmed up.

We've found two problems with the way most software is developed:

- ✔ **Some developers intentionally design products for themselves.** This results in products that are made by geeks and intended for fellow geeks. The average user then has no idea how to use the product.

- ✔ **Some developers just can't help designing products for themselves.** They intend to make a product for the user, but they can't help tweaking it into a confusing behemoth of a program.

We solved the first problem by declaring our intent in the Firefox manifesto: "The interface will not be geeky nor will it have a hacker-focus. The idea is to design the best Web browser for most people." Solving the second, however, requires an understanding of how non-developers look at and use software, and that isn't easy to come by.

Enter my mother. I started working on Firefox toward the end of high school, after many years of jogging down the hall to help her with computer problems. That hall bridged the generation gap and opened my eyes to how "normal" people use and understand computers.

Every Firefox developer has a story like that. Some observe their friends and family struggling; others sit down with strangers in book stores and coffee shops. We want to understand what's wrong with your Web experience and how we can fix it. In the following sections, I discuss the main complaints we've gathered.

"I can't stand all the clutter."

Buttons. Menus. Windows. Popups. Technology is supposed to help people, so why does it always stand in your way? We want Firefox to be practically invisible, so if we've done our job properly, you shouldn't notice it. Popup ads and other nuisances are blocked silently and automatically, and only the features you need are included.

One of those features is called *tabbed browsing,* and it will change the way you surf the Web. Tabbed browsing is the kind of thing that's hard to explain

A Firefox by any other name

In an industry built on Windows, it's hardly surprising that the question I'm asked most often concerns Firefox's unusually eye-catching name. In fact, Firefox has gone by three names throughout its short lifetime.

When we started work on the Firefox project in 2002, we called it Phoenix after the mythical bird that is reborn from its own ashes. This was a tongue-in-cheek reference to the fact that the product was being reborn out of the ashes of Netscape, the very first Web browser. Because Firefox is based on much of the same underlying code as Netscape, this was an apt metaphor. It was also a playful jab at a company that, we felt, had stopped adequately serving its customers, and desperately needed to be reborn.

Unfortunately, we were a very small — and very broke — team in those days, and we didn't have the money or the wherewithal to do any sort of legal inquiry into the name. As Phoenix grew more popular, we were contacted by a company who claimed ownership of the trademark. To avoid legal problems, we changed the name to Firebird, a synonym for Phoenix that evokes the same imagery. Of course, we still didn't have any money, and we just wanted to get back to work on the browser. So we didn't bother inquiring about this name, either.

We soon learned that a database project was already using the name Firebird, and the encroachment was even worse this time, because the project was open source and community-developed — just like Firefox. Oops.

Because Firebird had grown fairly popular by this point, we wanted to keep the Fire moniker for continued name recognition, and spent about three months just bouncing ideas off each other:

- ✔ Fireblast?
- ✔ Fireworks?
- ✔ Firefox?
- ✔ Firesoup?

Bingo! Firesoup it was. No, just kidding. We did, of course, pick Firefox, and this time we made sure we had rights to the name. Contrary to popular belief, a Firefox is actually not a fox — it's a Chinese red panda, as shown in the figure.

Of course, our community wasn't going to let us off the hook so easily — especially after we poked fun at Netscape with our first two names. Soon after this final name change, a volunteer created an extension called Firesomething that randomly assigns a new name to Firefox each time you start — like Firecat or, yes, even Fireblake. What goes around comes around.

but easy to fall in love with. (Figure 1-2 shows you tabs, and Chapter 7 tells you more about them.) When you work with tabs, you enjoy multiple Web pages in the same window, just a click away from each other! No more littered taskbar!

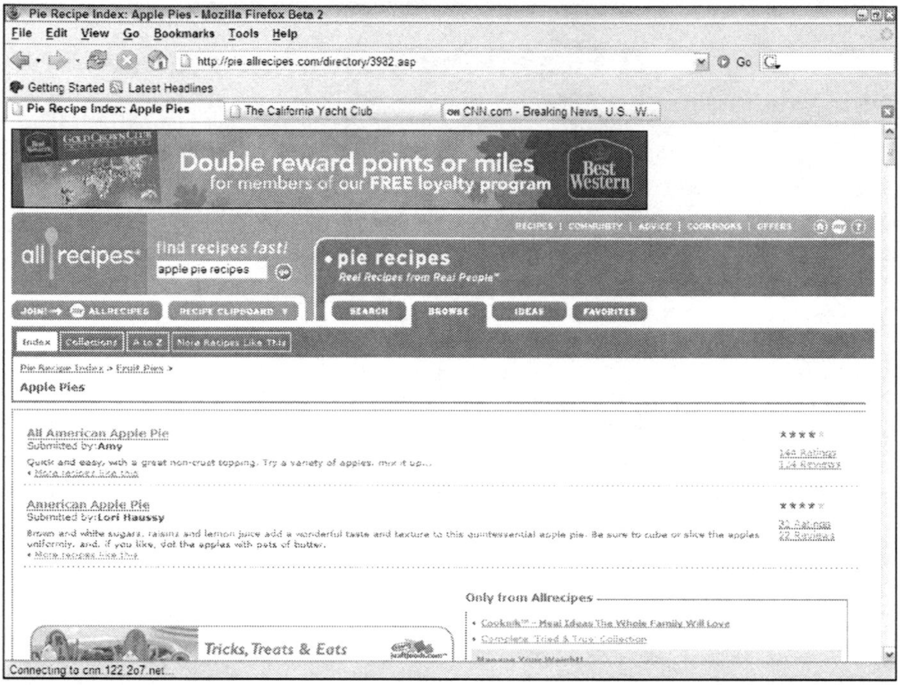

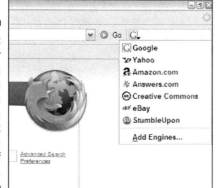

Figure 1-2:
Firefox
pioneers
a new,
clutter-free
method of
surfing
called
tabbed
browsing.
It's a
favorite
among
users.

"I can never find what I'm looking for."

And who can blame you? There are over 12 billion pages on the Web. The
Search Box in the upper-right corner gives you direct access to a handful of
top search engines from wherever you are (see Figure 1-3) and allows you to
add engines to that list (see Chapter 4). When you find a relevant page, use
the Find Bar to drill down even further (see Figure 1-4). Chapter 4 outlines
how Firefox helps you find what you're looking for.

Figure 1-3:
Search for
anything
from
anywhere
by using the
Search Box
in the
corner of
Firefox.

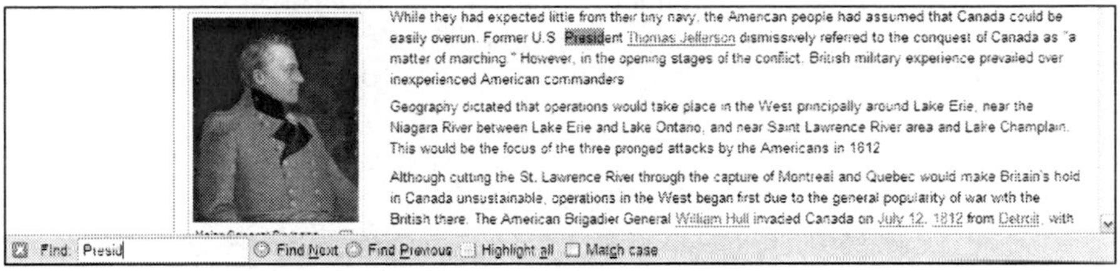

Figure 1-4:
Firefox's
revolutionary
Find Bar
automatically
finds text on
a page as
you type.

While they had expected little from their tiny navy, the American people had assumed that Canada could be easily overrun. Former U.S. President Thomas Jefferson dismissively referred to the conquest of Canada as "a matter of marching." However, in the opening stages of the conflict, British military experience prevailed over inexperienced American commanders

Geography dictated that operations would take place in the West principally around Lake Erie, near the Niagara River between Lake Erie and Lake Ontario, and near Saint Lawrence River area and Lake Champlain. This would be the focus of the three pronged attacks by the Americans in 1612

Although cutting the St. Lawrence River through the capture of Montreal and Quebec would make Britain's hold in Canada unsustainable, operations in the West began first due to the general popularity of war with the British there. The American Brigadier General William Hull invaded Canada on July 12, 1812 from Detroit, with

Find: Presid   Find Next   Find Previous   Highlight all   Match case

"The Internet is a scary place."

Every day, the media warns you about rampant identity theft, yet the world's most-used browser — Internet Explorer — has the worst security track record of any product. Firefox was built with your security in mind and forbids the technologies that make Internet Explorer so exploitable. Hundreds of thousands of volunteers across the globe test for problems before Firefox reaches your computer.

Firefox also gives you complete control over the information it stores while you're surfing, such as browsing history and saved passwords. You can choose how long Firefox remembers this information, and you can clear it all at once with a simple keystroke: Ctrl+Shift+Delete in Windows (see Figure 1-5; see Chapter 14).

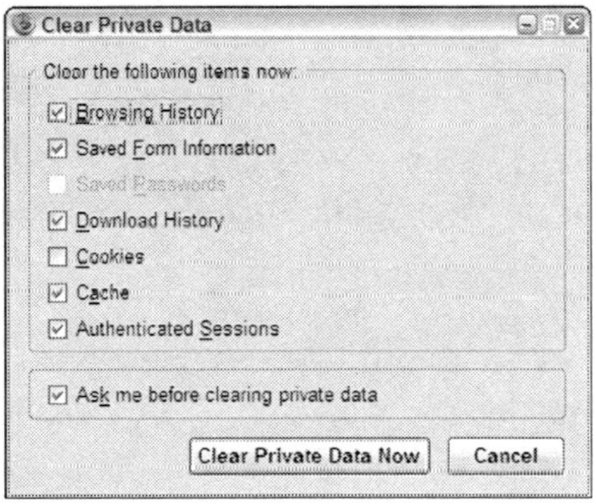

Figure 1-5:
Firefox's
Clear
Private Data
feature lets
you clear
all your
browsing
records with
a keystroke.

Clear Private Data

Clear the following items now:

☑ Browsing History
☑ Saved Form Information
☐ Saved Passwords
☑ Download History
☐ Cookies
☑ Cache
☑ Authenticated Sessions

☑ Ask me before clearing private data

Clear Private Data Now   Cancel

"The Internet is slow."

Over the past five years, a plague called *spyware* has infected computers worldwide. Spyware is a kind of software that creeps onto your machine and watches what you're doing so it can display supposedly relevant advertisements. It isn't just a distraction; it's an invasion of your privacy, and it slows your computer to a crawl. Research indicates that much of the spyware on computers today comes through Internet Explorer. Firefox helps you avoid these annoying pests. When you cut down the spyware on your computer, your Internet connection speeds up.

"Computers are stubborn."

Sometimes it seems like you have to obey software and not the other way round. Firefox knows who's boss: *You are.* Build your dream browser through glamorous themes (see Figure 1-6; check out Chapter 17 for more info) and powerful extensions that reshape, redesign, and enrich Firefox (see Figure 1-7 and Chapters 20 and 22). You can also customize your toolbars to your heart's content, as I explain in Chapter 18.

Themes change the appearance of toolbars, buttons, and windows.

Figure 1-6:
Who said
software
had to
be ugly?
Choose from
hundreds
of Firefox
themes.

Figure 1-7:
Extensions
add new
features,
such as
weather
information,
to Firefox.

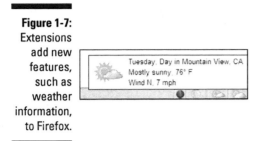

"I can't find the files I downloaded."

It's amazing that you can retrieve files from all over the world, but if you can't find them on our own computers after you download them, you have a problem. Firefox integrates a Download Manager that offers one-click access to your downloaded files (see Figure 1-8; see Chapter 11).

Figure 1-8:
The
Download
Manager
makes
it easy to
keep an eye
on your
downloads
and open
them when
they finish.

"Staying up-to-date is stressful."

As wonderful as the Internet is, it can be overwhelming. Some people track so many sources of information that it's impossible to keep up. Firefox brings the news to you through a feature called Live Bookmarks — bookmarks that can update themselves. Whether you want to stay on top of the headlines, the weather, or your sister's blog, Firefox keeps you connected automatically.

Figure 1-9, for example, shows the latest batch of headlines from BBC News. Firefox creates and updates this list automatically. (See Chapter 5 for more about bookmarks and live bookmarks.)

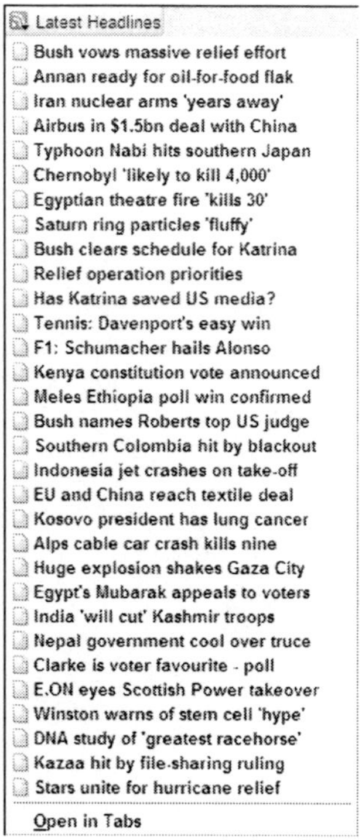

Figure 1-9:
Firefox can update your bookmarks automatically, so stay where you are: The info comes to you.

Latest Headlines
Bush vows massive relief effort
Annan ready for oil-for-food flak
Iran nuclear arms 'years away'
Airbus in $1.5bn deal with China
Typhoon Nabi hits southern Japan
Chernobyl 'likely to kill 4,000'
Egyptian theatre fire 'kills 30'
Saturn ring particles 'fluffy'
Bush clears schedule for Katrina
Relief operation priorities
Has Katrina saved US media?
Tennis: Davenport's easy win
F1: Schumacher hails Alonso
Kenya constitution vote announced
Meles Ethiopia poll win confirmed
Bush names Roberts top US judge
Southern Colombia hit by blackout
Indonesia jet crashes on take-off
EU and China reach textile deal
Kosovo president has lung cancer
Alps cable car crash kills nine
Huge explosion shakes Gaza City
Egypt's Mubarak appeals to voters
India 'will cut' Kashmir troops
Nepal government cool over truce
Clarke is voter favourite - poll
E.ON eyes Scottish Power takeover
Winston warns of stem cell 'hype'
DNA study of 'greatest racehorse'
Kazaa hit by file-sharing ruling
Stars unite for hurricane relief
Open in Tabs

Firefox is developed by people who care

The greeting card writers are calling me now, but I don't know how else to say it: Firefox developers *care.* You've heard this sales pitch from companies before, but there are two differences here: We aren't selling anything, and we aren't a traditional company.

Firefox is a free product that is guided by a non-profit organization. Unlike most other software projects, Firefox is developed by a global network of volunteers through a development model called *open source.* This model ensures that the project remains open and guided by its principles, not by the ambitions of any one individual or corporation. There are no riches to be had and no stocks to be sold; Firefox developers are here because they want to create a better browser.

If you aren't using Firefox, you're probably using Microsoft Internet Explorer. And like most other people I've talked to, you probably aren't thrilled with the experience. Maybe it's the incessant popup ads or the weekly security updates. Maybe your computer moves more slowly than your teenage son on Monday morning. Maybe you can't pinpoint the problem; the browser just *feels* inadequate.

Firefox solves these problems, but I don't waste pages in this book giving you a feature-by-feature comparison. Feature charts are for marketing departments (yawn), which we Firefox developers don't have to worry about (woo!). Instead, I talk about motivations. I look at what drives the people behind these products.

Internet Explorer is developed by a company that exists, first and foremost, to make money for its shareholders. This is not an attack; it's just the reality of a public company. Using Internet Explorer wasn't always so painful. But after it became mainstream over four years ago, Microsoft stopped developing it. After all, why upgrade a free product? Since then, sleazy salespeople have come up with a horde of new tricks to bother you online, but Microsoft has had no financial reason to combat them. Internet Explorer has thus become outdated and inadequate.

Firefox began as a hobby, not a corporate expenditure. I started it with Dave Hyatt, a co-worker of mine at Netscape, another browser company, when Netscape stopped seeing users and started seeing dollar signs. We aren't driven by revenues or competition. Our users are our only shareholders, and they are the ones we need to satisfy.

You have nothing to lose

It takes just a couple minutes to start using a browser that could save you hundreds of hours and dozens of gray hairs. Your bookmarks, saved passwords, browsing history, and other information are transferred automatically from your old browser to Firefox. And it's free. Why not?

Chapter 2

Finding Your Way Around Firefox

*N*ew software is overwhelming, and not just for the person using it. When my mother tries a new program, I don't get to sleep for weeks. Although the other Firefox developers and I have tried to make Firefox self-explanatory, any change involves a learning curve. This chapter explains the basics of the Web and the Web browser, and then shows how they apply in a Firefox world. Most importantly, it walks you through the buttons and toolbars you will use in your day-to-day surfing.

Wandering the Web

The Web began as an arcane communications tool for scientists and government officials, but today a half-billion people have usurped it for everything from shopping to photo swapping. I won't bore you with a longwinded description of what the Internet is and how it came to be, but I do want to share some of the fundamental concepts that I explore throughout this book.

The Web is a global network of billions of pages. In the real world, this would be an organizational nightmare. Can you imagine the filing cabinets? But the Web offers a radical solution: There is no solution. Rather than being neatly categorized and indexed, the Web is literally one giant mess. Pages come and go at random, and no central authority keeps tabs on them.

If this is a weakness of the Web, it's also its greatest strength. Because there's no Web authority, nobody censors, controls, or monopolizes content. Anyone with an Internet connection can broadcast his or her message around the world.

Looking for links

The glue that holds the Web together is the *link,* a clickable target on a page that takes you to a new page or elsewhere within the same page. In the early days of the Web, most links were underlined blue text, but today almost anything can be a link — even pictures. Perhaps the best part about links is that they don't discriminate; they can bridge a sports page to a pasta recipe or connect a news site to your family photos. A typical Web site (such as `www.onlinecomics.net`) might contain dozens of links to other pages, as shown in Figure 2-1.

Increasing your search engine savvy

In a medium as chaotic as the Web, where do you begin? Let a search engine be your guide. *Search engines* are tools that try to make sense of the Web's information. The most popular ones, such as Google (`www.google.com`) and Yahoo! (`www.yahoo.com`), can reveal thousands of useful pages on any topic in under a second, as shown in Figure 2-2. Many people confuse search engines and browsers, but the two are quite different; see the section "A Browser Is Not a Search Engine," later in this chapter.

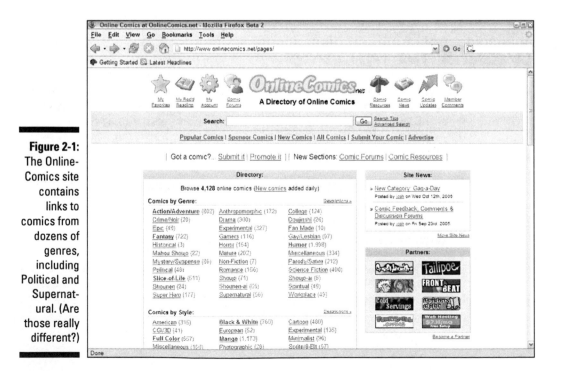

Figure 2-1:
The Online-Comics site contains links to comics from dozens of genres, including Political and Supernatural. (Are those really different?)

Figure 2-2:
The most popular search engine, Google, can find thousands of useful pages on any topic imaginable.

Feeling at home with Web addresses

Just as each home in your city has a unique address, each page on the Internet has an address that people can use to access it. Fortunately, Internet addresses don't require directions. ("Turn right, then left, continue on for 4 million pages. . . .") Unfortunately, Internet addresses are absurdly complicated and serve as daily reminders that the Internet wasn't originally designed for normal folk. Even the simplest ones look like gibberish:

```
http://www.dog.com/
```

The .com suffix here means that the Web site at this address belongs to a commercial entity (indeed, this is a dog supplies outfit). Other suffixes include .org for organizations and .net for Internet providers.

In general, understanding the meaning of Web addresses isn't important. As long as you know where to type them, you can get where you want to be.

The home page is where the heart is

When it comes to browsing, the *home page* is a Web site that loads automatically when you start your browser and serves as your browsing launch pad. Many companies aggregate news, sports scores, and other information onto a single *portal* page. As an example, Figure 2-3 shows the My Yahoo! page, at `http://my.yahoo.com`. Some people set portals as their home pages, and others prefer to start their browsing with a search engine. By default, Firefox caters to the second group by offering a Google home page, but it's easy to change (see Chapter 16).

Figure 2-3: My Yahoo! combines many types of information onto a single page that you can set as your home page.

The Back, Forward, Reload, and Stop commands

Before you go onto the Web, you should understand four basic browsing commands. These commands have been around since the dawn of the Internet:

- ✔ **Back** returns you to the last Web site you visited. If you go to the CNN Web site, click the Sports link, and then click Back, you're back at the CNN front page. Now you can click **Forward** to return to the Sports page.

- ✔ **Reload** fetches the newest version of the Web site you're currently viewing. For example, you might want to leave the CNN Web site open and reload it occasionally to see the latest headlines.

- ✔ Web sites take a little bit of time to load, but you can **Stop** loading them at any time.

A Browser Is Not a Search Engine

It's a reasonable mistake to confuse your browser with a search engine because most daily browsing begins with a search. However, whereas a search engine finds Web sites, a browser displays them. Think of the browser as your window to the Web. It doesn't have specific knowledge about the scenery (like a search engine), but you need to look through it to see what's out there.

In addition to displaying Web sites, the browser provides tools to help you navigate among them. Most browsers include many features, like the Bookmarks feature, which helps you keep track of your favorite pages. Successful browsers hide the complex underpinnings of the Web and make surfing pleasurable and easy.

Using the Firefox Interface

Before diving into specific areas of Firefox, I walk through the main interface (see Figure 2-4) you'll use each day, identifying features by the names I use throughout the book.

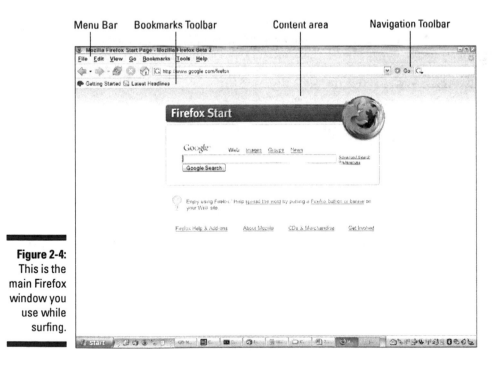

Figure 2-4:
This is the main Firefox window you use while surfing.

The Content area

When you first launch Firefox, you see the Firefox Start page shown in Figure 2-4. This page offers fast access to Google searches for news, images or general content, and the reason you're seeing it now is because it's the default home page. Take note of the box that holds the home page. This is called the Content area, and all of the Web sites you visit will load here.

The toolbars

Three toolbars sit above the Content area. The first is the standard Menu Bar, which you're probably familiar with from other programs. The Menu Bar, shown in Figure 2-4, offers access to virtually everything you can do in Firefox, and I discuss each command in depth in Appendix A.

Below the Menu Bar is the Navigation Toolbar, also known as the primary toolbar. By default, the Navigation Toolbar, shown in Figure 2-4, offers only those commands you'll need while browsing, such as Back and Forward. It also includes the Location Bar, where you can type in the address of a page you want to load. You can use the Search Box at the far right to search popular sites such as Google, Amazon, and eBay from anywhere on the Web.

The Bookmarks Toolbar, shown in Figure 2-4, provides a place to house your most frequently used bookmarks. By default, Firefox includes two bookmarks on this toolbar: Getting Started (a Firefox help page) and Latest Headlines (an automatically updated list of news stories). Chapter 5 shows you how to delete these items and add your own.

The Status Bar

Firefox also includes a Status Bar that sits at the very bottom of the window. The Status Bar, shown in Figure 2-4, displays information about the page you're currently viewing. For example, as a Web site loads, the Status Bar displays progress information via a progress meter. When you move the mouse pointer over a link on a Web site, the Status Bar displays the address of the linked page. The Status Bar also displays information about the security of a Web site, as I discuss in Chapter 15.

Sidebars

Firefox displays certain types of content in *sidebars* that open on the left side of the screen. A sidebar doesn't replace the Web site you're viewing; it just shoves it over to make room, as shown in Figure 2-5. This location makes it an ideal access point for things you might need while surfing. For example, Chapter 6 demonstrates displaying browsing history in a sidebar (shown in Figure 2-5) so you can keep track of where you are and return to old sites quickly. You can also display your bookmarks list and even arbitrary Web sites in sidebars, as I discuss in Chapter 5, and as shown in Figure 2-6.

Figure 2-5:
The History
Sidebar
displays
your history
list so you
can keep
track of
where you
are and
revisit sites.

The History Sidebar

Figure 2-6:
The
Bookmarks
Sidebar
allows you
to access
and search
your favorite
sites quickly.

The Bookmarks Sidebar

The Find Bar

The Find Bar (see Figure 2-7) is a thin toolbar that appears above the Status Bar when you need to find text in a page. It replaces the Find window that most other applications use, and we think it's a much faster and less intrusive way to search. Chapter 4 discusses the Find Bar in depth.

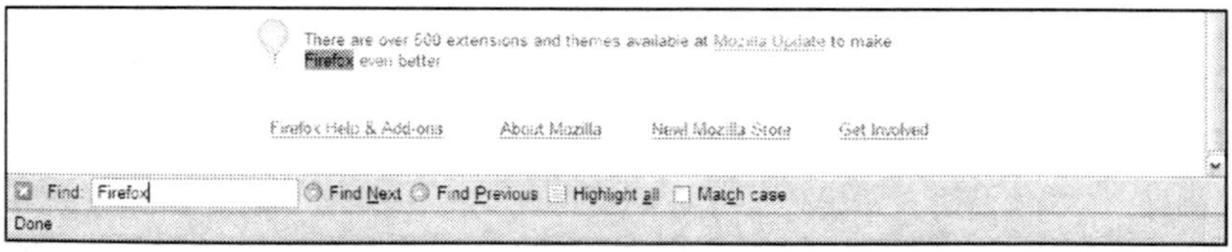

Figure 2-7:
The Find Bar
opens at the
bottom of
the window,
so it never
gets in the
way of your
searching.

Chapter 3

Setting Up Firefox

* *

* *

*I*nstalling Firefox is as easy as using it. After you install Firefox, the handy Import Wizard allows you to import your settings and bookmarks from other browsers — like switching flights but having your luggage transferred automatically. Whether you use Windows or Macintosh, this chapter tells you everything you need to know to get started.

System Requirements

You should check to make sure that your computer is powerful enough to handle Firefox before installing it. If you bought your computer in the past three or four years, it should be fine.

To install Firefox on Windows, we recommend using Windows XP, although other flavors of Windows (such as Windows ME or Windows 2000) are supported as well. Your computer should also have at least a 500 MHz processor and 128MB of RAM.

To install Firefox on the Macintosh, we recommend using OS X 10.1 or later. For best performance, your computer should also have at least a 667 MHz PowerPC G4 processor with 256MB of RAM and 72MB of free hard drive space.

Getting Firefox

Firefox is available both on CD from the Mozilla Store and as a free download from the Firefox Web site.

Downloading Firefox

If you already have an Internet connection, the best way to get Firefox is by downloading it for free from our Web site. It's a small file, so it should only take a few minutes to download — even on the slowest of Internet connections. To download the setup file:

1. **Navigate to the Firefox Web site** (www.getfirefox.com).

2. **Click the Free Download link and save the Firefox Setup file to your computer's Desktop.**

3. **When the download finishes, double-click the Firefox Setup file on your Desktop.**

For Windows

If you are using Windows, the Setup Wizard appears and walks you through the installation process, as shown in Figure 3-1. For detailed instructions, see "Installing Firefox with the Setup Wizard," later in this chapter.

For the Mac

If you are using a Macintosh, a folder containing a Firefox icon appears, as shown in Figure 3-2. Simply drag the icon onto your desktop, then double-click it to launch Firefox.

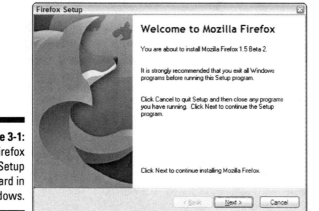

Figure 3-1:
The Firefox
Setup
Wizard in
Windows.

Figure 3-2:
The Firefox
disk image
on a
Macintosh.

Using a Firefox CD

If you don't yet have an Internet connection, or if you want to install Firefox on your friends' computers (remember, it's free and open source!), you can order Firefox on CD for just a few bucks from the online Mozilla Store. Orders must be placed via the store's Web site, so if your Internet connection isn't working yet, you can use a friend's computer.

1. **Navigate to the Mozilla Store Web site** (www.store.mozilla.org).

2. **Click Software & Guides in the left sidebar.**

3. **Add the Firefox CD to your cart.**

4. **When you finish shopping, click Check Out. If this is your first time using the Mozilla Store, you will need to create an account. The Store Web site walks you through this painless process.**

5. **When the CD arrives in the mail, put it in your computer's CD tray.**

For Windows

If you are using Windows, the Setup Wizard appears and walks you through the installation process, as shown earlier in Figure 3-1. For detailed instructions, see "Installing Firefox with the Setup Wizard."

If you're using Windows and the Setup Wizard does not appear automatically, you can open it manually. Double-click the My Computer icon on your Desktop, double-click your CD drive, and double-click the Firefox Setup file.

For the Mac

If you're using a Macintosh, a folder containing a Firefox icon appears, as shown in Figure 3-2. Simply drag the icon onto your desktop, then double-click the icon to launch Firefox.

Installing Firefox with the Setup Wizard

On Windows, the Firefox Setup Wizard walks you through the installation process. (The procedure on a Macintosh is a simple drag-and-drop operation as described in the previous section.)

1. **The first screen of the Setup Wizard welcomes you to Firefox. Click Next to continue to the End-User Software License Agreement.**

2. **Select "I Accept the Terms of the License Agreement" and click Next.**

   You'll probably just skip past End-User Software License Agreement without reading the actual text, but it's worth a read if you enjoy the fine language of legalese. The Software License Agreement tells you, among other things, that you can use Firefox free of charge, but if something goes wrong, the Mozilla Foundation isn't legally liable. Of course, in that unlikely situation, we're here to help.

3. **The Setup Type screen appears, allowing you to select either a Standard or Custom setup. If you have no preference where Firefox installs and don't need advanced tools, just accept the Standard option and click Next.**

   The Custom option allows you to choose:

   - Where Firefox gets installed on your computer. For example, maybe you have several hard drives and you don't want Firefox setting up shop on the C drive.

   - Whether Firefox installs advanced tools, like the Document Inspector for analyzing Web site code. These tools are for advanced users.

   - Where Firefox should put its flashy, foxy icons. This option is available in case you don't like clutter on your Desktop or in your Start menu.

   The Summary screen confirms what you've decided to install and where it will be installed.

4. **Click Next to begin installation.**

   The Install Complete screen appears when Firefox is installed.

5. **Click Finish to launch Firefox.**

   By default, the Firefox Home Page is Firefox Start, which offers fast access to Google Search. If you've installed Firefox before and would rather keep your old home page, deselect the Use Firefox Start as My Home Page check box.

Importing Your Information

When you first launch Firefox, the Import Wizard appears and walks you through the migration process. You can also access the wizard at any time by choosing File➪Import.

Firefox supports importing information from any of the following browsers:

- ✔ Microsoft Internet Explorer
- ✔ Netscape
- ✔ Opera
- ✔ Apple Safari
- ✔ OmniWeb
- ✔ Camino
- ✔ And, of course, earlier versions of Firefox

The import process is short and sweet, and when you're finished, Firefox looks and acts like your previous browser. Where possible, importing *adds* to your Firefox information rather than replacing it. For example, if you used Firefox for a week before deciding to import, the bookmarks or passwords you saved during that time won't be lost, as you see in the following steps:

1. **Open the Import Wizard by choosing File➪Import.**

2. **Select the browser to import from, and then click Next.**

   The first screen of the wizard lists the browsers currently installed on your computer, as shown in Figure 3-3. If you aren't ready to import, click Cancel.

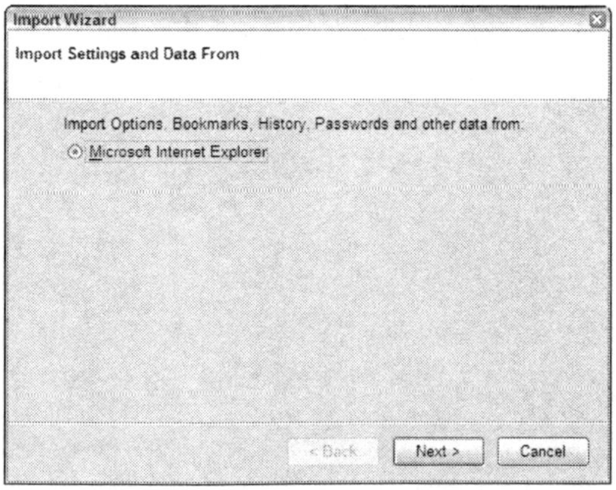

Figure 3-3: The Import Wizard automatically finds and displays the browsers installed on your computer.

Import Wizard

Import Settings and Data From

Import Options, Bookmarks, History, Passwords and other data from:

⊙ Microsoft Internet Explorer

< Back   Next >   Cancel

3. Select the information to import, and then click Next.

Several options are available, as shown in Figure 3-4. The available options depend on the browser from which you are importing.

- **Internet Options:** Transfer your former browser's settings to Firefox. Firefox can only transfer the settings it supports.

- **Cookies:** Transfer the cookies that are used in the other browser. A *cookie* is a piece of information that a Web site stores on your computer, such as your preferences for that site. Cookies make it easier for a site to remember you if you have visited it before.

- **Browsing History:** Transfer the history of Web pages you've visited. Transferring your history allows you to revisit the sites you visited with your former browser.

- **Saved Form History:** Transfer the form information collected by your former browser's form-filling mechanism. This way, you can get access to form information, such as Internet searches, that is saved in your other browser.

- **Saved Passwords:** Transfer passwords your former browser saved when you logged in to Web sites.

- **Favorites/Bookmarks:** Transfer your list of bookmarks (also called Favorites).

By default, Firefox imports everything it can, but you can deselect any type.

If you choose to import settings, Firefox will be configured as much like your former browser as possible. Naturally, Firefox can't support every setting available in another browser, but it inherits the ones it can.

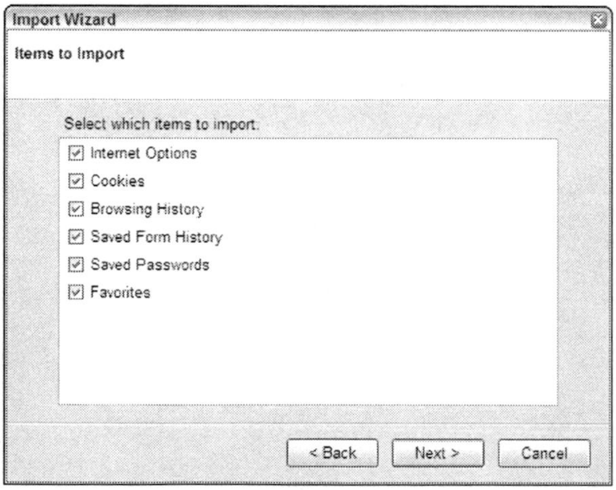

Figure 3-4:
Firefox can
practically
replicate
your
previous
browser by
importing
everything
from
bookmarks
to saved
passwords.

Import Wizard	
Items to Import	

Select which items to import:

- ☑ Internet Options
- ☑ Cookies
- ☑ Browsing History
- ☑ Saved Form History
- ☑ Saved Passwords
- ☑ Favorites

[< Back] [Next >] [Cancel]

When you click Next, the import process begins. It should take less than a minute.

4. **The final screen (see Figure 3-5) shows you the information that Firefox has imported. Congratulations! Click Finish to start using Firefox.**

You can make Firefox look even more like your old one by customizing the Firefox toolbars to match the other browser's toolbars, as I discuss in Chapter 18.

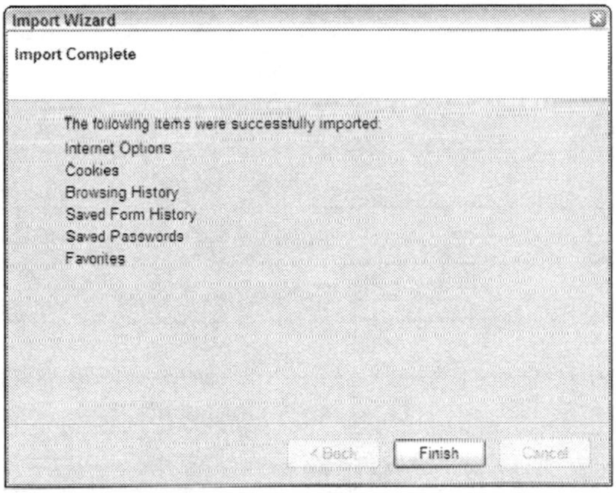

Figure 3-5: It normally takes less than a minute to import your data. When you see this screen, you're ready to use Firefox.

> **Import Wizard**
>
> Import Complete
>
> The following items were successfully imported:
> Internet Options
> Cookies
> Browsing History
> Saved Form History
> Saved Passwords
> Favorites
>
> < Back   Finish   Cancel

Switching from Internet Explorer

The Windows version of Firefox is designed for an easy transition from Internet Explorer. It supports nearly all of the Internet Explorer 6.0 keyboard shortcuts and offers similar toolbars, menus, and colors.

Keyboard shortcut differences

There are just two minor keyboard shortcut differences to be aware of if you're switching from Internet Explorer, as you see in Table 3-1.

Table 3-1	Keyboard Shortcut Differences	
Action	*Internet Explorer*	*Firefox*
Select Location Bar	Ctrl+Tab	Ctrl+L, Alt+D, F6
Open Location	Ctrl+O	Ctrl+L, Alt+D, F6

Terminology differences

A rose by any other name might work for Shakespeare, but computers are less forgiving. Table 3-2 describes some of the differences in terminology between Internet Explorer and Firefox.

Table 3-2	Differences in Terminology
Internet Explorer	*Firefox*
Internet Options	Options
Temporary Internet Files	Cache
Favorites	Bookmarks
Address Bar	Location Bar
Refresh	Reload
Links Bar	Bookmarks Toolbar
Explorer Bar	Sidebar
Copy Shortcut	Copy Link Location
Save Target As	Save Link As
Set as Background	Set as Desktop Background

Feature differences

Firefox does not support these Internet Explorer features:

- ✔ Content Advisor
- ✔ Privacy Report
- ✔ Synchronize
- ✔ Web Content Zones

Switching from Apple Safari

Just as the Windows version of Firefox is tailored to former Internet Explorer users, the Macintosh version is designed for Safari fans.

Keyboard shortcut differences

The Macintosh version of Firefox sticks to Safari's keyboard shortcuts as faithfully as possible, but there are a few differences to be aware of, as shown in Table 3-3.

Table 3-3	Keyboard Shortcut Differences	
Action	*Safari*	*Firefox*
Open Download Manager	Option+⌘+L	⌘+Y
Load Home Page	Shift+⌘+H	Option+Home
View Source (Code)	Option+⌘+U	⌘+U
Open Bookmarks Sidebar	Option+⌘+B	⌘+B
Select Next Tab	Shift+⌘+]	⌘+Page Down
Select Previous Tab	Shift+⌘+[	⌘+Page Up

Terminology differences

There's not much in terms of terms that are different except for the following: What Safari calls the Address Bar, Firefox calls the Location Bar.

Feature differences

Firefox does not support certain Safari features by default. However, in many cases, you can download an extension that will add the same capabilities to Firefox, and I note the extensions that are available. See Chapter 21 for more information about installing and using extensions. Firefox does not support the following Safari features:

- Snapback
- Bookmarks Synchronization (try the Bookmarks Synchronizer extension)
- Spell Check (try the SpellBound extension)
- Edit⇨Special Characters
- Send Page (however, the Send Link command, which sends a link to a Web page, is available from the Firefox File menu)
- Activity window
- Edit⇨Autofill (however, Firefox autocompletes as you type)

A tale of two browsers

I spend much of this chapter discussing feature, keyboard, and terminology differences among browsers, but the most important difference is in how browsers decide to lay out Web pages. Although Web pages are fully interactive and often beautifully designed documents by the time they reach your screen, they are in fact a jumble of computer instructions under the hood. How a Web page looks on your screen depends on how your particular browser decides to interpret these instructions.

To ensure consistency among browsers, an open standards organization called the World Wide Web Consortium (W3C) oversees the development of technical specs that govern the interpretation of these instructions. Unfortunately, from 1995 through about 2001 — the very time period that launched the Web — the two dominant browser vendors largely ignored the W3C. Engaged in the software industry's version of the Space Race, Microsoft and Netscape created their own Web "standards" in-house and evangelized them to Web developers. Each vendor hoped, of course, that more developers would adopt its respective standard, thereby locking out the other — since Web pages wouldn't load properly in the other's browser.

Unfortunately, this devious strategy worked. More unfortunately, it worked to the favor of Microsoft, which now enjoys a monopoly on the Web. The lock-in strategy is viciously cyclical: If most developers are developing for Microsoft's browser, users have to use that browser to display Web sites properly. And if most users are using Microsoft's browser, developers want to develop for it. In a world like this, why would developers follow the W3C's standards? As rosy as a global Web standard sounded, practical developers coded to Microsoft's *de facto* standard.

Part of the reason Firefox exists is to break Microsoft's hold on the Web. This kind of monopoly is harmful to all of us, because it locks us into Microsoft devices and leaves us at the whims of an enormous public company that ultimately answers to shareholders. Case in point: In 2001, Microsoft abandoned development of Internet Explorer, the most used software application in the world, because the company had no incentive to upgrade a free product after winning the browser war against Netscape. Good move for Wall Street, but perhaps not such a good move for you, if you were one of the 500 million Internet Explorer users left to fend for themselves.

Firefox adheres closely to the W3C standards to promote a Web that works on any device, any platform, anywhere. When we first began the project, we faced the difficult and often futile challenge of convincing developers not to use Microsoft's proprietary Web standards. However, now that Firefox has won over 10 percent of the browsing market — over 50 million users — developers are starting to change course.

So what does this mean for you today as you switch to Firefox? It means that about 97 percent of the 12 billion (and counting) Web sites out there should render perfectly well in Firefox today, and that number continues to rise as Firefox's global market share increases. If you come across a Web site that doesn't look or work properly in Firefox, you can let us know by following the directions in the "Reporting Broken Web Sites" section of this chapter.

Reporting Broken Web Sites

Every browser interprets and displays Web sites in different ways. Some Web sites will look better in Firefox, but others might look worse or work improperly. This is rare, but when it happens, it's usually due to a programming error in the Web site (assuming you haven't yet tweaked the Firefox display options I discuss in Chapter 19).

Firefox includes a tool you can use to notify us when you encounter a broken Web site. We examine each submission to make sure it doesn't indicate a defect in Firefox itself. To help us, the reporting tool sends basic information about your version and configuration of Firefox, as shown in Figure 3-6. If you provide personal information, such as an e-mail address, it is not shared with anyone outside the core Firefox team. Anonymous version information is published to our extended development community.

If no Firefox defect is found, we notify the owner of the broken Web site and help him or her fix the errors so the Web site works properly. After the Web site is fixed, it starts working in your version of Firefox; you don't need to download anything.

To report a broken Web site:

1. **Navigate to the broken Web site.**

2. **Choose Help⇨Report Broken Web Site.**

3. **If this is the first time you're accessing the Reporting Wizard, select the check box underneath the policy to indicate your agreement, and then click Next.**

   The first time you access the Reporting Wizard, it displays the Mozilla Reporting Privacy Policy, as shown in Figure 3-6. You must agree to these terms to continue.

4. **The next and final screen of the Reporting Wizard (see Figure 3-7) asks you to describe the problem:**

   • **Web Site URL:** The address of the Web site is already prefilled. If the site requires a password, select the Web Site is Password-Protected option. (Your login information is *not* sent to us.)

   • **Problem Type:** Select the option that best describes the problem you're seeing or select Other if none match closely.

   • **Describe Problem:** Enter a brief description of the problem. For example, if you think part of the page is missing, indicate what you expect to see and where you expect it.

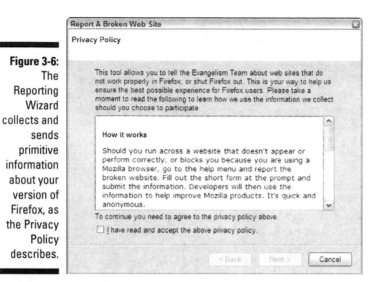

Anything you enter into this field will be published, so don't include personal information (such as name or e-mail address) here. (The Email text box, however, is not published.)

- **Email (Optional):** Enter your e-mail address if you'd like the Firefox team to follow up on your report. This address isn't shared with anyone and is used only to contact you regarding this particular report. For example, we might contact you if we need additional information about the problem or when the site has been fixed.

5. **Click the Submit Report button to send the problem report.**

   When the submission is complete, the Reporting Wizard displays the Report Sent screen, as shown in Figure 3-8.

   The Mozilla Web site might go down from time to time. If you encounter an error while submitting your report, try again later.

6. **To see the information included in the report, click Show Details; to close the Reporting Wizard, click Finish.**

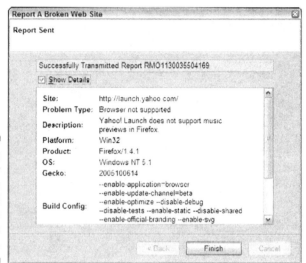

Figure 3-8: Click Show Details to see the full report once it has been sent.

Part II
Ready, Aim, Firefox

The 5th Wave   By Rich Tennant

Hang on! I keep entering a search for "squishy red orb next to the lungs", and this dumb browser keeps taking me to sites for rubber balls, Silly Putty, and chew toys.

In this part . . .

So you already had "the talk" with your former browser and you're ready to dig in deep with Firefox. This part delivers the goods. This part begins with a tour of Firefox's innovative search capabilities in Chapter 4 and then dives into powerful bookmark features in Chapter 5. Be sure to pause at the end of Chapter 6 and give your surfing habits a proper eulogy, because Chapter 7 shows you the new way to get around the Web: tabbed browsing.

There's plenty of other fun to be had along the way, including an exploration of Firefox's history and downloading features. Oh, and don't mind that music in the background. It's just the sweet, sweet sound of popup blocking. Enjoy!

Chapter 4

Finding Information Online

*T*rying to find your car in a parking garage is hard enough as it is. Now imagine that the parking garage has 12 billion cars, and all you know about yours is that it's white.

Finding the information you want on the Internet can be equally frustrating if you don't know where to begin. So-called search engines, such as Google and Yahoo!, map the Web's information for you to make it searchable. Firefox works closely with these search engines to help you find information quickly and easily.

Searching the Web with Firefox

Finding information on the Web is as easy as "telling" a search engine what you want to find, clicking a button, and combing through the information the engine returns. The trick is in the telling. A search engine can't understand sentences the way a human does, so follow these tips to get better results:

  ✔ **Be succinct.** Search only for the keywords that define what you want. For example, if you're looking for ski resorts in Lake Tahoe, try *ski resorts Lake Tahoe* instead of the more conversational *"Where can I find ski resorts in Lake Tahoe?"* Many engines, however, are getting better at understanding the latter format.

  ✔ **Be specific.** Although being succinct is important, you also need to strive to be as specific as possible. Use distinct, targeted words that precisely describe what you're looking for. For example, *Lake Tahoe Karaoke* returns about a tenth of the results as *Lake Tahoe night life,* as does *Lake Tahoe comedy club.*

✔ **Don't worry about case.** Virtually all search engines ignore the casing of your search phrase, which means that *Lake Tahoe* is equal to *lake tahoe*.

✔ **Use quotes for phrases.** By default, search engines look for pages that contain any of the words you enter. When you want to search for a phrase that consists of multiple words, you can enclose it in quotation marks, and the engine finds only pages that contain the entire phrase. For example, searching for *"Lake Tahoe"* returns only pages that contain the full phrase. Web sites that contain only *Lake* or only *Tahoe* are not returned.

Searching for keywords and phrases at the same time is okay. For example, to find a healthy restaurant near Lake Tahoe, you could search *healthy restaurant "Lake Tahoe"*. You probably wouldn't want to include *healthy restaurant* in quotation marks because most sites wouldn't include that phrase word for word. Instead, they'd have *restaurant* at the beginning of the review, and *healthy* elsewhere.

Because searching is such a common activity, you're never more than one click away from a search box where you can type your keywords in Firefox.

Searching from the default Firefox home page

By default, Firefox offers a slightly modified version of Google — the leading Internet search engine — as its home page (see Figure 4-1). This means that as long as you don't change your home page, you'll be ready to begin searching each time you start Firefox.

To perform a search from the default home page, follow these steps:

1. **Click within the Google search box.**

2. **Type in your search keywords (for example,** *ski resorts Lake Tahoe***).**

3. **Click the Google Search button (or press Enter) to begin your search.**

   Google returns a list of Web sites that are (hopefully) relevant to your search.

Searches usually take less than a second, but they could take longer on slower Internet connections. The Firefox Tabbed Browsing feature makes it easy to navigate this list quickly; see Chapter 7 for more information.

Figure 4-1:
The default
Firefox
home page
offers
instant
access to all
kinds of
Google
searching.

Searching from the Search Box

If you have changed your home page to something other than Google or if
you have navigated to a different Web site, you can still begin a search immediately through the handy Firefox Search Box. It's located on the right side of
the primary toolbar, to the right of the Location Bar and the Go button, as
shown in Figure 4-2.

Figure 4-2:
You can
search by
using the
Search Box
in the
upper-right
corner of
the window.

The Google icon

Search Box

The Search Box works just as you would expect: Simply type in one or more search terms and press Enter to see a list of Web sites that contain relevant information.

To begin your search without having to reach for the mouse, press Ctrl+K in Windows or ⌘+K on the Mac. This shortcut quickly takes your cursor to the Search Box. Pressing Alt+Enter instead of Enter in Windows, or Option+Return on the Mac, loads the search results in a new tab when searching from the Search Box.

Swapping Search Box engines

As with the home page, the Search Box uses Google by default because it is widely considered to be the fastest and most accurate general-purpose engine currently available. However, just as you can change your home page to whatever you'd like, you can also change the engine used by the Search Box. This is useful if you prefer another general-purpose engine, such as Yahoo!, or if you're looking for a specific type of information, such as a word definition, and want to switch to an engine better equipped to handle it, such as a dictionary.

To change your Search Box engine, follow these steps:

1. **Click the icon to the left in the Search Box (refer to Figure 4-2).**

   The Firefox Search Box uses Google by default, so the icon you see is the Google icon.

2. **Choose a new engine from the menu that appears (see Figure 4-3).**

   Firefox remembers which engine you select and defaults to it in all future windows.

   To switch engines with the keyboard, press Ctrl+↓ within the Search Box.

Figure 4-3:
You can choose from a variety of search engines by clicking the icon.

Choose a new engine from the menu.

Firefox offers several high-quality engines in its Search Box, and I summarize them in Table 4-1.

Table 4-1	Search Engines for the Search Box
Engine	*Specialty*
Google	General purpose
Yahoo!	General purpose
Amazon	Retail books, movies, computer software, and more
Answers.com	A variety of reference tools, including a dictionary, a thesaurus and an encyclopedia
Creative Commons	Photos, music, and text you can reuse without having to pay or ask the author's permission
eBay	Auctions selling any possible item imaginable

Adding an engine to the Search Box

You can add engines to the list you see in Figure 4-3 (shown earlier) so you can search with them from the Search Box. Here's how:

1. **Click the icon to the left of the Search Box.**

2. **Choose Add Engines.**

   This step loads the Firefox Central Web site.

3. **Under the Add New Search Engines heading at the bottom of the page (see Figure 4-4), find the engine you want to add.**

   If you don't see the engine you want in the list, click the last link — Find Lots of Other Search Engines — to load a list of engines, all neatly organized into categories (such as Reference and Shopping).

   Hundreds of search engines are available to choose from. I outline some of my favorites in Table 4-2.

4. **When you find the engine you want, simply click it and then click OK in the Firefox confirmation window.**

   Your new search engine is immediately available from the Search Box.

Figure 4-4:
Here's
where you
can select a
different
search
engine
for the
Search Box.

At the present time, you cannot remove a search engine from the Search Box list (shown earlier in Figure 4-3).

Table 4-2	Additional Search Engines to Choose
Engine	**Specialty**
Wikipedia	Wikipedia is an encyclopedia with information on nearly every topic imaginable — and in dozens of languages, from Arabic to Vietnamese. As if that weren't enough, the articles are written entirely by volunteer experts in each subject area. Because every volunteer has a voice, no article is subject to the kind of bias — intentional or otherwise — you can often detect in articles written by a single author.
IMDB	What shade of green is Luke Skywalker's lightsaber? Which hand did ET use to phone home? IMDB is the online version of your nerdy friend who knows all the movie trivia — and I mean that in a good way. It includes descriptions, cast information, trivia, user ratings, and pictures of millions of films, many of which haven't even hit screens yet.
Google News	Stay up-to-date with the latest headlines from over 4,500 popular news sources worldwide.

Firefox developers felt lucky

We fiercely debated whether to conduct a traditional Google search or Google's I'm Feeling Lucky search as the default search method for the Location Bar. All other browsers at the time conducted normal searches, but the Firefox development team eventually decided that the benefits of an I'm Feeling Lucky search far outweighed the break with consistency. Two benefits in particular motivated our decision:

✔ **Many of us on the Firefox team share a strong (if naïve) desire to rid the world of the arcane site addressing system.** We believe `http://www.fordvehicles.com/` is a ridiculous bunch of gibberish that no sane human being should ever have to remember. What was that address again? Ford.com? Fordtrucks.com? Ford-vehicles.com? Or was there no dash? And what does all that `http://` stuff mean, anyway? Did somebody's cat walk across the keyboard? This addressing system is just one of the many painful reminders that the Internet was originally designed for military officials, scientists, and other similarly technical crowds.

Choosing the I'm Feeling Lucky search as the default search method in Firefox's Location Bar, then, was our first tentative step toward bypassing this arcane addressing system. Instead of having to remember an address, you simply have to remember a couple keywords that describe what you're looking for and have faith that Google and Firefox will find it for you. For example, instead of worrying about whether there's a dash in `http://www.fordvehicles.com/`, you can type **"Ford trucks"**, **"Ford vehicles"**, **"Ford SUVs"**, **"Ford cars"**, or even **"Ford vehicle info"** and be on your way. Or take the example of the horror flick *The Ring:* Is the site address `http://www.thering.com`, `theringmovie.com`, or `the-ring.com`? Actually, it's none of those. It's `ring-themovie.com`. But if you have trouble remembering that, just type **the ring** into the Location Bar and press Enter.

✔ **The Location Bar is very much a place of action, whereas combing through search results is traditionally a more casual and longer-term approach.** Internet surfers are all accustomed to using the address bar to get somewhere *quickly*, and the other developers and I wanted to uphold that.

Searching from the Location Bar

Firefox allows advanced users to search the Web from the Location Bar — the box in which you typically enter the address of a Web site to visit. This can be useful if, for example, you have hidden the Search Box to conserve space.

Simple searching with Location Bar keywords

At the simplest level, searching from the Location Bar requires no additional work on your part. If you enter a series of keywords into the box and press Enter (or click Go), Firefox automatically treats the phrase as a search request. Unlike a traditional search, however, you don't see a list of relevant Web sites. Instead, Firefox automatically takes you to the page that most likely contains what you're looking for. Firefox does this neat trick by using Google's I'm Feeling Lucky technology, which automatically redirects you to the very first Google search result for your search phrase.

Specialized searching with Location Bar keywords

Firefox also allows you to conduct searches from the Location Bar by using Search Keywords. Rather than typing an address, you type the keyword that represents the search engine you want to use, followed by the phrase to search for. By default, Firefox includes four Search Keywords that you can use from the Location Bar. (You can also add your own special words, but this is a very advanced topic beyond the scope of this book.) I outline these in Table 4-3.

Table 4-3	Firefox Search Keywords	
Keyword	*Action*	*Example*
google	Searches for a word or phrase on Google	google New York
dict	Retrieves the definition of a word on Answers.com	dict facetious
wp	Searches for a word or phrase on Wikipedia, a community-edited encyclopedia	wp war of 1812
quote	Retrieves trading information for a stock ticker on Google's stock quote service	quote GOOG

For example, suppose you want to look up a company's trading information on the stock market. You would simply:

1. **Click within the Location Bar.**

2. **Type** quote *stocksymbol* **(but replace** *stocksymbol* **with the stock's symbol).**

   For example, you can type **quote GOOG** and find out the current value of Google stock (see Figure 4-5).

3. **Press Enter or click Go.**

   Firefox displays the latest stock quote information.

Finding Text within a Page

Unfortunately, finding the Web page you're looking for is often just half the battle. The other half is finding the specific bit of information you're looking for within that page. Fortunately, Firefox offers a powerful tool called the Find Bar, which makes searching pages easy.

In search of a better Find feature

Because the Find Bar is a radical departure from the standard Find features in other programs, it was also the subject of much debate during early Firefox development. The concern wasn't that Firefox searched as you typed, but rather that the Find feature now lived within a toolbar instead of a window, and that this toolbar lived at the bottom of the window instead of the top.

The problem with the standard Find window is that it invariably gets in the way by obscuring the very phrase you were trying to find. Some programs, such as Microsoft Word, try to alleviate the problem by moving the Find window out of the way automatically, but we found this behavior even more annoying: Suddenly your windows are playing musical chairs without your consent. We modeled an alternate solution whereby the Find feature was instead housed in a toolbar at the bottom of the window and asked some people to try it out. Their reaction was so positive that we decided the break with tradition was warranted.

Software development is a tricky business, however, and we overlooked one subtle flaw in our model testing: Rather than allowing our test users to discover the toolbar on their own, we pointed them to it. Had we instead observed them in their natural course, we would have immediately discovered a problem that only came to light much later on: Many people didn't notice the Find Bar's appearance after they opened it! We received many reports of the Find in This Page option being broken.

That discovery came rather late in the development process, and we needed to ship Firefox 1.0 soon, so our options were limited. We considered moving the toolbar to the top of the window alongside all other toolbars, where it would be less likely to go unnoticed. However, the reason we placed it at the bottom in the first place was to prevent the entire Web site from shifting up or down to make room for the toolbar each time you opened or closed it. Moving it to the top would mean introducing a long-term annoyance just to fix a short-term problem of discovery. That didn't seem right.

We ultimately converged on a solution that, although less than ideal, was suitable given our time constraints. We decided that the first two times the Find Bar is opened, its text box would flash bright yellow to draw the user's attention. So, no, you're not crazy. It really did blink!

Using the Find Bar

The Find Bar is a thin toolbar that appears along the bottom of a Web page when you choose Edit➪Find in This Page or when you press Ctrl+F (Windows) or ⌘+F (Mac). Like the finding capabilities in most other programs, the Find Bar allows you to jump right to the spot on a Web page that contains a certain word or phrase. Unlike most other programs, however, Firefox searches as you type the phrase, enabling you to stop typing as soon as you find it, and ultimately saving you time. Let's see how this works.

1. **Navigate to** www.getfirefox.com.

   You can simply type **get firefox** in the Location Bar and press Enter! (Be sure to see the earlier section, "Searching from the Location Bar," to find out more about this.)

2. **Choose Edit➪Find in This Page or press Ctrl+F (Windows) or ⌘+F (Mac).**

3. **In the Find Bar at the bottom of the window, type the word or phrase you want to search for (see Figure 4-6).**

   For example, you can search for Thunderbird, the name of the e-mail program produced by the Mozilla Foundation (the same organization that develops Firefox).

   Don't include quotation marks unless you're searching for a phrase that contains them.

By default, searches are case-insensitive, which means `thunderbird` and `Thunderbird` and `THUNDERBIRD` are treated as if they were all the same word. To have Firefox treat them distinctly, select the Match Case check box on the Find Bar.

Notice that even before you finish typing the word, Firefox has already found the first instance of it, scrolled to it, and highlighted it (see Figure 4-6). For my Thunderbird example, you could stop typing at `Thunder` or even `Thu`!

Now try typing **Thunderfox**. As soon as you type the *f,* Firefox highlights the search box in bright red and displays `Phrase not found` on the right (see Figure 4-7). Because `Thunderf` isn't found on the page, no additional letters are going to yield a match, and you can stop typing. Even when you're looking for something that isn't to be found, Firefox saves you time.

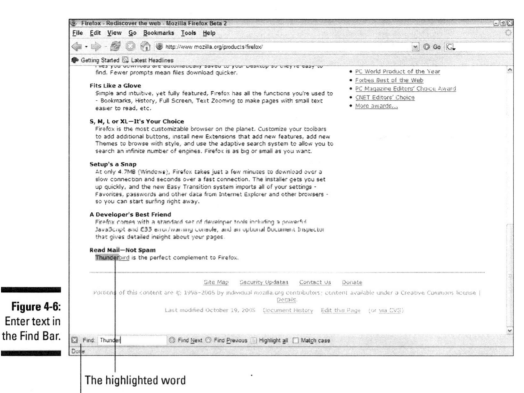

Figure 4-6:
Enter text in
the Find Bar.

The highlighted word

The Find Bar

Moving among multiple Find Bar results

If a page contains multiple instances of your search phrase, Firefox makes it easy and intuitive to move among them. To move to the next phrase, click the Find Next button or just press Enter. To move to the previous phrase, click the Find Previous button or press Shift+Enter.

Because we wanted to minimize distraction, Firefox doesn't display an error message when you reach the end of a Web page in your search. Instead, you see a message appear on the right side of the toolbar: `Reached end of page, continued from top`. (See Figure 4-8.) If you choose Find Next at this point, Firefox restarts your search from the beginning of the Web page.

When you finish searching, you can close the Find Bar by clicking the Close button (the one with the X in it) at the far left or by pressing Esc.

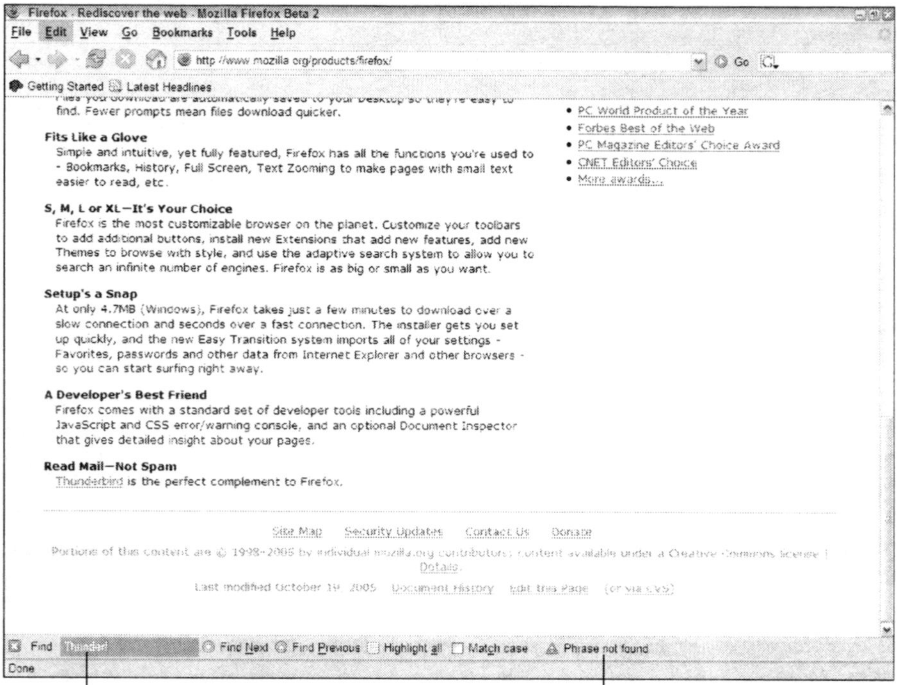

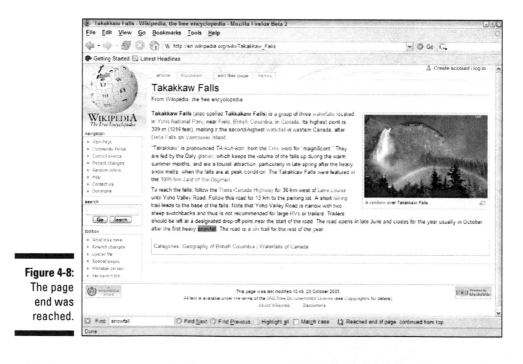

Figure 4-7:
This phrase
isn't found.

The Find Bar highlights the search box in red . . . and displays the message.

Figure 4-8:
The page
end was
reached.

Chapter 5

Bookmarking Great Sites

*F*irefox strives to make the Web easy to use for everyone, but it can't avoid one aspect of the Web: the complicated addressing system. Suppose your friend Julie maintains a Web site at www.therosenbergfamily.com/julie/start.html, and you visit it frequently to see how she's doing. Why should you have to remember such a long and seemingly absurd string of letters? Why should you need to recall that the *j* in Julie is lowercase, contrary to what you were taught in school?

You shouldn't. And although Firefox can't do away with such addresses altogether, it *can* remember them so you don't have to. Like many other browsers, Firefox allows you to bookmark a Web site so you can easily return to it later on — much as you would bookmark pages in a book. In the Internet Explorer browser, these bookmarks are called Favorites. Firefox also offers sophisticated but easy-to-use organizational tools to keep your bookmarks in order whether you have 5 or 500.

Creating and Accessing Bookmarks

Bookmarking a Web page is about as easy as bookmarking a page in a book. You just need to tell Firefox what to call the bookmark and where you want to put it. By default, bookmarks appear in a list accessible from either the

Bookmarks menu or the Bookmarks Sidebar, which is a small panel that opens on the left side of the screen (see the section "The Bookmarks Sidebar," later in this chapter). However, you can also organize bookmarks into folders and subfolders so you can access them in a manner that suits you.

Creating a bookmark

To bookmark an interesting Web site, follow these steps:

1. **Navigate to the Web site you want to bookmark.**

2. **Choose Bookmarks⇨Bookmark This Page to open the Add Bookmark window.**

   You can open this window more quickly by pressing Ctrl+D (Windows) or ⌘+D (Mac).

3. **In the Name text box, enter the name you would like to use for the bookmark or accept the default name that appears there.**

   The name will appear in the Bookmarks menu and in the Bookmarks Sidebar. By default, Firefox uses the title of the Web site you're book-marking as the name, as shown in Figure 5-1.

4. **Select the folder in which you'd like to place the bookmark by using one of the following methods:**

   • Select a folder from the Create In drop-down list. This list contains the last five folders in which you filed a bookmark.

   • If you don't see the folder you want, or if you want to create a new folder, click the button next to the Create In list (the down arrow, as shown in Figure 5-1). The full list of folders appears. Select the one you want to use or click the New Folder button at the bottom to create a new folder. The folder is created within whichever folder you selected.

   By default, Firefox places all new bookmarks in the main Bookmarks folder, so the new bookmarks appear alongside folders in the main list and not within any particular subfolder.

5. **Click OK to create the new bookmark.**

   The bookmark appears immediately on the Bookmarks menu and in the Bookmarks Sidebar in the location that you chose in Step 4.

Figure 5-1:
Bookmark
sites to
return
to them
quickly.

Add Bookmark

Name: CNN.com

Create in: Bookmarks

OK   Cancel

Creating multiple bookmarks at once

If you browse with tabs (see Chapter 7 for more information), you can bookmark multiple open tabs at once into a single bookmarks folder. Later, you
can open each bookmark individually in the usual way — by opening the
folder and clicking it — or you can open all the bookmarks in the folder at
one time, as I discuss in "Opening multiple bookmarks at once," later in this
chapter.

To bookmark your open tabs, follow these steps:

1. **Open each page you want to bookmark in a separate tab within the
   Firefox window.**

2. **Choose Bookmarks⇨Bookmark All Tabs to open the Bookmark All
   Tabs window.**

3. **Enter a folder name. Firefox creates a new folder to contain the
   bookmarks.**

4. **Choose a location for the new folder.**

   By default, Firefox creates the folder in your Bookmarks list alongside
   regular bookmarks. However, you can also choose to create it inside
   another folder (that is, you can make it a subfolder).

5. **Click OK to create the new folder and bookmarks.**

Creating a bookmark that auto-updates

Bookmarks are a great way to access your favorite Web sites quickly, but in
some ways, they're a curse. You might find yourself visiting Web sites for
updates five or six times a day just because they're so easy to access. Thanks

to an emerging technology called Really Simple Syndication (RSS), Firefox can bring the updates to you from any Web site that supports RSS. Bookmarks in special folders can update automatically to show you new content, which saves you time.

These so-called *live bookmarks* are based on the simple idea that a Web site is really a type of folder. CNN.com, for example, is nothing more than a collection — or folder — of various items, which in this case are news stories. Similarly, your friend's *blog* (short for *Web log,* which is an online journal or diary) is like a folder of journal entries.

You already know that you can organize your bookmarks into folders. But you can also create live bookmark folders of any RSS-enabled Web site. Firefox automatically fetches new items posted to the Web site — including news stories, journal entries, and so on — and presents each new item to you as a separate bookmark. You access these live folders the same way you do all other folders. The only difference is that the bookmarks in the folder change as the Web site it points to is updated with new content.

Firefox comes with a live bookmark folder by default so you can see how they work. It's called Latest Headlines, and it sits on your Bookmarks Toolbar. The folder contains the latest news headlines straight from BBC News, an RSS-enabled Web site.

To subscribe to additional Web sites in this fashion, follow these steps:

 1. **Visit the Web site for which you want to create a live bookmark.**

    If the Web site supports RSS, you see the orange-and-white subscribe image to the right of the Location Bar, as shown in Figure 5-2. If this image does not appear, the Web site doesn't support RSS, and you can't create a live bookmark. Plenty of sites these days support RSS. For an example, try www.cnn.com.

 2. **Click the subscribe image.**

    A menu appears containing the list of information sources, or *feeds,* that the Web site offers.

    For example, CNN allows you to subscribe to all recent stories or only the top stories.

 3. **From the menu, choose the feed to which you want to subscribe.**

    In some cases, the available feeds have arcane names such as *RSS 2.0* and *Atom 2.0.* These names refer to the varying subscription technologies that the Web site supports; the actual information carried by each feed is the same, so you can choose either one without worrying about the technical details.

    After you choose from the menu, the standard Add Bookmark window appears.

4. **At this point, the process is the same as for all other bookmarks, so follow the instructions I provide in the "Creating a bookmark" section earlier in this chapter.**

Note that what you're actually creating here is a bookmark *folder,* not a single bookmark, that will represent the Web site. Firefox automatically fills the folder with new bookmarks as new items become available on the Web site. Therefore, the name you supply in the Add Bookmark window is actually the name of the folder that Firefox will create.

Figure 5-2:
Some Web sites offer self-updating news feeds.

RSS symbol

Opening a bookmark

You can access bookmarks in three ways: from the Bookmarks Toolbar that sits just above the Web sites you visit, from the Bookmarks menu at the top of the window, and from the Bookmarks Sidebar that can appear on the left side of the screen. Each location offers different advantages depending on how frequently you access a given bookmark and how conservative you are with your screen's real estate:

- ✔ **The Bookmarks Toolbar** is useful for fast access to the bookmarks you visit most frequently. The bookmarks on the toolbar are always visible and are always one click away. The toolbar occupies a thin horizontal strip and can show six to ten bookmarks comfortably on a normal-sized screen.

- ✔ **The Bookmarks menu** is useful if you don't access bookmarks very often and don't want to waste screen space. If you have a lot of bookmarks, you're better off using the Bookmarks Sidebar, which scrolls more easily and has a search feature.

- ✔ **The Bookmarks Sidebar** is useful for people who have lots of bookmarks and need to access them frequently. It offers a quick-search feature and can be opened or closed quickly by pressing Ctrl+B (Windows) or ⌘+B (Macintosh).

I discuss each of these tools further in the following sections.

The Bookmarks Toolbar

The Bookmarks Toolbar (shown in Figure 5-3) is designed for people who visit a small set of Web sites so frequently that they want these Web sites to be one click away at all times. You can put as many bookmarks onto the Bookmarks Toolbar as you can fit, and if you run out of space, Firefox automatically creates a menu at the end of the toolbar to offer access to the remaining bookmarks, as illustrated in Figure 5-4. Click a bookmark to visit it.

The Bookmarks Toolbar can display about 6 to 10 bookmarks at a time. You can make better use of the space by creating folders on the toolbar and putting frequently accessed bookmarks inside those folders. To create a folder on the Bookmarks Toolbar, simply right-click on empty space within it, and then choose New Folder. When the New Folder window appears, enter a name for the folder and click OK. To add bookmarks to a folder, simply drag and drop them onto the folder.

You can also conserve space on the Bookmarks Toolbar by giving your bookmarks shorter names. To rename a bookmark, right-click it and choose Properties. When the Properties window appears, enter a new name for the bookmark and click OK.

The Bookmarks Toolbar includes two bookmarks by default: a Getting Started bookmark that introduces you to Firefox, and a live bookmark folder that contains the latest BBC News headlines (see "Creating a bookmark that auto-updates," earlier in this chapter).

If you don't use the Bookmarks Toolbar and want to reclaim the space it uses, you can hide the toolbar by choosing View⇨Toolbars⇨Bookmarks Toolbar.

The Bookmarks Toolbar

Figure 5-3:
The
Bookmarks
Toolbar.

Figure 5-4:
These
bookmarks
overflowed.

So how do you get a bookmark onto the Bookmarks Toolbar? The toolbar automatically displays any bookmarks you have placed in the special Bookmarks Toolbar Folder. You can add bookmarks to this folder just as you would to any other folder: by choosing it from the list in the Add Bookmark window, as I describe in Step 4 in the earlier section, "Creating a bookmark." As soon as you add the bookmark to the folder, it appears on the toolbar.

There's a faster way to add Web sites to the Bookmarks Toolbar. Visit any Web site and look to the left of the Web site's address in the Firefox Location Bar. In most cases, you see the Location Bar icon. In some cases, you see a special image representing the Web site you're viewing (for example, when you're visiting CNN.com, you see the CNN logo). In either case, the image that appears represents a link to the Web site you're viewing. You can drag the image into an e-mail to send a link to the page to your friend. In this case, it also means you can drag the image down to the Bookmarks Toolbar to create a bookmark to the page.

The impersonal toolbar

The Bookmarks Toolbar seems so simple and innocent — you'd hardly guess it was the cause of many a shouting match at Netscape, the original browser company. Because the toolbar is prominent yet largely empty by default, it was an appetizing target for Netscape marketers with dollar signs on the brain. After all, why not fill the bar with advertising links? Asking the Marketing department to leave the toolbar alone was like asking them to pass up a Super Bowl ad or leave the side of a bus blank — it just wasn't happening. Instead, the Netscape 6 browser shipped with a bevy of advertising and other buttons that didn't behave like regular bookmarks and were difficult to remove manually. Now for the ultimate irony — the bar was known as the Personal Toolbar.

In Firefox, we drew a line in the sand early on that the bar would be *your* bar and no one else's. The bar includes two bookmarks by default: a Getting Started link and a live bookmark that contains the latest BBC News headlines. The first helps you get comfortable with Firefox, and the second introduces you to our innovative Live Bookmarks technology (which I discuss elsewhere in this chapter). Neither makes us money, and you can remove them just like any other bookmark — by right-clicking and choosing Delete. We've also retired the tragically ironic Personal moniker and called it what it is: your Bookmarks Toolbar.

Changing the bookmarks displayed on the toolbar

Firefox allows advanced users to change which folder's bookmarks the Bookmarks Toolbar displays. This can be handy if you have a lot of bookmarks and you've already organized them thoroughly into folders. For example, suppose you have a folder called News Sites and you want the bookmarks in this folder to be displayed on the Bookmarks Toolbar. You can simply designate the News Sites folder as the folder to use for the Bookmarks Toolbar:

1. **Choose Bookmarks⇨Manage Bookmarks to open the Bookmarks Manager.**

2. **In the pane on the right, select the folder you want to designate as the Bookmarks Toolbar folder.**

3. **Choose Edit⇨Set as Bookmarks Toolbar Folder.**

    The Bookmarks Toolbar immediately updates to display this new folder's bookmarks.

    Note that after you do this the first time, the Bookmarks Toolbar Folder still has the same name, but it is just a regular folder now; its bookmarks aren't reflected in the toolbar. Be sure to rename this folder to avoid confusion.

Deleting bookmarks from the Bookmarks Toolbar

The Bookmarks Toolbar merely displays the contents of the Bookmarks Toolbar Folder by default. Thus, to remove a bookmark from the toolbar, you simply remove it from the folder as you would any other bookmark (see "Deleting bookmarks and folders," later in this chapter). You can also right-click any bookmark on the toolbar and choose Delete.

Be aware that deleting a bookmark from the Bookmarks Toolbar also removes the bookmark from the Bookmarks Toolbar Folder (or from whichever folder you've assigned to the toolbar).

The Bookmarks menu

The Bookmarks menu (shown in Figure 5-5) is designed for people who use a large number of bookmarks and access them relatively infrequently.

Accessing a bookmark is as simple as opening the Bookmarks menu, finding the bookmark in the list or in a folder, and clicking it. Of course, the more bookmarks you have, the longer the list gets — and the longer it takes to find the one you're looking for. If you run into this problem, organize your bookmarks into folders (see "Organizing Your Bookmarks," later in this chapter), or use the Bookmarks Sidebar, which scrolls more easily and offers a search feature.

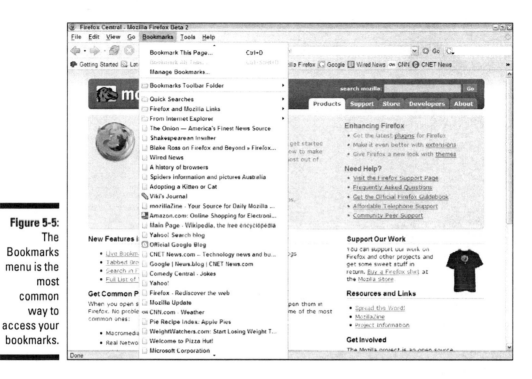

Figure 5-5:
The
Bookmarks
menu is the
most
common
way to
access your
bookmarks.

By default, the menu contains two folders: *Quick Searches* and *Firefox and Mozilla Links.* The first is used in conjunction with the Search Keywords feature, which I discuss in Chapter 4 (see the section on searching from the Location Bar) and should be ignored. The Firefox and Mozilla Links folder contains a number of bookmarks to Firefox resources that will prove useful as you get to know the browser's ins and outs.

The Bookmarks Sidebar

The Bookmarks Sidebar (shown in Figure 5-6) is designed for those people who have a large amount of bookmarks and need to access or organize them frequently. The Sidebar is a thin panel that appears on the left hand side of the screen, and it will stay open as you navigate from site to site. It contains a search bar so you can find the bookmark you want more quickly.

You can also drag links into the Bookmarks Sidebar to bookmark them.

You can open the Sidebar in three ways:

- Choose View⇨Sidebar⇨Bookmarks.
- Press Ctrl+B (Windows) or ⌘+B (Mac).
- Click the Bookmarks button on your toolbar. See Chapter 18 for instructions on how to add the Bookmarks button to your toolbar as well as other information about customizing toolbars.

Figure 5-6:
The
Bookmarks
Sidebar
provides
quick
access to all
your
bookmarks.

> **Bookmarks**
> Search:
> ⊞ ☐ Bookmarks Toolbar Folder
>
> ⊞ ☐ Quick Searches
> ⊞ ☐ Firefox and Mozilla Links
> ⊞ ☐ From Internet Explorer
> ☐ The Onion — America's ...
> ☐ Shakespearean Insulter
> ☐ Blake Ross on Firefox an...
> ☐ Wired News
> ☐ A history of browsers
> ☐ Spiders information and p...
> ☐ Adopting a Kitten or Cat
> ✎ Viki's Journal
> ☐ mozillaZine - Your Sourc...
> ☐ Amazon.com: Online Sh...
> ☐ Main Page - Wikipedia, t...
> ☐ Yahoo! Search blog
> ☐ Official Google Blog
> ☐ CNET News.com -- Tech...
> ☐ Google | News.blog | CN...
> ☐ Comedy Central - Jokes
> ☐ Yahoo!
> ☐ Firefox - Rediscover the ...
> ☐ Mozilla Update
> ☐ CNN.com - Weather
> ☐ Pie Recipe Index: Apple ...
> ☐ WeightWatchers.com: St...
> ☐ Welcome to Pizza Hut!
> ☐ Microsoft Corporation
> ☐ Firefox Central

To access a bookmark from the sidebar, simply locate and click it. If you can't find the bookmark you're looking for, try the simple Search function at the top of the sidebar. Enter a word or phrase that you believe to appear in the name of the bookmark. As soon as you stop typing, even if you stop typing in the middle of a word, Firefox searches your collection and displays any matches, as shown in Figure 5-7.

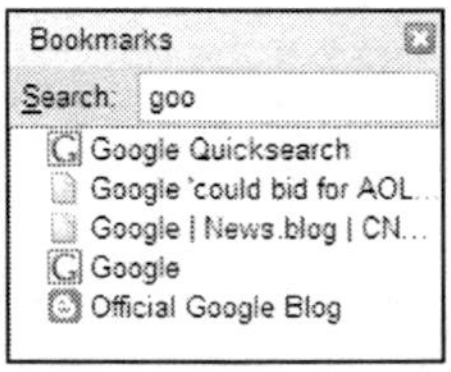

Figure 5-7:
You can
search your
bookmarks
from the
Bookmarks
Sidebar.

> **Bookmarks**
> Search: goo
> ☐ Google Quicksearch
> ☐ Google 'could bid for AOL...
> ☐ Google | News.blog | CN...
> ☐ Google
> ☐ Official Google Blog

You can also use the Bookmarks Sidebar for rudimentary bookmark organizing. For example, you can drag and drop items to new locations or right-click them to access their properties or delete them. For more information about bookmarks organization, see "Organizing Your Bookmarks," later in this chapter.

Opening multiple bookmarks at once

Unlike most other Web browsers, Firefox allows you to open all the bookmarks in a folder at once. Each bookmark loads in a separate tab (see Chapter 7 for more information about tabs). This feature is most useful for switching between two activities quickly.

For example, suppose you begin the day by reading the news on five different news Web sites. You could quickly access all five sites by opening your news folder in the Bookmarks menu and choosing Open in Tabs. Then, when it comes time to begin work, you could instantly access all your work-related resources by opening your work folder and choosing Open in Tabs. This option always appears at the bottom of the folder's bookmark list, as shown in Figure 5-8. If you use the Bookmarks Sidebar or the Bookmarks Toolbar rather than the menu, you can still access this feature by right-clicking the folder and choosing Open in Tabs.

Figure 5-8:
Open
multiple
bookmarks
with the
Open in
Tabs
command.

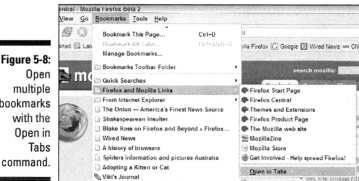

When you open multiple bookmarks at once in Firefox, Firefox loads the bookmarks in any tabs you already have open, thus replacing the Web sites you're viewing. If you open more bookmarks than you have tabs open, Firefox opens additional tabs.

Opening bookmarks with keywords

If you prefer using the keyboard over the mouse, be sure to assign brief keywords to your bookmarks and use those keywords to access the bookmarks from the Location Bar. For example, if you bookmark Blockbuster's Web site, you might assign the bookmark a keyword of bb. You could then type **bb** into the Location Bar at any time to go instantly to www.blockbuster.com.

Using multiple bookmarks as your home pages

Instead of using a single home page, you can have several home pages by setting Firefox to open multiple bookmarks whenever you start Firefox. The condition is that they all have to be in the same folder. Here's how you set up this option:

1. **Choose Tools⇨Options.**

   The Options window appears.

2. **Click the General icon at the top of the window if it isn't already selected.**

3. **Under Home Page, click the Use Bookmark button.**

   The Set Home Page window appears.

4. **Select the folder that contains the bookmarks you want Firefox to load on startup.**

5. **Click OK to close the Set Home Page window.**

6. **Click OK to close the Options window.**

The next time you open a Firefox window or click the Home button on the main Firefox toolbar, the bookmarks in the selected folder open in tabs.

Here's how you assign a keyword to a bookmark:

1. **Right-click the bookmark to which you want to assign a keyword and choose Properties.**

   The bookmark's Properties window appears.

   You can do this from the Bookmarks Sidebar, the Bookmarks Manager, or the Bookmarks Toolbar. If you're using Windows, you can also right-click the bookmark in the Bookmarks menu.

2. **In the Keyword text box, enter the keyword you want to use (for example, bb).**

3. **Click OK to close the Properties window.**

4. **Try out your new keyword by typing it into the Firefox Location Bar and then press Enter.**

You can't specify a keyword for a bookmark from the Add Bookmark window. You must open the bookmark's properties after adding it.

Opening bookmarks in a sidebar

Have you ever come across a Web site that feels too lightweight to be taking up so much room on your screen? If you've bookmarked a sports site, should you really need to leave the site you're currently viewing and load an entire

Web page just to see the latest score of the basketball game? In Firefox, you can choose to view any bookmark in a sidebar that appears next to — rather than in place of — whichever site you're viewing, as shown in Figure 5-9.

To open a bookmark in a sidebar, follow these steps:

1. **Right-click the bookmark you want to open in a sidebar and choose Properties.**

   The bookmark's Properties window appears.

   You can do this from the Bookmarks Sidebar, the Bookmarks Manager, or the Bookmarks Toolbar. If you're using Windows, you can also right-click the bookmark in the Bookmarks menu.

2. **Select the Load This Bookmark in the Sidebar check box.**

3. **Click OK to close the Properties window.**

   The *next* time you open the bookmark, it loads in the sidebar, as shown in Figure 5-9 (using Amazon Search as an example).

This feature is especially useful if you put the bookmark on your Bookmarks Toolbar, as I describe earlier in this chapter, in the section "The Bookmarks Toolbar." You can close the sidebar by clicking the X in the top-right corner (of the sidebar, not of the Firefox window).

Figure 5-9:
Firefox allows you to display any Web site in a sidebar so you don't have to leave the Web site you're viewing.

The slimmer, trimmer trend

When you try opening sites in the sidebar, you might notice that as convenient as it is, many Web sites simply don't fit in such a small box. Firefox displays vertical and/or horizontal scrollbars to help alleviate this problem. However, this feature works best when you find Web sites that are designed to fit in small spaces. Many Web sites link to versions of their content that are specially designed for cell phones; these pages tend to work very well in the Firefox sidebar as well. Better still, many companies provide Web sites specifically tailored to fit inside browser sidebars and offer easy installation of these pages.

For example, CNN offers a slender list of the latest headlines. Opera Browser's Web site (`http://my.opera.com/community/customize/panel`) includes a directory of sidebars. When you select a sidebar to install from the directory, Firefox automatically opens the Add Bookmark window. The bookmark that is added is just like any other bookmark, except it is configured to load in the sidebar by default.

Opening bookmarks in new windows or tabs

When you choose to open a bookmark, Firefox loads it in place of whichever Web site you're currently viewing. If you'd rather open a bookmark *in addition to* your current page, you can choose to open the bookmark in a new tab or a new window. This is as easy as right-clicking the bookmark and choosing Open in New Tab or Open in New Window from the menu that appears. You can right click on a bookmark in the Bookmarks Manager, the Bookmarks Toolbar or the Bookmarks Sidebar. If you're using Windows, you can also right-click a bookmark directly from the Bookmarks menu.

If your mouse has a middle button — or a scroll wheel that doubles as a button — simply middle-click any bookmark to open it in a new tab.

Organizing Your Bookmarks

Anyone who uses a filing cabinet knows the grim reality of organization: It doesn't last long. Sure, that first week you've got your stack of brand new manila folders and pens and you're eager to file. But by the second week, you're starting to stick papers in the wrong folders just to get them out of your sight. By the time a month has passed, the stack of junk on your desk is now a stack of junk in an oversized Miscellaneous folder.

As I discuss earlier, in the "Creating a Bookmark" section, Firefox makes it easy to organize your bookmarks by helping you file them into folders from the start. However, it also offers a sophisticated manager so you can go back and organize your collection at any time. To access this tool, open the Bookmarks menu and choose Manage Bookmarks.

The Bookmarks Manager, shown in Figure 5-10, is divided into two panes. The left pane contains a list of folders, and the right pane contains the items in whichever folder you've selected. By default, the Bookmarks folder — which contains all your bookmarks and folders — is selected.

The Bookmarks Manager offers one-click access to all the organizational capabilities you need. Note that you can perform many of the actions that I discuss in the following sections, such as deletion and movement, on multiple bookmarks and folders at one time. For example, you can select multiple bookmarks and then drag them all into a folder. To select multiple items, Ctrl+click (Windows) or ⌘+click (Mac) them.

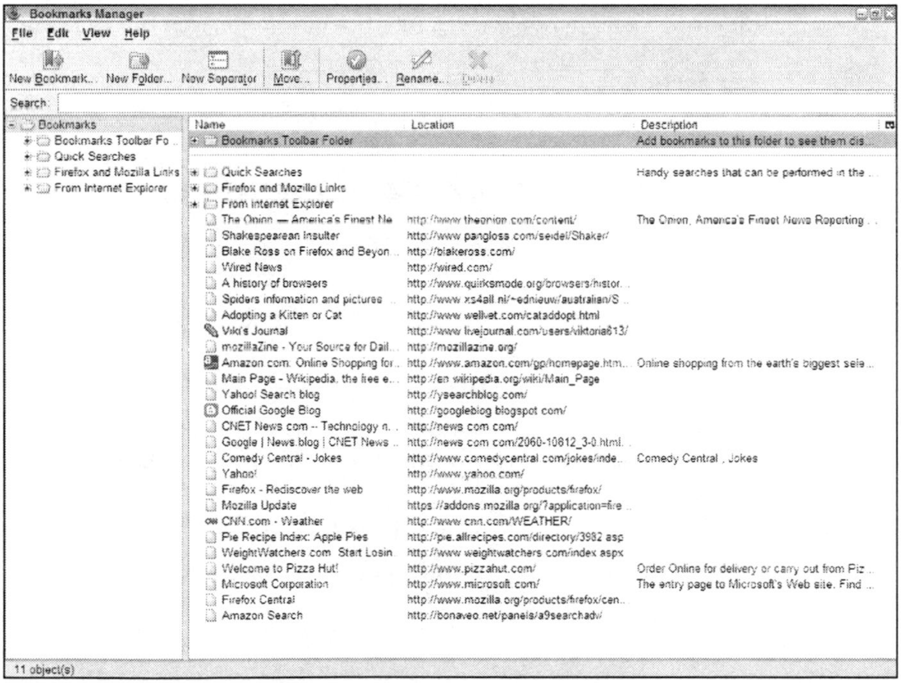

Figure 5-10: The Bookmarks Manager is a simple interface for managing your bookmarks.

Creating bookmark folders

Firefox helps you file a bookmark into a folder at the moment you create the bookmark. This is the best way to stay organized, but you might not see the need for a folder until you've accumulated a group of related bookmarks over time. Therefore, Firefox lets you create bookmark folders at any time, and then you can move existing bookmarks into them.

To create a bookmarks folder, follow these steps:

1. **Choose Bookmarks⇨Manage Bookmarks to open the Bookmarks Manager.**

2. **Click the New Folder button on the toolbar at the top of the window.**

   The New Folder window appears.

3. **Enter a name for the new folder.**

   You can also enter a description that will be displayed alongside the folder in the Bookmarks Manager, as I discuss in "Describing bookmarks and folders," later in this chapter.

4. **Click OK to create the new folder.**

To move existing bookmarks into the new folder, simply drag and drop them onto the new folder, as I discuss in "Moving bookmarks and folders," later in this section.

Renaming bookmarks and folders

To rename a bookmark or folder, follow these steps:

1. **Choose Bookmarks⇨Manage Bookmarks to open the Bookmarks Manager.**

2. **Select the bookmark or folder you want to rename.**

3. **Click the Rename button on the toolbar at the top of the window. Alternatively, you can right-click the bookmark and choose Properties.**

   The bookmark's Properties window appears.

4. **Type the new name you want to use in the Name text box.**

5. **Click OK.**

Deleting bookmarks and folders

When it comes time to clean house, Firefox makes it easy to delete those old and unused bookmarks. Follow these steps:

1. **Choose Bookmarks⇨Manage Bookmarks to open the Bookmarks Manager.**

2. **Select the bookmark(s) or folder(s) you want to delete.**

   Hold down the Ctrl key (Windows) or the ⌘ key (Mac) to select multiple bookmarks.

3. **Click the Delete button on the toolbar at the top of the window or press Delete on your keyboard.**

   If the item you have selected is a folder, all the bookmarks it contains are deleted.

Firefox won't ask you to confirm your decision to delete. However, if you change your mind after doing so, you can undo the action by choosing Edit⇨Undo. After you shut down Firefox, you cannot undo your changes.

The Quick Searches folder that comes with Firefox holds your Search Keywords. See the section in Chapter 4 about searching from the Location Bar for information about quick searches using Search Keywords.

Moving bookmarks and folders

Moving bookmarks in the Bookmarks Manager is easy. Simply drag the bookmarks you want to move to the desired location. You can select multiple bookmarks by holding down the Ctrl key (Windows) or the ⌘ key (Mac) as you click them.

You can also use the standard cut-and-paste method of movement. To cut bookmarks or folders, simply select them and choose Edit⇨Cut or press Ctrl+X (Windows) or ⌘+X (Mac). To paste them elsewhere, select the new destination and choose Edit⇨Paste, or press Ctrl+V (Windows) or ⌘+V (Mac).

Sorting bookmarks

By default, Firefox displays your bookmarks in the order you added them. Your most recently added bookmarks are at the bottom of the list, and the bookmarks you created longest ago are at the top. However, you can instruct

Firefox to sort your bookmarks alphabetically at any time. Simply right-click a bookmark in the Bookmarks Toolbar, Sidebar, or (in Windows) menu and choose Sort by Name. It doesn't matter which one you right-click because Firefox maintains a single bookmarks list across all three interfaces, and thus your bookmarks will be sorted alphabetically in all of them.

Note that if you sort by right-clicking one of the bookmarks in the main bookmarks list, Firefox sorts only the main bookmarks list. It does not sort bookmarks within folders; those will continue to be in chronological order. To sort the bookmarks within a particular folder, right-click the folder and choose Sort by Name.

This kind of sorting is useful if it's easier for you to find and access bookmarks that are sorted alphabetically. However, if you want to sort your bookmarks temporarily for the purpose of managing and organizing them more easily, the Bookmarks Manager offers a variety of sorting options, such as sorting by last visited date or by location. These options are available from the View menu in the Bookmarks Manager and do *not* affect the Bookmarks Toolbar, Sidebar, or menu.

Describing bookmarks and folders

You can give bookmarks and folders brief descriptions that can serve as reminders to you later on about why you bookmarked a particular page or what a particular folder contains. Descriptions appear in the Description column of the Bookmarks Manager, and you can also view them in the Properties window (right-click the bookmark or folder and choose Properties).

Follow these steps to enter a description:

1. **Choose Bookmarks⇨Manage Bookmarks to open the Bookmarks Manager.**
2. **Select the bookmark or folder you want to describe.**
3. **Right-click the bookmark or folder and choose Properties, or click Properties in the toolbar at the top of the window.**

   The bookmark's Properties window appears.
4. **Enter the description in the Description text box.**
5. **Click OK.**

Creating separators

Separators are horizontal lines used to divide related bookmarks and folders into groups. For example, if you have a group of sports-related bookmarks and a group of recipe bookmarks, you could use separators to differentiate the groups visually in the Bookmarks menu, Sidebar, and Toolbar.

Here's how you make separators:

1. **Choose Bookmarks⇨Manage Bookmarks.**
2. **Select the bookmark or folder above which you want to create a separator.**
3. **Click the Separator button on the toolbar at the top of the window.**

 You can give separators names that will appear in the Bookmarks Manager and in the Bookmarks Sidebar (although they don't appear in the Bookmarks menu). Simply select the separator, click the Rename button on the toolbar at the top of the window, then enter the name and click OK.

Importing and Exporting Bookmarks

Can you imagine if you had to start all over again each time you bought a new filing cabinet? You'd have to start filing your hair away because you'd be tearing it out by the handful. Luckily, Firefox provides an easy Import Wizard that migrates your bookmarks from your former browser. You can import your bookmarks when you first launch Firefox or at any time thereafter. Firefox stores the bookmarks in one of two locations depending on when you import them, as I discuss in the following sections.

Firefox also allows you to export your bookmarks to a file on your computer for use in other browsers or for your own personal backup.

Importing on your first launch

When you launch Firefox for the first time, the Import Wizard opens. If you choose to import bookmarks at this point, Firefox imports the bookmarks directly into your bookmarks list. In other words, when you open your Bookmarks menu, you see all your existing bookmarks just as they were in your previous browser.

Chapter 3 provides instructions for importing bookmarks and other data the first time you start Firefox.

Importing after the initial launch

Importing favorites works fine if you're launching Firefox for the first time, but what happens if you have used it for a couple of months — and built up a new bookmarks collection — before deciding to import? In this case, rather than mixing your old bookmarks with your new collection, Firefox places all your old bookmarks in a new folder named From *Previous Browser*. For example, if you're importing Internet Explorer Favorites, the folder is called From Internet Explorer. The imported bookmarks are still organized into the same folders (if any) as they were in your previous browser, but they will be contained entirely within this new folder.

1. **Choose Bookmarks⇨Manage Bookmarks.**

2. **In the Bookmarks Manager, choose File⇨Import.**

3. **To import from another browser, select the name of the browser.**

   Firefox supports importing bookmarks from Internet Explorer, Apple Safari, Opera, Netscape 4.0 through 8.0, Camino, iCab, earlier versions of Firefox, and OmniWeb. Only the browsers that are installed on your computer are displayed.

4. **Click Next to import the bookmarks and then click Finish to close the wizard.**

Firefox allows you to import bookmarks from a file located on your computer. The file must be in the Firefox bookmarks/HTML format. Choose From File, in the Import Wizard, click Next, and then locate the file that contains the bookmarks you want to import.

Exporting bookmarks

If you need to get bookmarks *out* of Firefox instead of into it, Firefox can help you with that, too. Firefox can export your bookmarks — that is, store them in standard HTML format on your computer — for backup purposes or so that other browsers are able to retrieve them. This feature is generally useful only for advanced users. Here's how:

1. **Choose Bookmarks⇨Manage Bookmarks.**

2. **In the Bookmarks Manager, choose File⇨Export.**

3. **Navigate to the directory in which you would like to store the exported bookmarks and enter the name of the file to create, and then press Enter.**

   By default, Firefox uses the filename `bookmarks.html`.

Now that your bookmarks exist in an HTML file on your computer, you can import them into any browser that understands the HTML bookmarks format. If you're using the file as a backup, you can import your bookmarks back into Firefox later by using the Import Wizard, as I discuss at the end of the preceding section.

Experimenting with social bookmarks

A new phenomenon is taking the Internet world by storm — the concept of *social bookmarking*. The pioneers behind social bookmarking argue that if people will just share their bookmarks with the world, everyone can enjoy a bookmarking experience that is exponentially better than the one that exists now. Why is that?

By aggregating millions of individual bookmark collections, computer algorithms can begin to identify trends that would otherwise be difficult to chart. For example, computers could notice that a certain Web site has been bookmarked by 500,000 people. Because people tend to bookmark pages that they find interesting or informative, you could reasonable conclude that this Web site is extremely interesting or informative. You can publish a list of such Web sites, but more importantly, you can incorporate this knowledge into search engines and use it to bump these Web sites higher in the rankings. Think of it as the world's bookmarks.

In many cases, social bookmarking algorithms confirm what is already known from Web sites statistics about the top Internet destinations. Sites like CNN and Yahoo! rule the Web (no surprises there). Where social bookmarking really starts to get interesting is when it exposes diamonds in the rough — valuable Web sites that are being passed around fervently on small word-of-mouth networks but aren't yet known to the world at large. Social bookmarking can find local stars — Web sites that are circulating among certain communities — and turn them into worldwide hits overnight.

One of the earliest and most popular social bookmarking sites to arise was `http://del.icio.us` (think *delicious*). Using Delicious is about as easy as using the built-in Firefox bookmarking feature. The difference is that instead of accessing your bookmarks through Firefox, you access your bookmarks through your personal page on the Delicious Web site. By using Delicious, you contribute to the social body of knowledge. Other people can see what you found interesting on the Web, and better yet, you can find new and interesting Web sites you've never seen before. Delicious has clear, step-by-step instructions for getting started.

One additional benefit of social bookmarking is that you can also access your bookmarks from any computer around the world. The downside, of course, is that your bookmarks are publicly viewable by anyone. But although some people consider this a privacy violation, others find it a valuable way to leverage the expertise of others. You probably know of people who are experts in their field, whether it's computers, knitting, or biology. When you're looking for information about their subjects of expertise, wouldn't it be great if you could "get inside their minds" and know what *they* find important?

Chapter 6

Returning to Sites You've Visited

*H*ave you ever had one of those dreams that hops from one scene to another without any logic to fill the gaps? You know the type. One minute you're eating breakfast, the next minute you're a flying coconut, the next minute *you're* breakfast and the flying coconut is eating you.

Sometimes surfing the Web feels the same way. One minute you're reading ESPN, and the next minute you're shopping for pants. The Internet is a random patchwork of information loosely joined by hyperlinks. If you're not careful, it's easy to get lost.

But Firefox is there for you. Its powerful yet simple history controls track your every move and allow you to swiftly return to any spot in your journey. You decide how much history Firefox remembers and when to empty out the history.

In real life, you have two kinds of memory: short-term and long-term. (Or perhaps you don't — where are those keys?) Firefox's memory works the same way. Your short-term history on the Web consists of the last ten Web sites you visited in the current browsing session, and your long-term history consists of all the sites you visited in the past nine days — or however many days you choose.

And, yes, those jeans look great on you — now get back to the sports page!

Navigating Short-Term History

If you've used the Web for any amount of time, you're already intimately familiar with navigating short-term history in Firefox. You know how to go back to the page you looked at previously (click the Back button), and you know how to go forward again (click the Forward button). Through deductive reasoning, you've probably also figured out how to go back and forward more than one page: Just click each respective button repeatedly until you get to the page you want.

If you prefer the keyboard, you can press Alt+← and Alt+→ in Windows (or ⌘+[and ⌘+] on a Mac) to go backwards and forwards, respectively.

But Firefox exists to rid your life of every last extraneous click, especially with something as common as going back and forth. Seconds here and there quickly add up to hours every month. Firefox thus offers two additional ways to jump immediately back to a page you visited recently. I explain each way in the following sections.

Going back and forth with the Back and Forward menus

The first method of navigating short-term history is to use the menus attached to the Back and Forward buttons:

1. **Right-click the Back or Forward button, depending on the direction in which you want to navigate.**

   Rather than right-clicking, you can instead click the arrows next to the Back and Forward buttons.

   The button must be lit up (not grayed out) for you to use it. Figure 6-1 illustrates the difference between a lit up button and a grayed out button. After clicking, a menu appears, and it contains up to the last ten Web sites you visited in the current browser window (see Figure 6-2). Note, however, that after you go back ten pages, you can then go back another ten. In other words, the menu displays only the last ten Web sites at a time so it's not overwhelming, but Firefox stores dozens of pages in your short-term history.

   If you're using tabbed browsing (see Chapter 7), the menu contains only those Web sites you visited in the current tab. In other words, short-term history is tied to individual tabs if you're using them; otherwise, it is tied to individual windows.

2. **Choose the Web site you want to revisit from the history menu.**

Navigating history more quickly with the Go menu

The second method of navigating short-term history is to use the Go menu at the top of every Firefox window. Like the Back and Forward menus, the Go menu offers quick access to the last ten Web sites you visited. But unlike the Back and Forward menus, the Go menu isn't tied to any particular tab or window, and it remembers your recently visited sites even if you restart Firefox. In that sense, it's more like "medium-term" history.

An example should illustrate that this is less confusing than it sounds. Open a new Firefox window and navigate to CNN.com, then to ESPN.com, and then to Google.com. Right-clicking the Back button offers quick access back to ESPN.com.

Now open a new Firefox window. You can see that the Back button is no longer lit up; that's because you haven't visited any Web sites *in this particular window* yet, so you have no Web sites to go back to. Even so, when you open the Go menu in this new window, you see CNN, ESPN, and Google near the top of the Go menu.

Unlike the Back and Forward menus, the Go menu abides by the history setting with respect to how many days' worth of history to remember. (I discuss this setting at length in "Extending, shortening, or disabling long-term history," later in this chapter.)

In other words, the Go menu is a great tool when you know you visited a Web site recently but you aren't sure if it was in this window or that window, this tab or that one, or even today or yesterday.

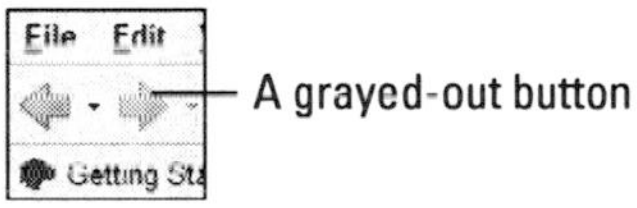

Figure 6-1:
The Back button is lit up, but the Forward button is grayed out.

File   Edit
◄ · ► · ───── A grayed-out button
● Getting St

Figure 6-2:
Right-clicking the Back button opens a menu of sites you've visited recently.

File   Edit   View   Go   Bookmarks   Tools   Help
◄ · ► · 🔄 ⊗ 🏠 │ http://www.nba.com/

Major League Baseball : The Official Site
Home | The Onion - America's Finest News Source
Funny Pet Pictures - Pictures of Cats, Dogs, Birds & Other Animals!
Google Image Search
Mozilla Firefox Start Page

Delving into Long-Term History

Many browser designers seem to think that because short-term history is the one you'll be accessing most frequently, it's okay to turn long-term history into the abandoned, dusty wing in the library basement — you can trek down there every so often and get what you need, but it won't be easy. The problem with this approach is that it's ridiculously simple to access the last 10 pages you visited but nigh impossible to get to that 11th.

Firefox puts your long-term history at your fingertips so you can quickly return to that elusive page you found last week. By default, every Web site you visited in the past nine days is stored; to change this setting, see the later section "Extending, shortening, or disabling long-term history." You access long-term history from the History Sidebar (shown in Figure 6-3), which you can open by choosing Go⇨History or by pressing Ctrl+H (Windows) or ⌘+Shift+H (Mac). The History Sidebar offers two means of finding the page you're looking for: browsing through a list or, if you remember part of the page title, searching for it.

Figure 6-3:
The History Sidebar allows you to search and access all of the Web sites you have visited in the past nine days.

Browsing long-term history

The History Sidebar uses the familiar concept of folders to organize your history and allows you to switch among five views via the View button next to the Search text box:

- **Date and Site (default):** Web sites are organized into folders, first by the date you visited them (for example, *Yesterday* or *4 days ago*) and then alphabetically by the site addresses themselves (for example, *www. cnn.com*).

- **Site:** Web sites are organized into one long, alphabetical list by site title. Folders are not used.

- **Date:** Web sites are organized into alphabetical lists by site title and grouped into folders by the date you visited them. See Figure 6-4.

- **Most Visited:** Web sites are organized into one long list ordered by how frequently you visited them, with the most frequented page appearing at the top of the list. Folders are not used.

- **Last Visited:** Web sites are organized into one long list ordered by when you last visited them, with the most recently visited page appearing at the top of the list. Folders are not used. See Figure 6-5.

Figure 6-4:
The Date view organizes Web sites into alphabetical lists by title and groups them in folders by the date you visited them.

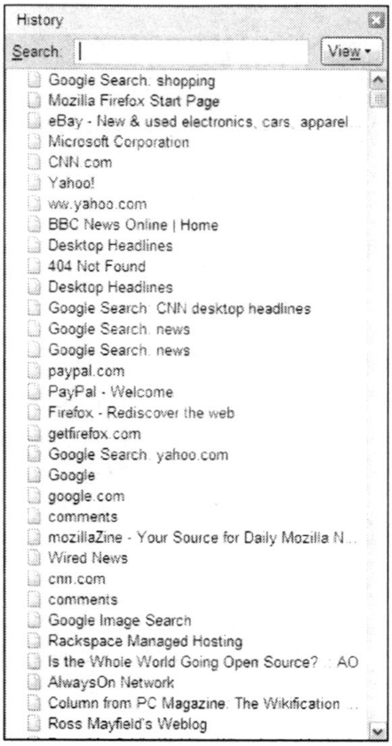

Figure 6-5:
The Last
Visited view
organizes
your Web
sites into
one long list
ordered by
when you
last visited
them.

It takes just one click to open a folder in the History Sidebar, although double-clicking will work as well. Likewise, to access a Web site from the History Sidebar, simply click it once.

Searching long-term history

If you remember a word or phrase that appears in the title of the Web site you want to revisit, you don't have to spend time browsing. Simply start typing in the Search text box at the top of the History Sidebar. As soon as you stop typing (or press Enter), Firefox searches long-term history and displays any matches — even if you are in the middle of a word, as demonstrated in Figure 6-6. (Searches are not case-sensitive, which means that *firefox* is considered equivalent to *FireFox*.)

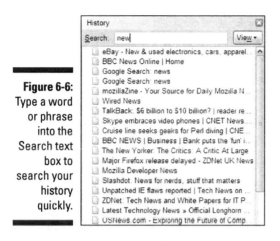

Figure 6-6:
Type a word
or phrase
into the
Search text
box to
search your
history
quickly.

Cleaning up long-term history

As convenient as it is to have computers remember things, it can also be unsettling to have your memories on display. After all, no matter how many times that darn brain forgets something important, it's still a pretty safe bet that anything you store in there is known to you and *only* you. However, anyone with physical access to your computer and (if you have one) to your computer login screen can view your long-term history. And the issues go beyond privacy: The larger your history gets, the more hard drive space Firefox requires.

To clear short-term history, you simply close the tab or window you were using to browse. Luckily, clearing long-term history is about as easy. You can delete specific records or clear the whole shebang.

Deleting individual entries from long-term history

Removing specific records from long-term history is easy:

1. **Choose Go⇨History to open the History Sidebar.**

2. **Right-click the record you want to delete and choose Delete from the contextual menu that appears. If you're using a view that organizes Web sites into folders, you can also right-click a folder and choose Delete to delete the folder and everything within it, as illustrated in Figure 6-7.**

Figure 6-7:
Right-click a
folder and
choose
Delete to
delete
everything
within the
folder.

History	
Search: [ ]	View ▾

⊟ 📂 Today
　　📄 funny-pet-pictures.com
　　　📄 Funny P   Collapse   ar...
　⊞ 📁 google.com   Delete
　⊞ 📁 mlb.com
　⊞ 📁 mlb.mlb.com
　⊞ 📁 nba.com
　⊞ 📁 stanford.facebook.com
　⊞ 📁 theonion.com
⊞ 📁 Yesterday

Deleting from history is not a reversible process; the Undo command won't
be available after you follow these steps. However, note that deleting a record
from history deletes only that particular entry. If you later visit that same
Web site, it again appears in your long-term history.

Clearing the entire long-term history

Firefox offers two ways to clear long-term history entirely. The fastest way
is to

1. **Choose Tools⇨Clear Private Data.**

2. **In the window that appears, ensure that nothing but Browsing History
   is selected (see Figure 6-8).**

   If the Browsing History check box is grayed out, long-term history is
   already empty, and you don't need to clear it again.

3. **Click the Clear Private Data Now button.**

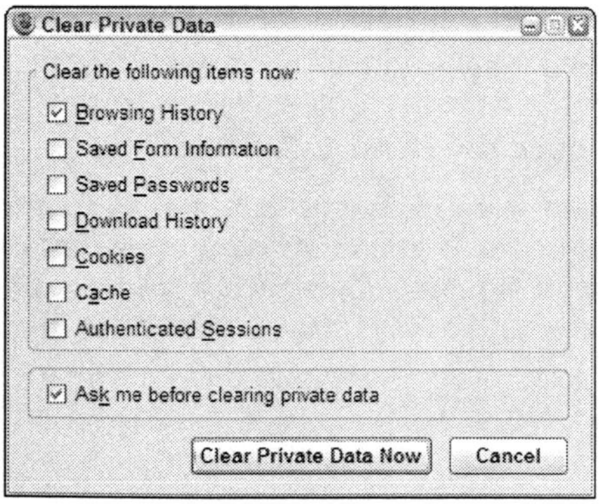

Figure 6-8:
The Clear
Private Data
window
allows you
to instantly
clear any or
all of the
info Firefox
stores about
your brows-
ing habits.

🌐 Clear Private Data	— □ ✕
Clear the following items now:	

☑ Browsing History
☐ Saved Form Information
☐ Saved Passwords
☐ Download History
☐ Cookies
☐ Cache
☐ Authenticated Sessions

☑ Ask me before clearing private data

[Clear Private Data Now]　[Cancel]

The Clear Private Data window offers quick access to clearing any types of information that Firefox remembers (see Chapter 14 for more information).

Clearing long-term history directly from the Options window

If you only ever use the Clear Private Data window to clear history, that method is the fastest way to do it. However, if you use it to clear a certain combination of information frequently — such as history, cookies, and saved form information — you might find it frustrating to have to continually change which check boxes are selected. In that case, Firefox allows you to bypass the Clear Private Data window altogether and clear browsing history directly:

1. **Choose Tools⇨Options.**

2. **Select the Privacy icon at the top of the window.**

3. **Select the History option.**

4. **Click the Clear Browsing History Now button to clear the long-term history.**

   If this button is grayed out, long-term history is already empty, and you don't need to clear it again.

   Clearing long-term history is not a reversible action; the Undo command won't be available after you complete this step. Furthermore, Firefox clears your history as soon as you click this button — without confirmation and without waiting for you to click OK in the main Options window.

5. **Click OK to close the Options window.**

Extending, shortening, or disabling long-term history

By default, Firefox remembers all the Web sites you visited in the last nine days. You can extend or shorten this length of time or turn off long-term history altogether so that Firefox no longer remembers any Web sites you visit:

1. **Choose Tools⇨Options.**

2. **Select the Privacy icon at the top of the window.**

3. **Select the History option.**

4. In the text box, enter the number of days for which Firefox should remember your history.

You can enter as many or as few days as you want. To disable long-term history entirely, enter **0**.

REMEMBER

If you disable long-term history, Firefox won't remember the Web sites you visit in the future, but any long-term history it has already accumulated will remain. See the earlier section, "Cleaning up long-term history," for instructions on clearing existing history.

5. Click OK to save your changes and close the Options window.

Is history an ancient concept?

The concept of history is one of the staples of the Internet. The very first browser ever released included Back and Forward buttons, and no browser since then has strayed too far from this iconic model. But many people are starting to do away with history altogether — how do they do this?

People first began to entertain the extinction of history with the advent of Google in the last five years. Before Google revolutionized the search industry, high-quality Web sites were rare and precious finds. If you came across one, you had to guard its location carefully — because the odds of your stumbling across it again, with billions of Web sites and poor search technology, were slim. Thus, long-term history became a critical part of the browsing experience. Paper notes with Web addresses scrawled illegibly were gradually replaced with automatic memory courtesy of the browser.

Google commoditized relevant content. You probably take it for granted today that you can enter a search term and find what you're looking for in under a second. If Google can't find anything relevant to what you're searching for, you no longer assume it's a shortcoming of the technology; instead, you might generally conclude that the answer just isn't on the Internet yet.

As a side effect of this new world, you no longer have to worry that the cream of the crop will slip away from you. Why crawl through long-term history when you could just search Google again for the same (or similar) words? Not only is searching Google often the fastest option, but Google is also much more forgiving. If you can't remember exactly what appeared in the title of the page you're looking for, you're out of luck in all Web browsers. But if you can tell Google so much as a synonym or a general description, it can hone in on what you want.

The only problem with this approach — as some of its proponents are discovering, much to their frustration — is that Google changes its search technology from time to time. In general, such changes benefit users because the changes improve the accuracy, relevance, and ordering of the search results. But when you're relying on a certain set of results, it can be quite vexing to discover that, for example, "the first term on the second page of search results" is no longer what you thought it was.

These kinds of issues make history invaluable for now. But one day, history might be history.

Chapter 7

Browsing with Tabs

. . . .

In This Chapter

▶ Getting comfortable with tabs

▶ Using tabs to set more than one home page

▶ Opening multiple bookmarks at once in tabs

. . . .

*T*abbed browsing is the feature for people tired of playing Whack-a-Mole on the Web. You know how it goes: You're halfway through a 5-hour surfing extravaganza and fast approaching 2×10^6 open Web sites, each in its own window. Suddenly, the buttons in your Windows taskbar are approaching atomic size. The Wally's Fish World button now reads "Wa . . . "; Sports Illustrated becomes "Spo . . . "; and CNN is just " . . . ". Switching back to the Web site you want becomes a guessing game. The taskbar itself is scrolling, which you didn't even know was possible!

Firefox has made that a thing of the past. This chapter shows how to take advantage of a revolutionary new way to browse the Web. It's called *tabbed browsing*, and it eliminates desktop clutter by allowing you to group all of your Web sites into a single window. Each Web site displays as a *tab* in a strip along the top of the browser's viewing area. Now you never have to close a Web site just to make room for more. Choosing between Wally's Fish World and CNN is a decision nobody should have to make.

Getting Started with Tabs

When you open multiple documents on your computer, you're probably accustomed to working with each document in a separate window. To switch between two windows, you click the button that represents the appropriate document on the Windows taskbar at the bottom of your screen. This method is similar to how things work in real life: You can lay multiple pieces of paper across your desk and focus your attention on any of them.

Most Web browsers follow this model, and Firefox can, too. But Firefox takes the perspective that Web sites are different from documents. When you open a document, you generally intend to spend a fair amount of time working on it. When you open a Web site, you might spend as little as 30 seconds reading it. And because Web sites take time to load, many people prefer to open multiple pages at once so they have more to read while other pages are loading.

Firefox offers tabbed browsing for users who maintain this kind of frantic and frenzied pace on the Web. Instead of being contained within a separate window as documents are, Web sites can be opened in tabs that appear along a tab strip along the top of the window, as shown in Figure 7-1.

Thus, instead of behaving like separate papers on your desk, each window (group of tabs) is essentially a folder containing multiple items. You can view all your Web sites in the same window or you can maintain multiple "folders" for keeping track of different types of Web sites. For example, a journalist might choose to have one window that houses all her research Web sites and another window that houses all her entertainment Web sites.

Click a tab here to access a site.

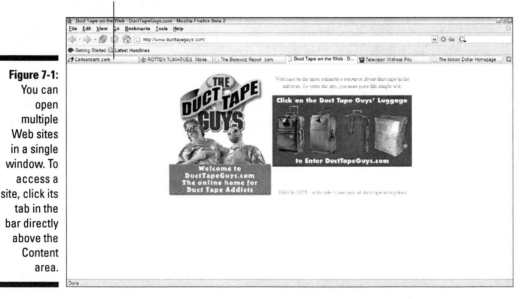

Figure 7-1:
You can open multiple Web sites in a single window. To access a site, click its tab in the bar directly above the Content area.

Some of the benefits of the tabbed approach are obvious. Your Windows taskbar is no longer cluttered with dozens of Web pages, each in its own window. Tabs open much more quickly than new windows. And unlike windows, they also open in the background, which means the tab you're currently looking at remains at the forefront. As you come across interesting links on the Web page you're reading, you can open them in new tabs for later viewing without getting distracted and losing your place.

Other benefits are more subtle and start to emerge only after you get immersed in the new rhythm of tabbed surfing. So, it's time to begin!

Opening a new site in a new tab

When you enter an address into the Location Bar at the top of the window and press Enter, the new Web page loads in place of the one you were previously looking at. If you want to keep the current Web page open and load a new Web page simultaneously, you can load the new Web page in a tab that appears next to the old Web page in the tab strip at the top of the window. Choose File⇨New Tab, and then enter the address of the page you want to visit into the Location Bar. It's that easy.

You can use the Ctrl+T shortcut in Windows (⌘+T on a Mac) to open a new, blank tab quickly. You can also open a site in a new tab by typing its address into the Location Bar and pressing Alt+Enter (Windows) or Option+Return (Mac). Or, if the tab strip is visible, you can double-click on any of its empty space (in other words, not on a tab) to open a new, blank tab. After the tab is open and selected, enter an address into the Location Bar to load a Web page in the tab.

Opening a linked site in a new tab

One of the biggest advantages of tabbed browsing is that it allows you to open linked Web pages in new tabs for later viewing without losing your spot on the Web page you're reading. For example, say you're reading a news article about allergy season that cross-references (with a link) a story about a major new medication. To read this story without tabbed browsing, you have two choices: You can click the link when you encounter it, read the new story, and then return to the original story. Or you can open the link in a new window, wait for the new window to load, and then switch back to the original window. Neither option is ideal because each steals your focus away from the original story. With tabbed browsing, you can choose to open the linked story in a background tab that never obscures the original story.

To open a linked Web page in a new tab, follow these steps:

1. **Right-click the link you want to open in a new tab.**

2. **Choose Open Link in New Tab from the menu that appears.**

   The linked page appears in a new tab at the end of the tab strip. A small image animates to the left of the page title until the page finishes loading, as shown in Figure 7-2. The current page remains the visible page, so you can continue reading without interruption.

3. **When you're ready to view the new Web site, simply click the tab.**

Opening links in new tabs can be a one-step process. If you have a middle mouse button, just middle-click the link you want to open. You can also middle-click a tab itself to close the Web site. Although most mice don't have traditional middle buttons, they typically offer a scroll wheel between the left and right buttons that doubles as a middle button when you press it. If your mouse doesn't have a middle button, you can hold Ctrl (or ⌘ on the Mac) while left-clicking a link to open it in a new tab.

The animation indicating the page is loading

Figure 7-2:
When you open a Web site in a new tab, an animation appears until the page has finished loading.

The ability to open linked Web pages in new tabs is perhaps most handy when you need to open a large number of links, such as when you're comparison shopping online or when you're navigating search results. For example, suppose you search Google for an analysis of *Hamlet*. In the prehistoric days before tabbed browsing, you'd probably click the first result and, if the resulting page wasn't what you wanted, go back and click the second result. Then you'd rinse and repeat until you found what you were looking for.

With tabbed browsing, you can open all the pages you find intriguing, each in its own tab, and keep the source page open in its original tab. Even if you open multiple pages in rapid succession, Firefox immediately gets to work on loading them simultaneously while you keep reading. By the time you're ready to look at the new tabs, they should be ready and waiting for you.

Navigating among Web sites in tabs

One important difference between windows and tabs is that each window gets its own toolbars, whereas tabs must share the same set. For example, the address in the Location Bar reflects the address of the current tab.

Navigation can be a little confusing at first. Firefox remembers the history of where you've been on the Web and allows you to go back and forth by using the Back and Forward buttons in the toolbar. The important thing here to remember is that Firefox remembers your history *for each tab* that you're using.

Consider the case where you have two tabs open, both displaying Google. If you switch to the second tab and load Yahoo!, you can click Back to return to Google. However, if you were to switch to the first tab, you would notice that you can't click Back, even though it's the same button you could click a moment ago. Firefox remembers your tracks in each tab but still allows the tabs to share the same button.

Rearranging tabs

When you open a new tab, Firefox positions the new tab to the right of all your existing tabs. However, you might often find that you want to group related tabs together to switch between them quickly. Changing a tab's position in Firefox is as simple as dragging the tab to a new location on the tab bar. As you drag the tab along the bar, a purple arrow indicates the new position of the tab should you decide to drop it there. (Figure 7-3, which appears later in this chapter, shows you the arrow.)

Closing tabs

What, closing tabs already? Has the magical journey ended? 'Fraid so. But this is why millions of people have fallen in love with tabbed browsing: It's so simple to understand, and yet it makes surfing the Web much more enjoyable.

Closing tabs is as easy as opening them, which is actually more important than it sounds — after all, tabbed browsing is about reducing clutter, and nothing leads to more clutter than your own unwillingness to do something about it. Isn't that why your garage is so messy?

Fortunately, cleaning up tabs is easier than cleaning your garage. First, click the tab that contains the Web site you want to close and then click the X button at the far-right end of the tab strip. You can also right-click the tab and choose Close Tab from the menu that appears.

If your mouse has a middle mouse button (or a scroll wheel that acts as a button), you can middle-click a tab to close it quickly.

When you close the currently selected tab, Firefox automatically selects the tab to its immediate left. If you don't like this behavior, you can install an extension called LastTab that instead selects the tab you used most recently. (See Chapter 20 for more information about installing and using extensions.)

Super Tabbing: Advanced Tips and Tricks

Okay, so you can open and close tabs in the blink of an eye. You fly through Google search results like it's your job. Don't get too cocky yet; the following sections show you how to truly exploit the power of tabbed browsing.

Tweaking tabs

Creating tabbed browsing was difficult for Firefox developers because we had to cater to two kinds of users: those who felt more comfortable with the normal way to surf and those who fell in love with tabs. We had to make some compromises and hide some tab features to ensure that we didn't over-whelm people with a radically new experience. But have no fear! If you're a tab junkie, you can tweak the behavior to your heart's content.

Navigate your way to the tabs options by choosing Tools⇨Options. Select the Tabs icon at the top of the Options window. You see the following options, which allow you to specify how Firefox handles tabs:

- ✔ **Open links from other applications in:** When other programs on your computer need to display Web sites, they launch Firefox. By default, Firefox loads these Web sites in a new tab within the Firefox window you used most recently. Here you can specify that these Web sites should instead open in a new window or in the most recent tab or window you used (thus navigating away from whatever Web site is displayed in that tab or window).

- ✔ **Force links that open new windows to open in:** Usually, when you click a link on a Web site, the linked page replaces the Web site you're viewing. However, a Web site owner can specify that a linked page must instead open in a new window. This setting allows you to override this behavior and open the link in a new tab or in the current tab or window (like a normal link).

- ✔ **Hide the tab bar when only one Web site is open:** By default, Firefox doesn't show the tab strip if you have only one Web site open because there are no tabs to switch between and it's a waste of space. Turn off this setting to keep the tab strip open permanently. You might want to do so if the flicker of the tab strip showing and hiding bothers you. Having the tab strip open is also handy because double-clicking any of its empty space (that is, anywhere but on a tab) opens a new, blank tab.

- ✔ **Select new tabs opened from links:** In the first section of this chapter, we looked at how to open linked Web sites in new tabs and noted that Firefox would open them *silently* without shifting your attention from your current Web site. This setting allows you to change this behavior so that Firefox automatically focuses on the new tab.

- ✔ **Warn when closing multiple tabs:** By default, Firefox warns you whenever you close a window that is displaying multiple Web sites in tabs. This setting lets you turn off that warning, but be careful when closing windows!

- ✔ **Extend tabbed browsing:** We've tried to deliver the best possible tabbed browsing experience out of the box, but remember that with Firefox's extensions mechanism (see Chapter 20), you don't have to settle. The official Firefox extensions site (http://addons.mozilla.org) contains an entire category of tabbed browsing extensions to customize the experience. One of my favorites is SessionSaver, which automatically remembers which tabs you have open when you close Firefox and reopens them the next time you start Firefox. Even if Firefox crashes, your tabs are restored.

There's no place like home pages

If you're like most other Web users, you probably begin your online journey at the same place every day. This is called your home page. Most browsers allow you to have only one home page, but this is like forcing you to choose just one section of the paper to read every morning. Firefox bucks the trend by allowing you to have as many different home pages as you want, each of which opens in its own tab — naturally — whenever you start the browser. However, Firefox can't fix your soggy cereal.

You can set multiple home pages in three different ways. I discuss each in the following sections.

Setting multiple home pages by entering addresses manually

If you know the addresses of the Web sites you want to set as your home pages, you can specify them manually. Follow these steps:

1. **Choose Tools⇨Options.**

2. **In the Options window, select the General icon at the top if it isn't already selected.**

3. **Enter the addresses of the Web sites you would like to use as your home pages. Separate each address with a | character.**

   For example, to use both CNN and Google as your home pages, enter **http://www.cnn.com | http://www.google.com**, as illustrated in Figure 7-3.

4. **Click OK to save your changes.**

   Your home pages now load in tabs in all future Firefox windows.

Figure 7-3:
If you have multiple home pages, each page opens in a separate tab.

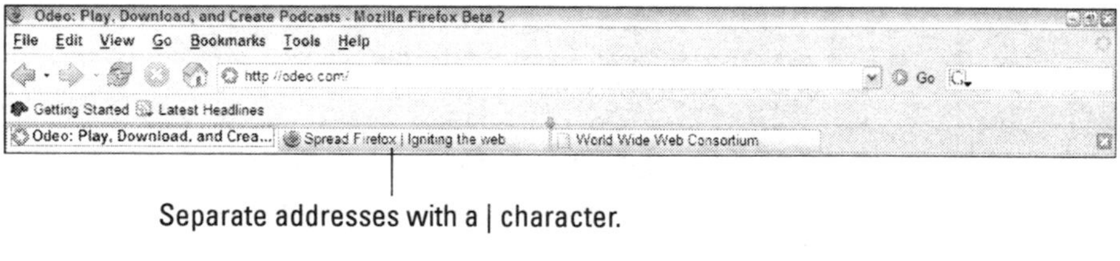

Separate addresses with a | character.

Setting the bookmarks in a folder as your home pages

Of course, Web addresses are strange beasts, and remembering them can be hard. If you've already bookmarked the pages you want to use in a bookmarks folder, you can instruct Firefox to use the folder by following these steps:

1. **Choose Tools⇨Options.**

2. **In the Options window, select the General icon at the top if it isn't already selected.**

3. **Click the Use Bookmark button.**

    A window appears containing a list of your current bookmarks.

4. **From the bookmarks list, choose the folder that contains the bookmarks you want to set as your home pages.**

    Choosing a bookmarks folder sets the bookmarks *currently* in the folder as your home pages. Adding a bookmark to or removing a bookmark from the selected folder in the future doesn't affect your home pages. If you add a bookmark to a folder and want to add it as a home page, you need to complete these steps again.

5. **Click OK to save your changes.**

As before, your home pages load in tabs in all future Firefox windows.

Setting a group of open Web sites as your home pages

You can also tell Firefox to use your current set of tabs as your home pages by following these simple steps:

1. **Open each Web site you want to set as one of your home pages in a new tab. Ensure that *only* the Web sites you want to set as your home pages are open in tabs.**

2. **Choose Tools⇨Options.**

3. **In the Options window, select the General icon at the top if it isn't already selected.**

4. **Click the Use Current Pages button.**

5. **Click OK to save your changes.**

As before, your home pages load in tabs in all future Firefox windows.

Opening multiple bookmarks simultaneously

Visiting your favorite sites should be a pleasurable experience. So why do people always look like they're having an ulcer when they have to venture into their Bookmarks menu? Perhaps it's because most people seem to have more bookmarks than there are pages on the Web. Firefox saves you time — and repetitive trips to the Bookmarks menu — by allowing you to open all bookmarks in a bookmarks folder at once, each in its own tab. Follow these steps (and don't have an ulcer):

1. **Open the Bookmarks menu.**

2. **Choose the folder that contains the bookmarks you want to open.**

   The contents of the folder appear in a new menu.

3. **Choose the Open in Tabs item at the bottom of the menu, as shown in Figure 7-4.**

   Each bookmark in the folder opens instantly in its own tab. As usual, each tab displays a spinning circle until its page finishes loading.

   Your bookmarks load in place of your open Web sites, and Firefox doesn't ask for any sort of confirmation. So if you have 12 tabs open and you open a group of 12 or more bookmarks, all your original 12 tabs are replaced with new pages. You can go to each individual tab and click Back to return to the previous page, but that's a big pain. Instead, make sure you're ready to leave your current pages *before* you open a group of bookmarks.

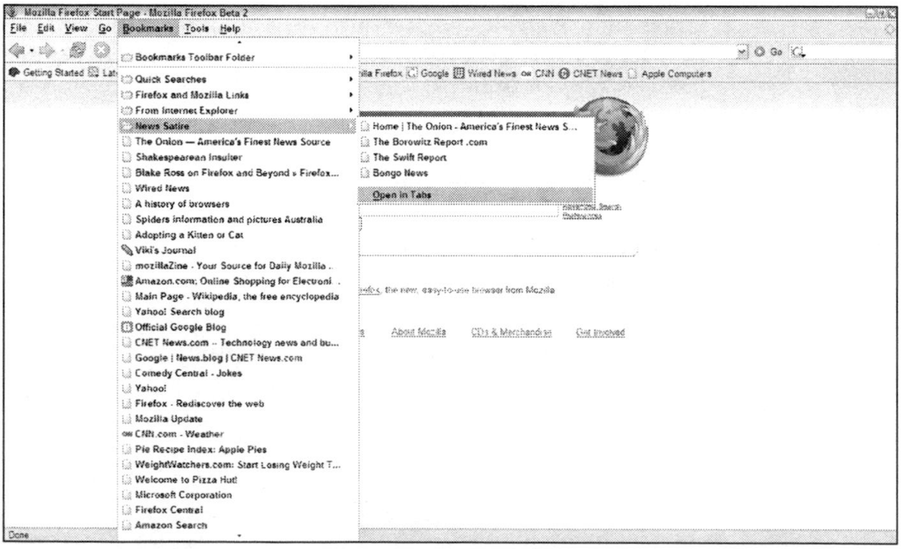

Figure 7-4: You can open all the bookmarks in a folder at once by choosing the Open in Tabs menu item at the bottom.

If your mouse has a middle button or clickable scroll wheel, you can middle-click a bookmark folder to achieve the same result.

This feature is incredibly useful if you find yourself needing to switch quickly between different tasks on the Internet. For example, say you're playing a bunch of games online, and your boss comes in. (This is hypothetical.) You can quickly open your Bookmarks menu and choose to open all your Work Web sites (that is, all the sites you have grouped in your hypothetical Work folder).

Bookmarking open tabs

Taking the preceding section's games pages versus work pages example one step further, what happens if you actually want to save your games pages for later? If you just choose the Work folder, your games pages are lost. To take care of this ultra-important case, Firefox allows you to bookmark all open tabs at once into a bookmarks folder.

1. **Load each Web site you want to bookmark into a tab.**

2. **Choose Bookmarks⇨Bookmark All Tabs.**

   The Bookmark All Tabs window appears so you can enter information about the new bookmarks folder that will contain the open tabs.

3. **Enter the name you want to use for the new folder.**

4. **(Optional) From the Create In drop-down list, you can select a folder within which the new folder will be created.**

   The Create In drop-down list displays your most recently used bookmarks folders. If you don't see the folder you're looking for, click the button with the down arrow next to it to see a list of all your folders, and then select the desired folder from the list.

   By default, the new folder is displayed directly in the bookmarks list itself.

5. **Click OK to create the new folder.**

Put that on my tab!

Tabbed browsing is a favorite new feature among the Firefox developers, so perhaps it's no surprise that support for the feature is woven throughout Firefox. For example, if your mouse has a middle button or a clickable scroll wheel, you can middle-click virtually anything that loads a Web site to instead load it in a new tab: the Back, Forward, and Home buttons as well as bookmarks and history items. You can also right-click bookmarks and history items, and then choose the Open in New Tab option from the menu that appears.

Chapter 8

Filling In Forms Quickly

In This Chapter

▶ Saving time with Firefox's form-filling feature

▶ Saving and managing passwords in Firefox

▶ Using a Master Password to protect saved passwords

*I*n your online adventures, you've probably encountered Web sites that require you to register for their services by providing personal information. Basic information, such as a username and password, are generally necessary to identify you in the Web site's network. However, Web site operators like extended registration because it allows them to learn more about you, which helps them deliver advertising more closely matched to your interests. (As charitable as that sounds, the endgame, of course, is getting you to click the advertisements.)

Registration probably isn't as rosy from your perspective. It requires you to enter the same information — such as ZIP code — again and again across multiple sites, and it forces you to remember the login information you use at each Web site. Repetitive tasks and long-term memory — isn't that what computers were supposed to *help* you with?

Firefox comes to the rescue with two handy features:

▶ **Automatic form filling:** Enter a piece of information once, and Firefox helps you fill it in again in the future.

▶ **Automatic login filling:** This feature remembers your username/password combinations at Web sites that require you to log in.

I give you the details about both of these features in this chapter.

Saving Your Sanity with Saved Forms

By default, Firefox automatically saves information you enter into online forms, such as search phrases, addresses, and ZIP codes. When you begin typing the same information into another form, Firefox automatically suggests your previous entries in a list below the form, as shown in Figure 8-1. To see the complete list of suggestions without beginning to type, double-click within the empty form field or press the down-arrow key. If no suggestions are available, either you haven't entered the information previously, or Firefox can't understand what the field is asking for (as I describe a little later). To select a suggestion, click it or navigate to it with the down-arrow key and press Enter.

Firefox compares apples to apples when it makes form suggestions. For example, if your address starts with 3 and your telephone number starts with 3, Firefox won't suggest your address when you begin typing your telephone number. In general, this feature is convenient because it cuts down on silly suggestions and helps you choose the right one faster. However, it also requires that Firefox understand exactly what a form field is asking for, so it knows which of your previous entries to suggest. This is easier said than done because Web sites refer to the same piece of information (for example, a telephone number) differently (as in "phone number," "phone," "phone #," "home number," and so on). Firefox uses advanced algorithms to understand forms and make appropriate suggestions.

Don't be surprised if Firefox can't make suggestions from time to time even if you've entered the information previously. (Even advanced algorithms can't always be perfect.)

Keep in mind that Firefox offers two distinct form-filling features that function similarly but are controlled by different settings. The first, which I call *automatic form filling,* helps you fill out general form fields such as address, ZIP code, and birthday. The second, called *automatic login filling,* helps you log in to sites by remembering usernames and passwords and associating them together. For example, if you have multiple Amazon.com accounts, this feature remembers and suggests your login names and automatically fills in the correct password for the one you choose.

Here's a brief example to illustrate automatic form filling in action: Say you're registering for an eBay account. Like many other Web sites, eBay asks for a physical address, an e-mail address, and other information when you're registering. Ordinarily, filling this out would be a lengthy process. But with automatic form filling, Firefox helps you re-enter information you've entered in the past, as illustrated in Figure 8-1.

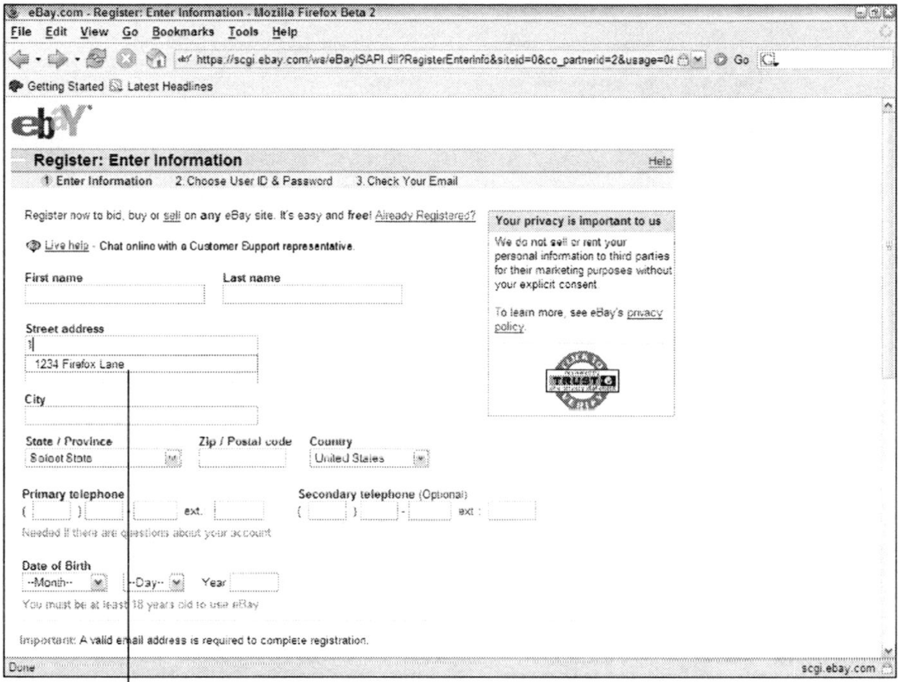

Figure 8-1:
Registering
for an eBay
account
takes just
a few
seconds
thanks to
automatic
form filling.

The address form-fill suggestion drop-down box

An online form doesn't necessarily have to resemble a typical form that asks for name, address, and phone number. Sometimes form fields are used for other purposes, such as search engines (see Figure 8-2). In general, any Web site that offers a text box and some sort of Submit button is using an online form, and Firefox saves the information you enter to make suggestions in the future.

Clearing saved form information

Real-world experience indicates that convenience often comes at the expense of privacy. Life would be much easier if everyone carried a national ID card that knows the holder's addresses, food preferences, favorite video rentals, and clothing sizes, but it would also mean that some company knows everything about everyone. Chapter 14 addresses online privacy in depth, but here I talk about it in terms of the form-filling feature.

The form-fill drop-down box

Figure 8-2:
Automatic
form filling
helps you
repeat
common
searches at
your favorite
search
engine.

Firefox saves form information directly to your computer, but other people with access to your computer can see it — sometimes inadvertently, if Firefox suggests one of your previous form entries as the person fills out a form. Thus, in Firefox, you draw the line between convenience and privacy by choosing when to clear saved form information and which information to clear. You can also disable the feature entirely, as you discover in the next section.

Firefox also remembers phrases you enter into the Search Box to the right of the Location Bar so it can suggest them when you use the Search Box in the future. The form-filling settings I discuss in the following steps also affect saved Search Box entries. For example, clearing saved form information clears the saved Search Box entries as well.

To clear all saved form information, follow these steps:

1. **Choose Tools⇨Options.**

2. **Click the Privacy icon at the top of the window that appears.**

3. **Click the Saved Forms tab.**

4. **Click the Clear Saved Form Data Now button.**

   The button becomes gray to confirm that Firefox has cleared saved form data, as shown in Figure 8-3. If the button is already gray, Firefox has not yet saved any form information to clear.

If you clear saved form information and other private information (such as browsing history) frequently, you can use Firefox's Clear Private Data feature to do so more quickly. You can also use the feature to have Firefox clear saved form information automatically each time you exit Firefox. See Chapter 14 for more information.

If you don't want to clear all of your saved form information, you can delete individual entries when Firefox suggests them. Follow these steps:

1. **Navigate to the form where Firefox makes a suggestion that you want to delete, and then select the appropriate field.**

   For example, if you don't want Firefox to suggest a particular search phrase you entered at Google in the past, navigate to Google and click the search field.

2. **Open Firefox's list of form suggestions.**

   You can do this step either by typing the beginning of the entry you want to delete or by leaving the field empty and double-clicking or pressing the down-arrow key to open the complete suggestions list.

3. **Select the suggestion you want to delete in the list using the down-arrow key.**

4. **When the appropriate suggestion is selected, press Shift+Delete to remove it from the list.**

   The entry is deleted immediately without confirmation.

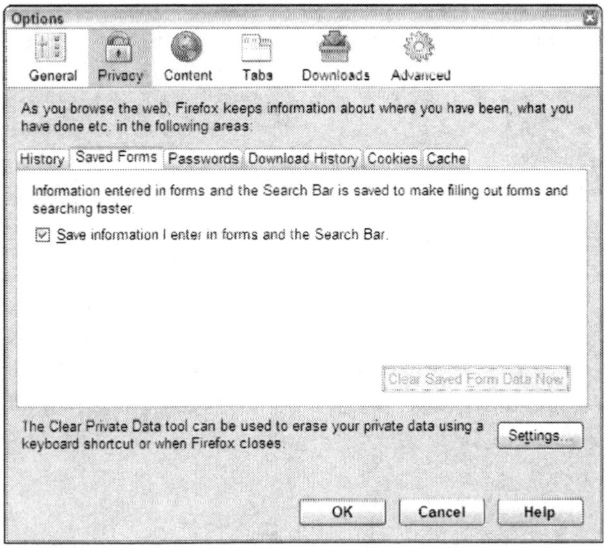

Figure 8-3:
Clearing
saved form
data.

Options dialog box showing Privacy tab with tabs: General, Privacy, Content, Tabs, Downloads, Advanced. Sub-tabs: History, Saved Forms, Passwords, Download History, Cookies, Cache. "Information entered in forms and the Search Bar is saved to make filling out forms and searching faster." Checkbox: Save information I enter in forms and the Search Bar. Clear Saved Form Data Now button. "The Clear Private Data tool can be used to erase your private data using a keyboard shortcut or when Firefox closes." Settings button. OK, Cancel, Help buttons.

Turning off automatic form filling

If you don't need the convenience of automatic form filling and want to keep form information private from others who use your computer, you can simply turn off the feature entirely:

1. **Choose Tools⇨Options.**

2. **Click the Privacy icon on the top of the window that appears.**

3. **Click the Saved Forms tab.**

4. **Select the Save Information I Enter in Forms and the Search Bar check box.**

Disabling the form-filling feature prevents Firefox from making suggestions when you fill out forms and from remembering any form information you enter after disabling the feature, but it does not clear the form information that's already saved. This means that someone could turn the feature back on and see your previous entries. To prevent this from happening, clear the form information that has already been saved by following the instructions in the earlier section, "Clearing saved form information."

Saving Login Information for Fast Access to Web Sites

Just as the automatic form-filling feature helps you fill out online forms quickly, the automatic login-filling feature helps you log in to Web sites quickly by keeping track of your usernames and their associated passwords. The first time you log in to a Web site with a username (or e-mail address) and password, Firefox asks you whether it should remember the password, as illustrated in Figure 8-4. You have three options:

- ✔ **Yes:** This option saves the password in the Password Manager. When you use the same username at the Web site in the future, Firefox automatically prefills the password. See the section "Viewing and clearing saved login info with the Password Manager," later in this chapter, for more information about viewing and removing saved passwords.

- ✔ **Never for This Site:** Click this button if you never want Firefox to save a password on any page of this Web site. This option is useful if you never want to save passwords for a particular site, perhaps because the site is especially private or sensitive (for example, your banking site). If you choose this option but later decide that you want Firefox to remember this site's login information after all, you can reverse this decision from the Password Manager. See "Viewing and clearing saved login info with the Password Manager," later in this chapter.

✔ **Not Now:** Click this button if you don't want to save the password now, but you want Firefox to continue to ask when you log in to this site in the future. This is useful if you have multiple accounts at the site and might want to save login information for some of them, but not this particular one. This might also be the case if, for example, your family shares one computer, and some members prefer not to use the automatic login filling feature.

Figure 8-4:
Firefox asks
whether
to save a
password
when you
log in to a
Web site.

If you choose to save the login information for a site, Firefox helps you fill it in quickly when you return. (This works in the same fashion as the automatic form filling feature, which I discuss at the beginning of this chapter.) As you begin typing a username into a login form field, Firefox makes suggestions based on the usernames you've used at the Web site in the past (see Figure 8-5). When you choose a username, Firefox automatically fills in the associated password.

For your convenience, the login filling feature goes one step further than general form filling. If Firefox only ever sees you use a single set of login information (username and password) at a particular site, it assumes that you want to use that information each time you visit, and automatically prefills the username and password fields for you, bypassing the suggestions list entirely. All you need to do is click the login button. As soon as you save another password on that site, Firefox stops this behavior and returns to offering a suggestions list rather than guessing which login you prefer to use.

Figure 8-5:
Multiple
saved user-
names at
Mozilla
Zine.org.

Using a Master Password

If multiple people share your computer, you might find it disconcerting that Firefox automatically prefills your passwords for them. Furthermore, these people will be able to see your passwords directly by using the View Saved Passwords option I discuss in "Viewing and clearing saved login information with the Password Manager," later in this chapter. On the other hand, you might appreciate the convenience of the feature when you're at your computer.

A Master Password provides a middle ground between security and convenience. Firefox asks you to enter the Master Password the first time you visit a login site for which Firefox has saved a password. If you enter the Master Password correctly, Firefox silently and automatically prefills all subsequent passwords until you shut down Firefox; the next time you launch Firefox, you will need to enter the Master Password again before Firefox starts regurgitating your saved passwords. Thus, with the minor inconvenience of entering the Master Password just once per browsing session, you can prevent other people with access to your computer from accessing your saved passwords.

Remember to shut down Firefox when you walk away from the monitor! If you leave Firefox open after entering the Master Password, the next person to use Firefox will have access to your saved passwords.

Bypassing Web site registration altogether

Nothing is more frustrating than a Web site that requires you to register just to see a particular article. By the time you finish registering and logging in, you probably could have read the article, transcribed it into beautiful calligraphy, and sent it to all your friends. Luckily, an enterprising group of people who were fed up with temporary registrations have set up a free service called BugMeNot.com to help you bypass them. The site is brilliant in its simplicity: Enter the address of the site offering the content you want to read, and BugMeNot spits out an anonymous login name and password you can use. The site even offers a Firefox extension you can use to log in to the sites automatically without having to sidetrack to BugMeNot. (See Chapter 20 for information about installing and using extensions.) Although some people might question the ethics of this service, you can't question its convenience. For more information, go to http://bugmenot.com.

To set the Master Password, choose Tools⬦Options, and click the Privacy icon, then click the Passwords tab. Then click the Set Master Password button, enter the password you want to use and then re-enter it (see Figure 8-6). A password quality meter indicates the relative security of the password you have chosen. Passwords that contain random mixtures of letters, numbers, and other symbols (such as $) are more secure because they're harder to guess, even with the help of automated guessing technology. See Chapter 15 for more advice about creating secure passwords.

If you decide to use a Master Password, make sure you remember it. If you ever forget your Master Password, there is no way to recover the passwords that are stored in the Password Manager.

Figure 8-6:
A Master Password gives you both automatic password entry and peace of mind.

Change Master Password

A Master Password is used to protect sensitive information like site passwords. If you create a Master Password you will be asked to enter it once per session when Firefox retrieves saved information protected by the password

Current password: (not set)

Enter new password: ••••••••••••

Re-enter password: ••••••••••••

Password quality meter

Please make sure you remember the Master Password you have set. If you forget your Master Password, you will be unable to access any of the information protected by it.

OK   Cancel

To change the Master Password later, simply click the same button, which now reads Change Master Password. Likewise, to remove the Master Password, click the Remove Master Password button. In either case, you need to first enter the current Master Password to prevent someone else with access to your computer from simply disengaging the feature and gaining access to your saved passwords.

Viewing and clearing saved login info with the Password Manager

From the Firefox Password Manager, you can view login information you've told Firefox to save and tell Firefox to forget that information and to stop recommending it whenever you visit the site. You can also view a list of Web sites at which you've told Firefox *not* to save login information and undo that setting so Firefox begins prompting you again when you log in at those sites.

Follow these instructions to use the Password Manager:

1. **Choose Tools⇨Options.**

2. **Click the Privacy icon at the top of the window that appears.**

3. **Click the Passwords tab.**

4. **Click the View Saved Passwords button.**

   The Password Manager window appears, as shown in Figure 8-7. It contains two tabs: Passwords Saved and Passwords Never Saved. The first tab shows the login names Firefox has saved and the associated Web sites. Passwords are not shown unless you choose to show them, as I discuss a little later in this section. The second tab shows the sites for which you've told Firefox not to save or offer to save login information.

Figure 8-7:
The
Password
Manager.

5. **From the Password Manager, you can do any of the following:**

   • **View the passwords Firefox has collected thus far.** If Firefox has prefilled your password for so long you've actually forgotten it, this is a good way to retrieve it!

   Make sure nobody's looking over your shoulder before you decide to show your passwords. Firefox shows every password it has saved.

   Click the Show Passwords button at the bottom of the Password Manager. If you have a Master Password, you need to enter it before you can access the stored passwords, even if you've entered it previously. This is for your security. Otherwise, Firefox asks you to confirm the decision. After you do so, your passwords are shown in a new Password column in the Password Manager's table of login information. To hide your passwords again, click the Hide Passwords button.

   • **Clear some or all of the stored login information.** If you want Firefox to forget a certain username and password combination so that it stops recommending the information when you visit the Web site, select the information in the Password Manager list and click the Remove button. To have Firefox forget all login information, click the Remove All button.

   • **Reverse an earlier decision to prevent Firefox from remembering login information on certain Web sites.** As I discuss in "Saving Login Information for Fast Access to Web Sites," earlier in this chapter, you can tell Firefox never to remember — or ask to remember — login information for certain sites. However, if you later change your mind and want Firefox to ask about saving login information at this site again, you can reverse your original decision from the Passwords Never Saved tab in the Password Manager. Simply click this tab, select the appropriate Web site in the list, and then click Remove. You can also click Remove All to undo the decision for all Web sites in the list.

   Unlike most other settings windows that you open from the Options window, the changes you make in the Password Manager take effect immediately, and are not undone even if you dismiss the Options window by clicking Cancel after closing the Password Manager.

6. **Click the Close button to close the Password Manager.**

7. **Click the OK button to close the Options window.**

Chapter 9

Blocking Popup Ads

*H*ow many times has a telemarketer called you during dinner? How many unsolicited catalogues have you received in the mail? The Internet was supposed to change all that. It promised to be a breakthrough communications medium that would be free of nuisances and readily available in the comfort of your own home.

Until Firefox came along, that promise was broken in a number of ways, particularly through a scourge that came to be known as *popup advertising*. If you've ever visited a Web site and encountered another, smaller window that contained a product advertisement obscuring the site you were trying to access, you have been a victim of popup ads. Luckily, Firefox enables you to block most unwanted popup windows and view only the ones you want or need. In fact, it does so for you right out of the box! This chapter walks you through the handful of ways in which you can customize this behavior.

Blocking Popup Windows

Firefox blocks popup ads by default, so you can start surfing the Web in peace without having to mess with configuration settings. However, there are a couple things you should know.

Firefox notifies you whenever it blocks a popup ad. The notification is designed to be obvious but far less unobtrusive and distracting than the popup ad itself. A thin bar appears right above the Web site that tried to open the popup as shown in Figure 9-1.

The notification bar

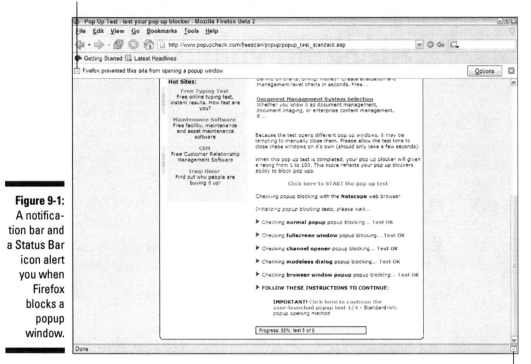

Figure 9-1:
A notifica-
tion bar and
a Status Bar
icon alert
you when
Firefox
blocks a
popup
window.

The Status Bar icon

You also see a small icon appear in the bottom-right corner of the window. This icon serves as an additional notification and offers access to the same options as the bar's Options button. It's useful if you decide to disable the bar from appearing when a popup is blocked, as I discuss later.

Some sites use popup windows for legitimate purposes — such as displaying a login form. The primary purpose of these notifications is to allow you to open popups that Firefox blocks. See the next section, "Viewing Blocked Popup Windows," for more information about how to unblock specific popup ads either temporarily or permanently, as well as how to disable popup blocking altogether.

To close the bar when it appears, click the red X button on the far right. The bar reappears the next time Firefox blocks a popup.

If you never want to see the bar again:

1. **Click the Options button — also on the far right.**

2. **Select Don't Show This Message When Popups Are Blocked in the menu that appears.**

The bar closes immediately and doesn't appear the next time a popup is blocked, but you will still be notified by the icon in the bottom-right corner of the window (refer to Figure 9-1).

If you later decide you want the bar back, click the icon and deselect the Don't Show Info Message When Popups Are Blocked option, as illustrated in Figure 9-2.

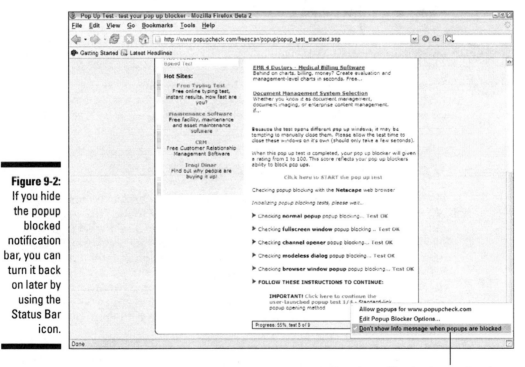

Figure 9-2:
If you hide the popup blocked notification bar, you can turn it back on later by using the Status Bar icon.

Turn the notification bar back on here.

Viewing Blocked Popup Windows

Although most popup windows are used to display advertising, some contain login forms or other legitimate contents that are necessary parts of a Web site. Because Firefox cannot tell advertisements apart from other content, it blocks all popup windows indiscriminately. However, you can open them manually, as I discuss in the following section.

So how can you tell which popups are legitimate without having to open all of them? A good rule is that if you're trying to do something that isn't working at the same time a popup is blocked (as indicated by the notification bar and icon shown earlier in Figure 9-1), you probably need to use the popup window to continue. For example, if you click a Web site's Log In button and nothing appears to happen, the Web site probably tried to open a popup login window that Firefox blocked.

 The directions in the following two sections assume that you have not disabled Firefox's popup blocking notification bar by choosing the Don't Show This Message When Popups Are Blocked option, as I describe in the preceding section. If you have disabled the bar, you can still do everything I outline here, but instead of clicking the Options button on the bar, you must click the popup icon at the bottom of the window (as shown earlier in Figure 9-2).

Opening blocked popup windows

Firefox allows you to specify that certain Web sites can *always* open popup windows. This feature comes in handy if you decide that a Web site opens only legitimate popups. In some cases, however, you might want to peek at a blocked popup window to confirm its legitimacy before making such a permanent decision. You might also want to do this if you don't intend to revisit the Web site later and you need just one-time access to the popup. To accommodate these cases, Firefox lets you open a blocked popup window without changing any long-term behavior. In other words, even after you decide to view a popup, all future popup windows from the Web site that opened it will continue to be blocked.

1. **Visit the Web site that tries to open the popup window you want to view.**

2. **When Firefox blocks the popup, click the Options button at the right end of the notification bar.**

3. **Choose the last option, which begins with the word *Show* and contains the Web address of the popup window that Firefox blocked.**

   If the Web site tried to open multiple popup windows, Firefox displays an entry in the menu for each one, as shown in Figure 9-3. Unfortunately, the only distinguishing factor between each menu item is the addresses that the Web site tried to load into each of the blocked windows. For example, in Figure 9-3, Firefox blocked three popups, and although each Show menu item appears identical, the Web addresses are slightly different. Because Web addresses are rarely helpful to mere humans, your best bet is to click each menu item to open and examine each blocked window individually.

When you choose a Show menu item, the popup window appears on your screen.

Allowing certain Web sites to open popup windows

If you frequent a Web site that uses a popup window legitimately — such as a bank that integrates one into its login process — you might find it inconvenient to have to open it manually each time by using the steps in the preceding section. Instead, you can permanently allow that particular site's popup windows to appear. Popup windows from other sites continue to be blocked.

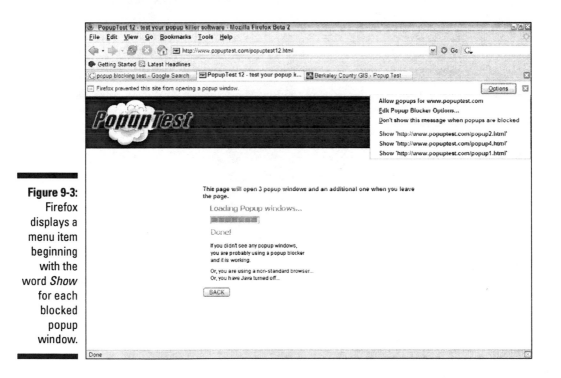

Figure 9-3:
Firefox displays a menu item beginning with the word *Show* for each blocked popup window.

Follow these steps to allow a Web site to open popup windows:

1. **Visit the Web site that tries to open the popup window you want to view.**

2. **When Firefox blocks the popup, click the Options button at the right end of the notification bar.**

3. **Choose the first option, which begins with the phrase "Allow popups for" and contains the Web address of the site you're viewing.**

Firefox doesn't show the popup it has already blocked. However, Firefox won't block any popup windows that the Web site tries to open in the future. To view the blocked window, follow the directions in the preceding section, "Opening blocked popup windows."

What do you do if you allow a site to show popups and later decide you don't want to see its popup windows after all? Firefox gives you direct access to the list of exception sites, so all you need to do is open it and remove the site:

1. **Choose Tools⇨Options.**

2. **Click the Content icon in the strip at the top of the Options window.**

3. **Click the Allowed Sites button next to the Block Popup Windows check box.**

4. **In the window that appears, select the address of the site whose popups you want to start blocking again (see Figure 9-4).**

5. **Click the Remove Site button at the bottom of the window.**

6. **Click the Close button to close the window, and then click OK to close the Options window.**

Figure 9-4:
Just say
"no" to
popups.
Select the
sites for
which you
want Firefox
to start
blocking
popups
again.

The next time you visit the site, Firefox once again blocks its popups.

Chapter 10

E-Mailing with Thunderbird

*B*rowsing without e-mail is like eating peanut butter without jelly, and I would be negligent if I failed to introduce Thunderbird, a first-class e-mail application that runs on your desktop. Thunderbird and Firefox serve two different purposes, but have plenty in common. Both are produced by the Mozilla Foundation, and both share the same goal: to make your life easier. And although they are two separate products, the experience is best when you use both because they integrate well.

Thunderbird is not an e-mail provider; it's an application you can use with your existing provider. If you use a Web-based e-mail program that you're satisfied with, it might not make sense to begin using Thunderbird. However, if you're currently using Microsoft Outlook, you should switch to Thunderbird because it offers superior search and spam-blocking capabilities. In this chapter, I walk you through the basics of Thunderbird and point you to additional resources should you decide to stick with it.

Getting Thunderbird

Like Firefox, Thunderbird is available both on CD and as a download. To order the CD, visit the Mozilla Store online (www.store.mozilla.org). To download the setup file, visit www.getthunderbird.com. The download takes just a couple of minutes on a high-speed Internet connection.

Installing Thunderbird

The installation process for Thunderbird is essentially identical to that of Firefox. If you're using Windows, a Setup Wizard just like the one from Firefox walks you through the brief installation process. If you're using a Macintosh, installation is the same simple drag-and-drop operation you use to install Firefox. (See Chapter 3 for instructions on installing Firefox from either the CD or the downloaded setup file.) Adapting the instructions to Thunderbird is easy, I promise, and if you get stuck, check out the list of online resources at the end of this chapter. The online resources offer step-by-step installation instructions.

Using the Import Wizard

Like Firefox, Thunderbird offers a simple Import Wizard to help you migrate your settings, address books, and old mail from your current mail application. Simply choose Tools⇨Import to open the Import Wizard. In the first screen of the wizard, select what kind of information to import, and in the next, select the e-mail application from which to import. You can return to the Import Wizard multiple times if you need to import more than one kind of information. I don't include extensive import instructions here because I suspect that you're taking more of a trial run with Thunderbird, and you might not be sure if you want to switch yet.

Setting Up Your E-Mail Account

The first thing you need to do after you download Thunderbird is set up your e-mail account. This is where you provide Thunderbird with a bunch of technical gibberish like your POP or IMAP server so it knows where to find your e-mail. When you first start Thunderbird, the Account Wizard opens to walk you through this process, as shown in Figure 10-1.

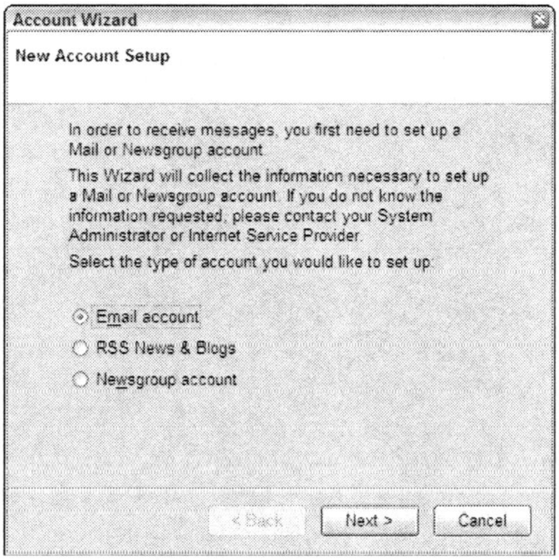

Figure 10-1:
The
Thunderbird
Account
Wizard.

To set up a Thunderbird e-mail account, follow these steps:

1. **Open Thunderbird by clicking the icon on your desktop.**

   Thunderbird opens and launches the Account Wizard.

2. **In the first screen of the wizard, select an account type and click Next.**

   Thunderbird offers three account types. The first option, Email Account, is used to receive and send e-mail. The second option is an RSS News & Blogs account, which allows you to subscribe to RSS-enabled Web sites (such as many blogs and news sites) and receive the latest articles in an e-mail–like interface. See Chapter 5 for a discussion of the RSS technology. The third option is a Newsgroup account, which allows you to participate in online forums about every topic imaginable.

3. **On the Identity screen, enter your name and e-mail address.**

   The Identity screen asks for your name and e-mail address so it can display this information in e-mails you send to others.

4. **On the Server Information screen, enter your current account server information and click Next.**

   To receive and send e-mail, Thunderbird needs to know certain technical details about your e-mail server, including account type (POP or IMAP — see the sidebar elsewhere in this chapter), incoming server (for example, mail.earthlink.net) and outgoing server (for example, smtp.earthlink.net). Your e-mail service provider typically offers this information on its Web site. Figure 10-2 shows how I set up Thunderbird to use my own e-mail provider, but of course, your settings are different.

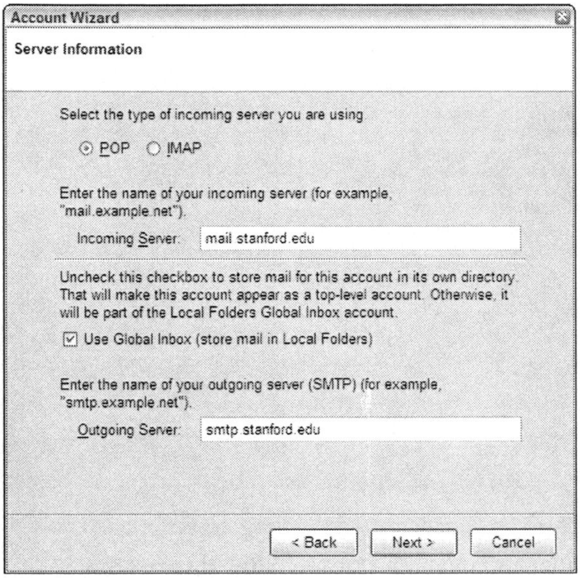

Account Wizard

Server Information

Select the type of incoming server you are using.

⊙ POP   ○ IMAP

Enter the name of your incoming server (for example, "mail.example.net").

Incoming Server: mail.stanford.edu

Uncheck this checkbox to store mail for this account in its own directory. That will make this account appear as a top-level account. Otherwise, it will be part of the Local Folders Global Inbox account.

☑ Use Global Inbox (store mail in Local Folders)

Enter the name of your outgoing server (SMTP) (for example, "smtp.example.net").

Outgoing Server: smtp.stanford.edu

< Back   Next >   Cancel

Figure 10-2:
The Server
Information
screen of
the Account
Wizard.

The Use Global Inbox check box is offered for people with multiple e-mail accounts. By default, Thunderbird combines e-mails sent to each account into a single Inbox for your convenience. If you intend to use multiple accounts and want to keep them separate, deselect this check box.

5. **On the User Names screen, enter your current account login information and click Next.**

   In addition to your account server information, Thunderbird also needs to know your e-mail account name for both incoming and outgoing mail (these are usually identical for most e-mail providers). Usually, but not always, your account username is the part of your e-mail address before the @ sign. For example, if your e-mail address is `jennysmith@earthlink.net`, your username is probably jennysmith.

6. **In the Account Name screen, enter a name for the new account and click Next.**

   People you e-mail cannot see this Account Name. It's for personal purposes, to allow you to identify this account if you create additional accounts in the future. By default, Thunderbird names the account by using your e-mail address.

7. **On the Congratulations! screen, verify the accuracy of the information you entered, decide whether to download messages now, and click Finish.**

   This screen provides an overview of the information you entered. If any information is wrong, click Back until you return to the screen where you entered the information, and then correct it. (You can modify account information in the future by choosing Tool⇨Account Settings.) Otherwise, you're finished with account creation. By default, Thunderbird downloads all the messages from your e-mail provider's server when you click Finish. If you'd rather download them later, deselect the Download Messages Now check box.

If you allow Thunderbird to download your messages here and you have a POP account, your messages will be removed from your e-mail service provider and will exist only in Thunderbird on your current computer. If you're just giving Thunderbird a trial run, this may not be the best idea. To instruct Thunderbird to leave the messages on the server, uncheck Download Messages Now and visit the Account Settings window, as I discuss in the sidebar "POP versus IMAP."

POP versus IMAP

I generally ignore the technical nitty-gritty when possible, but you should understand an important distinction between POP and IMAP accounts.

With a POP account, your e-mail remains on your e-mail provider's servers until you choose to download it to an e-mail program. After you download it, the e-mail is removed from the server and exists only on the computer and in the program to which you downloaded it. You would generally use this kind of account only if you use a single computer and e-mail program.

By contrast, with an IMAP account, your e-mail remains on your e-mail provider's servers until you manually delete it. This kind of account is a good choice if you need to access your e-mail from multiple computers because anywhere you go, your e-mail is available. As the world grows more connected and more people need this kind of access, IMAP accounts are becoming the clear favorite. If you use a Web-based mail server, you already enjoy the benefits of IMAP.

Unfortunately, not all e-mail service providers offer IMAP accounts. If that's the case with yours, you can still turn your POP account into a poor man's IMAP by instructing Thunderbird to leave your POP messages on the server even after you download them. Follow these directions:

1. **In the Thunderbird window, choose Tools⇨ Account Settings.**

   The Thunderbird Account Settings window appears.

2. **Under the name of your POP account in the left bar, click Server Settings.**

3. **Select the Leave Messages on Server check box.**

   The reason I call this a "poor man's IMAP" is because e-mail service providers don't offer POP accounts nearly as much space on their servers as they do IMAP accounts — after all, POP accounts aren't intended to be used in this way. To help alleviate this problem, use the For At Most ___ Days setting to instruct Thunderbird to remove messages from the server a certain number of days after it downloads them, and/or select the Until I Delete Or Move Them From Inbox option to have Thunderbird remove them from the server when you delete them on your computer.

4. **Click OK to save your changes.**

If you choose to download your messages now, Thunderbird prompts you for your e-mail account password as soon as you click Finish. Otherwise, it waits until the first time you try to receive new e-mail by clicking Get Mail on the toolbar. If you don't want to be prompted for the password every time you send or receive e-mail, select the Use Password Manager to Remember This Password check box, and Thunderbird remembers it for you.

After your password is accepted, Thunderbird downloads your messages from your e-mail server. If you have a POP account, there might be messages to download only if you have new mail, so don't worry if Thunderbird doesn't find any. If you have an IMAP account, Thunderbird needs to download every last message — and there might be thousands, depending on how frequently you delete mail. It might take a bit of time.

Receiving, Reading, and Searching E-Mail

Now that your e-mail account is set up, you're ready to begin receiving e-mail. You can manually check for new e-mail at any time by clicking the Get Mail button on the toolbar, and Thunderbird also checks automatically every 10 minutes. This interval is customizable.

To change how frequently Thunderbird checks for new e-mail or to disable automatic checking altogether, follow these steps:

1. **Choose Tools⇨Account Settings to open the Account Settings window.**

2. **Under the name of your account in the left bar, click Server Settings.**

3. **Do either of the following:**

   - In the text box that follows the check box beginning "Check For New Messages Every," enter the number of minutes representing how frequently Thunderbird checks for new e-mail.

   - To disable automatic checking, deselect the check box.

4. **Click OK to save your changes.**

If you have new e-mail when Thunderbird checks automatically, it plays a sound. If you are using Windows, it also shows an animated notification by your computer clock.

Reading e-mail

Take a minute and examine the main Thunderbird window. The window, shown in Figure 10-3, is divided into three panes. The Folders pane on the left contains the e-mail folders — such as Inbox, Sent (mail), and Trash — for your e-mail accounts. Your new e-mail appears in the Inbox folder.

When you select a folder in the Folders pane, the List pane in the top right shows you a list of the messages in the folder, ordered chronologically by default. Thunderbird packs a wealth of information about each message into this compact display — well beyond the traditional subject line and sender, as shown in Figure 10-4. You can quickly see the subject, sender and date, as well as whether the message has any attachments, is considered junk mail, or has been read.

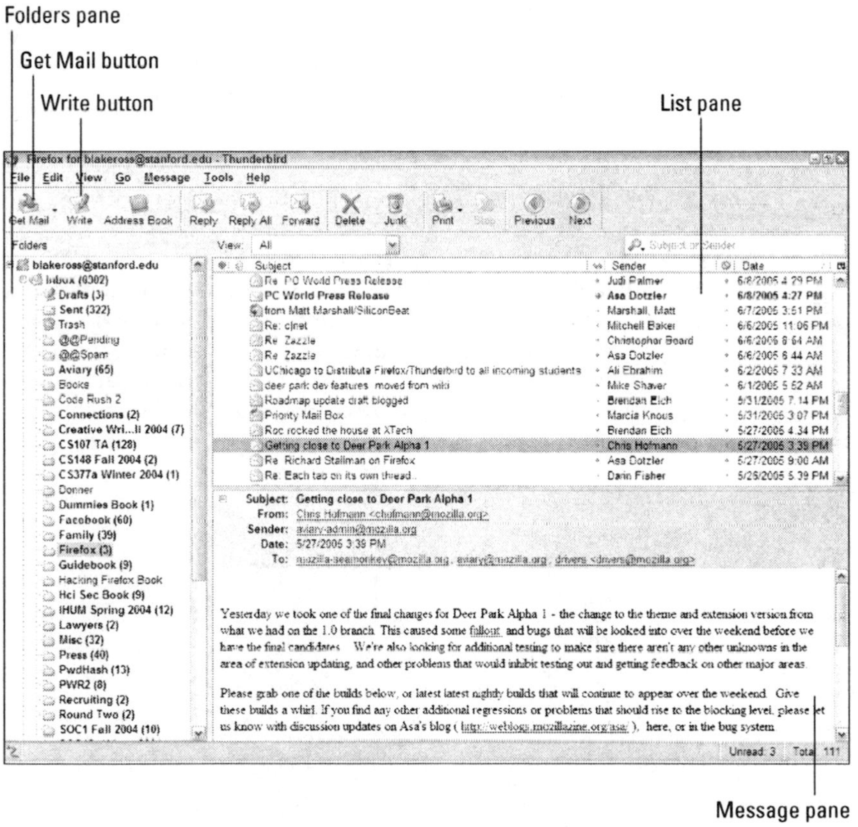

Figure 10-3:
The main
Thunderbird
window.

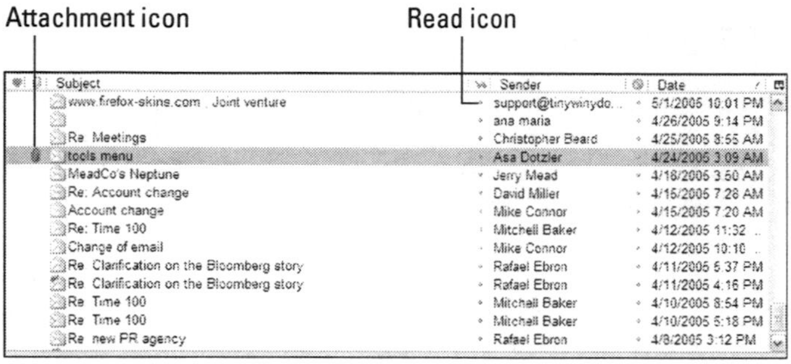

Attachment icon   Read icon

Figure 10-4:
The List
pane
contains a
wealth of
information
about each
message.

Subject	Sender	Date
www.firefox-skins.com Joint venture	support@tinywinydo...	5/1/2005 10:01 PM
	ana maria	4/26/2005 9:14 PM
Re: Meetings	Christopher Beard	4/25/2005 8:55 AM
tools menu	Asa Dotzler	4/24/2005 3:09 AM
MeadCo's Neptune	Jerry Mead	4/18/2005 3:50 AM
Re: Account change	David Miller	4/15/2005 7:28 AM
Account change	Mike Connor	4/15/2005 7:20 AM
Re: Time 100	Mitchell Baker	4/12/2005 11:32 ..
Change of email	Mike Connor	4/12/2005 10:10 ..
Re: Clarification on the Bloomberg story	Rafael Ebron	4/11/2005 5:37 PM
Re: Clarification on the Bloomberg story	Rafael Ebron	4/11/2005 4:16 PM
Re: Time 100	Mitchell Baker	4/10/2005 8:54 PM
Re: Time 100	Mitchell Baker	4/10/2005 5:18 PM
Re: new PR agency	Rafael Ebron	4/8/2005 3:12 PM

When you select a message in the List pane, the Message pane on the bottom right shows you the contents of the message. You can also double-click a message to open it in a separate window, which is handy if you want to open multiple messages at one time. After you select message in the List pane, you can use the toolbar buttons to reply to or forward the message, as I discuss in the following section. You can also click the Print and Delete buttons to — rather surprisingly — print or delete the selected e-mail.

Searching e-mail

Many e-mail programs bury their search capabilities in menus and windows that are difficult to access. Thunderbird takes the approach that search isn't just convenient in this networked world; it's an absolute necessity. As in Firefox, the search feature in Thunderbird is never more than one click away, thanks to a handy Search Box in the upper-right corner of the window (see Figure 10-5).

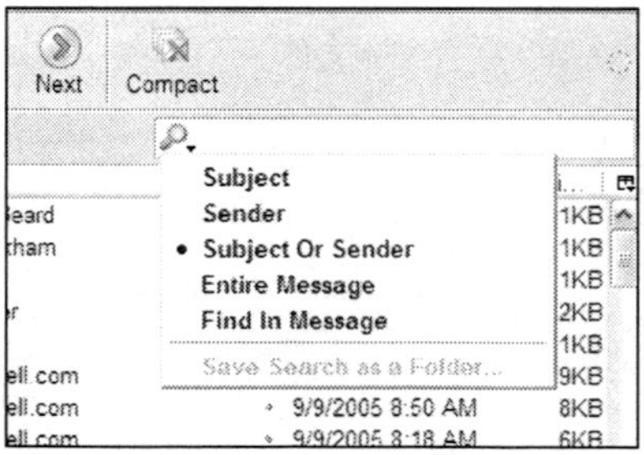

Figure 10-5:
Using the
Search Box,
you can
find that
old e-mail
quickly if you
remember
who sent it
or a phrase
it contains.

Next	Compact

Subject	1KB
Sender	1KB
• Subject Or Sender	1KB
Entire Message	2KB
Find In Message	1KB
Save Search as a Folder...	9KB
9/9/2005 8:50 AM	8KB
9/9/2005 8:18 AM	6KB

After you finish typing a phrase into the Search Box, Thunderbird automatically conducts the search and displays the results in the List pane. By default, Thunderbird searches on message sender and subject line, but you can choose from a number of other fields by clicking the magnifying glass icon in the Search Box, as shown in Figure 10-5. Searching certain fields, such as message body, can take a bit of time depending on how many messages you have.

The Search Box drop-down list includes two apparently similar options that actually do very different tasks. The Entire Message option searches all e-mails in the current folder for messages that contain the phrase you enter. Thunderbird displays all matching e-mails in the List pane. The Find in Message option searches only the e-mail currently displayed in the Message pane for the phrase you enter. Thunderbird highlights all instances of the phrase in the e-mail.

When matching messages appear in the List pane, you can work with them just as you work with all other List pane messages — respond to them, delete them, print them, and so forth. Click the red X button to the right of the Search Box when you're done so that the rest of your e-mail comes back into view.

Composing E-Mails

Reading e-mail is fun, but the real value is in the conversation. In Thunderbird, you can compose a new e-mail by clicking the Write button on the toolbar. To respond to an e-mail that somebody sent you, ensure that the e-mail is selected in the List pane and then click the Reply button. You can also forward an e-mail you receive to somebody else to show it to her by selecting the message and clicking the Forward button.

If you click Reply, your response is sent only to the sender of the original e-mail and not to any other recipients. To respond to both the sender and all of the e-mail's recipients (such as in a team conversation where every member should be kept in the loop), click the Reply All button on the Thunderbird toolbar.

In each of the cases, the powerful Compose window appears (as shown in Figure 10-6) so you can type, format, and send your message. The Compose window is organized into three primary sections to fill out before sending an e-mail, which I discuss in the following sections. I also tell you about attaching files to e-mails, spell-checking, and sending e-mails on their way.

The Firefox connection

Thunderbird is designed to feel comfortable to Firefox users. Its interface sports a similar menu bar and theme as Firefox, and also contains a Search Box in the upper-right corner. If Firefox and Thunderbird are your computer's default browsing and e-mail programs (as I discuss at the end of this sidebar), they also work together seamlessly to provide a complete Internet experience.

When you're in Firefox, you can access your Thunderbird mail quickly by choosing Tools⇨ Read Mail. You can also open an e-mail compose window (without even launching Thunderbird) by choosing Tools⇨New Message. To provide faster access to these commands, Firefox offers a Mail button that you can add to one of your Firefox toolbars, as I discuss in Chapter 18.

If you come across a link in a Thunderbird e-mail, you can click it to load the linked page in Firefox. By default, the link opens in a new tab of the last Firefox window you used, but you can configure this behavior from the Tabs category of the Firefox Options window, as I discuss in Chapter 7.

Note that the Firefox mail commands and the Thunderbird launch-in-browser feature work with your computer's default e-mail and browsing programs, respectively. If they aren't already your defaults, you can make Firefox and Thunderbird your default browsing and e-mail programs by using the General category of each application's Options window (Tools⇨Options).

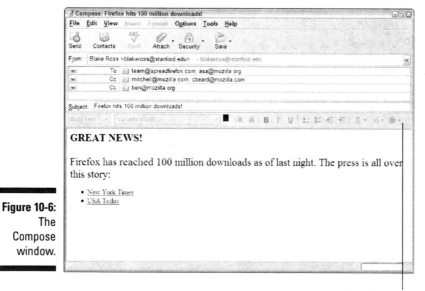

Figure 10-6:
The Compose window.

The Formatting Toolbar

Addressing e-mails

The first section you should fill out is the addressing area, where you indicate to whom the e-mail is being sent and in what way. The addressing area contains a list of rows in which you specify the addresses of the recipients. Each row that is in use begins with a drop-down list that contains the possible address types. Thunderbird supports the following forms of addressing e-mail:

- ✔ **To:** Sends e-mail directly to a recipient, who is the primary target of the e-mail.

- ✔ **Cc:** Sends a carbon copy to a recipient who might be interested in the e-mail but who is not its primary audience.

- ✔ **Bcc:** Sends a blind carbon copy to a recipient (which means that other recipients don't know that he or she is receiving it).

- ✔ **Reply-To:** Specifies the return address that recipients should use when responding to your e-mail. By default, the return address is the same address as the one you use to send the e-mail, but you might want to indicate a different one if you use multiple e-mail accounts or if the responses should go to a superior in your organization, to another e-mail member, or to some other party.

- ✔ **Newsgroup:** Specifies a newsgroup (an online forum) on which to post the e-mail message. This is an advanced feature that's beyond the scope of this chapter.

- ✔ **Followup-To:** This is to newsgroups what Reply-To is to e-mail: It redirects the conversation to a different newsgroup. This is an advanced feature that's beyond the scope of this book.

Begin by typing the To e-mail addresses into the top row. Separate multiple e-mail addresses by using a comma (for example, `bob@smith.com`, `emily@smith.com`).

If you want to specify additional types of recipients (such as Cc or Bcc), click Enter to insert a new row, and then use the drop-down list to the left of the row to specify the address type. Figure 10-6, earlier in this chapter, shows an e-mail addressed to a handful of recipients.

As you enter e-mail addresses, Thunderbird makes suggestions based on your address book. In fact, if you entered the recipient's name into your address book, you can start typing that instead, and Thunderbird can still recommend the right address. You can also add recipients from your address book manually by clicking the Compose window's Contacts button to open the Contacts Sidebar (shown in Figure 10-7), then double-clicking the recipients in the sidebar list. See "Creating an Address Book" later in this chapter for more information about creating an address book.

Contacts Sidebar

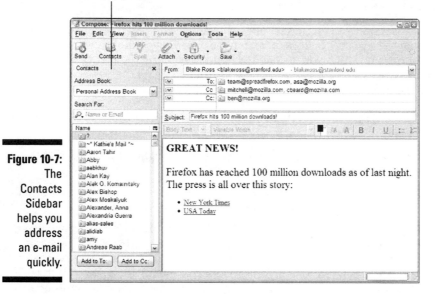

Figure 10-7:
The
Contacts
Sidebar
helps you
address
an e-mail
quickly.

Specifying an e-mail subject

Sending a new e-mail to someone is like beginning a conversation. It's a good idea to use the Subject line of the e-mail to indicate what you want to talk about (for example, "This week's sales meeting"). If, on the other hand, you're responding to or forwarding an e-mail you received, Thunderbird automatically uses the original e-mail's subject line, prefixed by Re: or Fwd:, respectively. You can still change the subject line, but I recommend you stick to these tried-and-true e-mail conventions.

Filling out the e-mail body

You've come to the fun part: typing the e-mail itself! If you're responding to an e-mail you received, Thunderbird automatically quotes the original e-mail in the message body, and you can type your response above or even within the quoted original. Otherwise, if you're starting fresh, you have a daunting white box to fill. Don't worry — Thunderbird offers a variety of handy tools to fill that box in interesting ways.

Thunderbird allows you to compose and send e-mails rich with colors, font styles, and images, much as Microsoft Word allows you to create stylized documents. These options are available on the Formatting Toolbar, as shown earlier in Figure 10-6, and might be familiar to you from other word-processing programs.

Composing an e-mail worthy of Van Gogh doesn't necessarily mean the recipients will receive it in all its glory. Your recipients' e-mail programs must support the so-called *rich* e-mail format that enables colors, fonts, and images to appear. These days, it's a pretty safe bet that this will be the case. However, if you use an unusual font that a recipient doesn't have, he or she will see your text in a plain font — so it's a good idea to stick to common fonts.

Attaching files

If you need to send a file along with an e-mail, you can attach it, and the recipients of the e-mail can download the file to their own computers when they receive the e-mail. To attach one or more files in Thunderbird, follow these simple steps:

1. **Click the Attach button on the toolbar of the Compose window.**

   The Attach File window appears so you can find and select the files to attach.

2. **Navigate to the folder containing the files to attach.**

3. **Select the file(s) to attach.**

   To select more than one file, hold Ctrl (Windows) or ⌘ (Mac) while clicking. To select a range of files at one time, hold Shift while clicking.

Thunderbird displays the e-mail's current attachments list in a box in the corner. (This box appears only when at least one file is attached, so don't worry if you don't see it yet.) You can add or remove files from the list at any time before sending the e-mail. To add files, repeat the preceding steps. To remove files, select the files in the list and press Delete. Removing an attachment does not, of course, delete or otherwise affect the file on your computer.

Spell-checking

So your e-mail is beautifully tricked out in colors and styles, and even contains some interesting prose, too. There's just one problem — that spelling of *mundain* doesn't look quite right, but you'd rather not use a more, uh, *boring* word. Fortunately, Thunderbird offers integrated spell-checking. Now you can focus on the e-mail itself, and not minor nuisances like the English language. Thunderbird identifies misspelled words as you type, and it can also guide you through the spell-checking process, which comes in handy for longer e-mails with more misspellings. I discuss both methods in the following two sections.

Spell-checking as you type

Like Microsoft Word and many other word processors, Thunderbird automatically checks your spelling as you type and underlines misspelled words with a dotted red line. When you right-click the word, Thunderbird displays a list of suggestions at the top of the contextual menu, as shown in Figure 10-8. You can choose a suggestion to replace the misspelled word or fix the word manually.

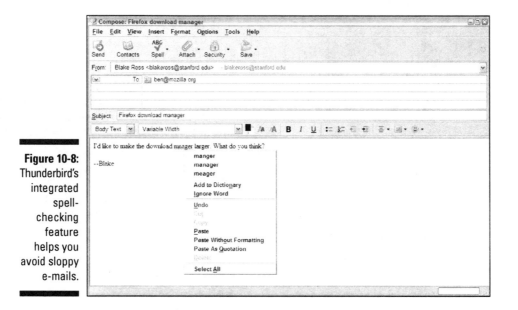

Figure 10-8: Thunderbird's integrated spell-checking feature helps you avoid sloppy e-mails.

Sometimes Thunderbird complains about words that are actually spelled correctly, such as slang, names, or other proper nouns. To prevent Thunderbird from complaining about occurrences of the word in this particular e-mail, right-click the word and choose Ignore Word from the contextual menu. To prevent Thunderbird from identifying the word as misspelled in this and all future e-mails, choose Add to Dictionary to add it to Thunderbird's dictionary.

Using the guided spell-checking feature

The method I describe in the preceding section is handy for a misspelled word or two, but might be cumbersome for long e-mails with many misspellings. If you prefer to have Thunderbird guide you through the spell-checking process, follow these simple steps:

1. **Click the Spell button on the toolbar.**

   The Check Spelling window appears to indicate the status of the spell-checking process. If Thunderbird finds no misspelled words, it says so.

In that case, click Close to close the window, and skip the remaining instructions. Otherwise, Thunderbird displays the first misspelled word in bold and offers a list of suggested corrections.

2. **If the word is in fact misspelled, select one of Thunderbird's suggested corrections, or type in your own correction in the Replace With text box.**

I say "if the word is in fact misspelled" because Thunderbird doesn't know your mother-in-law's name (and maybe that's a good thing) and some pop-culture lingo. You can use the Ignore buttons to ignore these words for this e-mail only. If you use the words often and don't want the spell-check feature to complain about them again, click the Add Word button to add the word to Thunderbird's dictionary.

If you enter your own correction, you can spell-check it by clicking the Check Word button.

3. **After you correct or ignore the misspelled word, click the Recheck Page button to continue spell-checking the rest of the e-mail. Repeat until Thunderbird indicates** No misspelled words.

Sending your e-mail

When your e-mail is spell-checked and ready to go, simply click the Send button to send it.

To send an e-mail quickly by using the keyboard, press Ctrl+Enter (or ⌘+Enter on the Mac). When you send an e-mail this way, Thunderbird asks you to confirm the send to make sure you didn't press those keys accidentally, so click Send in the confirmation window or press Enter. A check box in the window allows you to turn off the confirmation window for future sending.

Creating an Address Book

You can't even remember your mother-in-law's name, so how do you expect to remember her e-mail address? Thunderbird's address book helps you do what computers were made to do — remember mundane details for us. After you build up your address book, Thunderbird helps you compose e-mails to your friends, family and coworkers easily.

Creating an address book can be a chore, but Thunderbird simplifies the task by helping you build it automatically. Whenever you send an e-mail, Thunderbird automatically adds the e-mail's recipients to your address book. Even though you don't necessarily want everyone you e-mail in your address book, having them there doesn't really hurt anything because searching for an address later takes about the same amount of time even with a handful of unnecessary addresses.

If you want to manually add an address to your address book, you have two ways to do it. If the person you want to add sends you an e-mail, you can add his or her address from the e-mail itself. The Message pane already contains the sender's address, so just click it (with either the left or right mouse button) and choose Add to Address Book from the menu that appears, as shown in Figure 10-9.

Figure 10-9:
Build your
address
book quickly
and easily
from the
Message
pane.

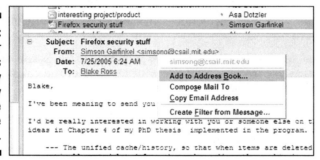

Otherwise, if you know the person's e-mail address, you can manually create a new *card* (which is like a record) in your address book by choosing File⇨ New⇨Address Book Card and filling out the window that appears. You can enter all sorts of information into an Address Book card, but filling out the first name, last name, and e-mail address is a good place to start.

After you add a name and address to your address book, Thunderbird can suggest it when you begin typing either one into the address field of an e-mail, as I discuss in the earlier section, "Composing E-Mails." You can also select it manually from the Contacts Sidebar of the Compose window, which I also discuss in that section.

Blocking Junk Mail

Every time I receive an e-mail from a friend in Peru, I stop to marvel at the amazing technological advances. But then the Viagra spam arrives, depriving the moment of its magic. Unsolicited e-mails — known bitterly as *spam,* or *junk mail* in Thunderbird — are a frustrating reality of the online experience. But Thunderbird takes broad and innovative strides to making them a thing of the past.

The system is simple and works like this: Thunderbird begins life stupid. It can't really tell the difference between a legitimate e-mail and junk e-mail, so you have to manually indicate the junk e-mail. However, as you identify junk e-mails, Thunderbird learns what junk looks like and begins to recognize it on its own. When you're confident in Thunderbird's ability to recognize junk e-mail, you can tell it to automatically move junk e-mail to a special Junk folder that you can quickly peruse when you have time (to ensure that no legitimate e-mails were misclassified). The Junk folder is displayed in the Folders pane alongside your other e-mail folders. When you're *really* confident in Thunderbird's abilities, you can have Thunderbird automatically empty the Junk folder at certain intervals. Thunderbird grows very smart pretty quickly, and it errs on the side of caution when it's uncertain about a particular e-mail, leaving that e-mail in your Inbox.

So there are just two things you have to know to take advantage of Thunderbird's junk mail capabilities: how to manually mark e-mails as junk mail to train Thunderbird; and how to make Thunderbird deal with junk e-mails automatically after it learns how to recognize them. I discuss both in the following two sections.

Marking e-mails as junk mail

Identifying an e-mail as junk mail is so easy it's almost criminal to devote a section to it. After you select the message in the List pane (so that you can now see the message in the Message pane), simply click the Junk button in the Thunderbird toolbar. A Junk Mail bar appears at the top of the Message pane indicating the junk mail status, and a tiny Trash icon appears next to the date in the List pane, as shown in Figure 10-10.

Junk Mail bar   Trash icon

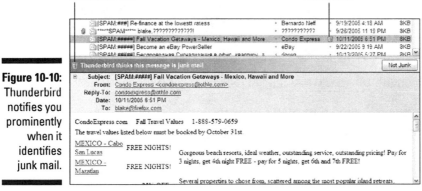

Figure 10-10: Thunderbird notifies you prominently when it identifies junk mail.

By default, marking an e-mail as junk mail doesn't affect the e-mail in any way; it just contributes to Thunderbird's education. However, you can tell Thunderbird to automatically move these messages to the Junk folder or delete them. This option affects only messages *you* mark as junk mail manually, not messages Thunderbird thinks are junk mail.

Follow these instructions to specify what Thunderbird does when you manually mark an e-mail as junk mail:

1. **Choose Tools⇨Junk Mail Controls.**

   The Junk Mail Controls window appears.

2. **Select the When I Manually Mark Message as Junk check box.**

3. **Select the Move Them to the "Junk" Folder or Delete Them option, depending on which action you want Thunderbird to take.**

4. **Click OK to save your changes.**

After you have manually marked a handful of e-mails as junk mail, Thunderbird begins identifying and marking junk mail on its own. You'll know when this happens because you'll start seeing messages flagged with the junk mail indicators (as shown in Figure 10-10) that you didn't flag manually. This doesn't mean it's time to stop marking junk mail manually, because Thunderbird is still learning, but it's a good sign — like a baby's first steps. Be sure to correct Thunderbird when it misidentifies legitimate e-mail as junk e-mail by clicking the Not Junk button in the toolbar.

Configuring automatic junk mail handling

When you're confident in Thunderbird's abilities to correctly distinguish legitimate mail and junk mail most of the time (it takes me about three weeks to train Thunderbird), you can instruct it to automatically move junk mail out of your way — which, after all, is the whole point. Thunderbird can move junk mail to a folder of your choosing, and optionally delete that folder at regular intervals you indicate.

To configure automatic handling of junk mail, follow these steps:

1. **Choose Tools⇨Junk Mail Controls.**

   The Junk Mail Controls window appears.

2. **Select the Move Incoming Messages Determined to be Junk Mail To check box.**

3. **To move junk mail to a folder named Junk, select "Junk" Folder On, and then select (by using the drop-down list) the account whose Junk folder you want to move it to.**

   This is an advanced option for people with multiple accounts.

   Thunderbird also lets you choose a different folder by choosing Other and then selecting the folder you want to use in the drop-down to the right.

4. **To have Thunderbird delete the junk mail folder you chose at regular intervals, select the check box beginning "Automatically Delete Junk Messages Older Than," and then enter the desired interval.**

   The default interval is 2 weeks.

5. **Click OK to save your changes.**

Getting Additional Help with Thunderbird

To keep a tight focus on Firefox in this book, I cut the Thunderbird discussion short here. However, if you like what you see so far, here are three great (and free) online resources:

- **Official Thunderbird Help:** The Mozilla Foundation's official Thunderbird support page, offering links to a Frequently Asked Questions (FAQ) page, free online support forums, and a list of tips and tricks. You can reach this page easily by choosing Help➪Mozilla Thunderbird Help in Thunderbird.

  ```
  www.mozilla.org/support/thunderbird
  ```

- **An Introduction to Thunderbird:** A wonderfully thorough, screenshot-laden online walkthrough of Thunderbird, beginning with installation.

  ```
  http://opensourcearticles.com/introduction_to_
          thunderbird
  ```

- **Harvard's Thunderbird Help Center:** Offers helpful tutorials for each of Thunderbird's primary features, with screenshots.

  ```
  www.fas.harvard.edu/computing/thunderbird/help
  ```

Chapter 11

Downloading and Saving Files

*T*he Internet is one of the most impressive engineering feats in human history, but it's also the largest wasteland ever created. Scattered carelessly across space and time, the Internet epitomizes mankind's tendency toward clutter. It is the collective closet of billions of people worldwide, and it's a *mess.* Just put those shoes anywhere.

But if that's the Internet's curse, that's also its charm. Because unlike your own closets, the mess that is the Internet is Someone Else's Problem. You fire up your browser and take what you need, and at the end of the day, you just shut it down.

It's only after you download stuff from the Internet to your computer that the clutter becomes *your* problem, and unfortunately, most browsers do little to temper it. Even the most casual downloaders soon find themselves overwhelmed with scattered files. The Firefox Download Manager is designed to help you organize and open the files you download so you don't have to spend your time searching for them. In other words, you can rest easy: Even your own clutter is now someone else's problem.

Downloading Music, Pictures, and Other Files

Many people these days have high-speed, always-on Internet connections. So what's the point of downloading a copy of something when you could access it live on the Internet? Admittedly, downloading has its roots in the quainter era of dial-up, when it was much cheaper to save a copy of that picture or song than keep reconnecting to the Internet to access it. Even today, though, there are plenty of reasons why you might want to download something:

✔ If you're a laptop user, you have access to the file when you're offline and on the road.

✔ Some types of media, such as video, play too slowly to enjoy live, even on a high-speed connection. Downloading these files first and playing them on your computer provides a less choppy and more pleasurable experience.

✔ If you want to edit a file (for example, suppose you have a team document at work that needs to be available to several coworkers), you should download it first so your changes are saved to your computer while you edit the file. You can later upload the finished version to the Internet.

Starting a download

How you download a file depends in part on how the Web site from which you're downloading is configured. In most cases, you can simply click a link or button — typically labeled Download. In other cases, the Web site asks you to wait while it begins the download on your behalf. Either way, Firefox displays the window shown in Figure 11-1 so you can decide how to download the file.

The name of the file   The file type

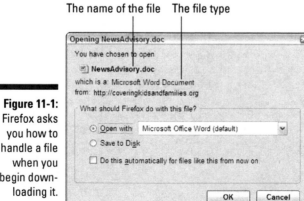

Figure 11-1:
Firefox asks you how to handle a file when you begin downloading it.

The text at the top of the window indicates the name of the file you are down-loading, as well as what type of file it is. For example, in this case, a family-oriented news advisory document is being downloaded, so the name of the file is NewsAdvisory.doc, and the file type is Microsoft Word Document.

Firefox asks you up front what you want to do when the file is finished trans-ferring. You have two options:

✔ Select **Open with** if you want to open the file as soon as it finishes trans-ferring. If you have an application on your computer that handles files of the type you are downloading, Firefox defaults to using it. To change the application that will be used, open the drop-down list next to Open With and select another application if one is available. If one is not available, you can select Other to find one on your computer, which is a fairly advanced feature.

✔ Select **Save to Disk** if you want to save the file directly to your desktop. (You can change the default download location or instruct Firefox to ask you for a location each time; see "Changing the default download loca-tion" later in this chapter for instructions.) When the file finishes down-loading, you can open it from the Download Manager (see the following section). However, Firefox doesn't open it automatically.

When the download begins, Firefox opens the Download Manager so you can track the progress of the download. See the later section "Using the Download Manager" if you want to disable this feature. Furthermore, Windows users are treated to an animated, nonintrusive notification in the bottom-right corner of the screen whenever a download ends, as shown in Figure 11-2. You can click it to open the Download Manager, or you can ignore it, and it will slide back down.

Figure 11-2:
This little window slides up above the Windows clock each time a download completes.

Open with caution

When downloading, using the Open With option has a subtle but important consequence that you should understand before selecting it. Open With is the option to select when you just want to view the file as quickly as possible and you don't expect to edit it or return to it later on. Firefox enforces this idea by downloading the file to a temporary location that's difficult to find and could disappear in the future if you or a cleaning application you use deletes the temporary folder to conserve space on your computer.

This might not seem like a big deal, but it's easy to wander into a trap. For example, say you choose to open the document with the intent to read it, but then decide you need to correct a few things. When you try to save the file, Word doesn't ask you where to save it because it

already exists at a temporary location. However, you certainly don't want to save your new copy to this location because it's hard to find and might be deleted later on!

You could work around that problem by choosing the Save As command in Word and saving the revised copy to a permanent location on your computer. But the best solution is to use the Save to Disk command in Firefox instead of Open With when you download a file that you need for long-term use. A good way to remember this is to think of Open With as writing the information you're downloading to a fortune cookie label. Would you save important information to that tiny strip of paper? Of course not! You'd save it to a memorable and easily accessible location, such as your computer's desktop.

Bypassing the download decision window

If you download frequently and stick with the same set of options, you might find the download decision window, which asks you how and where to download the file, to be too distracting. If so, select the check box at the bottom to instruct Firefox not to display the window again when you download files of the given type in the future. For example, if you select Open With: Microsoft Word for the document and then select this check box, Firefox automatically opens all future documents in Word without asking as soon as you choose to download them.

You can override this default behavior by right-clicking links to files you want to save and choosing Save Link As from the contextual menu as I discuss in "Overriding default actions with Save Link" later in this chapter.

If you change your mind later on, you can change which default action Firefox takes or instruct it to start asking you again:

1. **Choose Tools⇨Options.**

2. **Click the Downloads icon at the top of the window.**

3. **Under Download Actions at the bottom, select View & Edit Actions to open the Download Actions window, shown in Figure 11-3.**

Any files that Firefox handles for you automatically upon downloading are listed here. Notice that Firefox contains a long list of automatic actions by default; these are to enable the use of browser plug-ins, as I describe in "Plugging along with plug-ins" later in this chapter.

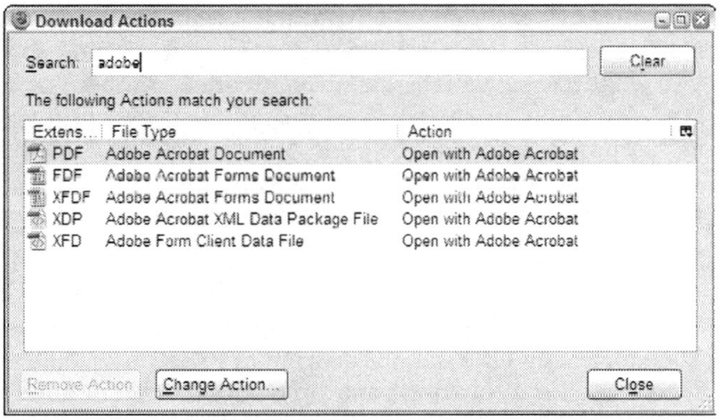

Figure 11-3:
The
Download
Actions
window
provides an
overview of
default
down-
loading
actions.

4. **Select the file type in the list whose default action you want to change.**

To find the item quickly in the list, type part of the file type. For example, type **word** for Microsoft Word documents. Note that search phrases must be lowercased.

5. **To remove the default action, click the Remove Action button at the bottom.**

Firefox asks you to confirm the decision; if you do so, it takes effect immediately. For example, if Firefox was set to open Word documents in Word automatically when you download them, Firefox will prompt you each time you download a Word document in the future.

Note that for the built-in file types that are handled by plug-ins, this button is unavailable. You can't remove the automatic handling for file types, although you can change how it behaves, as I describe in Step 6. See "Plugging along with plug-ins" later in this chapter for more information about plug-ins.

6. **To change the default action, click the Change Action button, and then select one of the following options in the window that appears.**

The first three options, although presented in a slightly different fashion, behave exactly like the Open With and Save to Disk options I discuss earlier, and the cautions apply.

- **Open Them with the Default Application:** Instructs Firefox to automatically open all files of the selected type in the program your computer typically uses, as soon as they finish downloading. For example, if you're changing the setting for document files and you have Microsoft Word installed as the default word processor, Firefox automatically opens documents you download in Word.

- **Open Them with This Application:** Instructs Firefox to automatically open files of the selected type in a program of your choosing as soon as they finish downloading. When you select this option, Firefox opens a Browse File window so you can find the program you want to use, which is a fairly advanced maneuver. For example, if you're changing the setting for document files and you would rather use WordPerfect to open downloaded documents instead of your system's default word processor, Microsoft Word, you can use this option to locate the WordPerfect program file.

- **Save Them on My Computer:** Instructs Firefox to automatically save files of the selected type to your hard drive as soon as they finish downloading. By default, Firefox saves files to the desktop. You can change the default download location or instruct Firefox to ask you for a location each time you download a file. See the following section for more instructions.

- **Use This Plugin:** Instructs Firefox to load files of the selected type using the specified plug-ins. If a plug-in that can handle the file type is available, Firefox displays it automatically. Otherwise, this option is unavailable. See the section "Plugging along with plug-ins," for more information.

7. **Click OK to save your changes.**

8. **Click Close to close the Download Actions window.**

9. **Click OK to close the Options window.**

Changing the default download location

Firefox allows you to either open or save downloadable files. If you choose to save, you might be surprised to discover that Firefox doesn't ask you *where* you'd like to save. Because most people tend to save files to a single location, Firefox bypasses this step to minimize distractions and save you time. By default, Firefox downloads all files to your computer desktop, where you can access them without having to search through your computer's file system.

Some people prefer to disable this behavior because their desktops can quickly get crowded if they're not careful. Others turn it off because sometimes they need to specify a different download location. However, neither of these reasons justifies turning off the feature entirely; instead, you can simply tweak the feature to accommodate each. You can resolve the first problem by changing the default location to a normal folder on your computer, and the second by using the Save Link mechanism to override the default location in the exceptional cases, as I outline in "Overriding default actions with Save Link," later in this chapter. You should turn off the feature entirely only if you want Firefox to ask you where to save each and every file you download.

To tweak or disable the default location behavior:

1. **Choose Tools➪Options.**

2. **Click the Downloads icon at the top of the window.**

3. **To change the default download location, click the Browse button and select the desired location, and then click OK.**

   To turn off the default download location altogether, select the Ask Me Where to Save Every File option.

4. **Click OK to save your changes.**

Plugging along with plug-ins

Saving or opening a file disrupts your flow by pulling you out of the Web browser. This disruption is expected for things like documents, but wouldn't it be nice if Firefox could play movie clips and songs without forcing you to divide your attention among multiple programs?

You're in luck. Firefox isn't designed to be a multimedia masterpiece in and of itself (that's what Web pages are responsible for), but it can emulate the experience through the use of browser *plug-ins.* Plug-ins are an advanced technology that most people should never have to worry about, but the basic idea is that you can literally insert programs into Firefox to give it newfound capabilities. Firefox can't play movies? No problem. Apple's QuickTime program can, so Firefox embeds QuickTime into the Content area. Now you've got the power of a full-fledged movie player with the convenience of in-browser playback. Your computer probably already contains most of the plug-ins you'll need, such as Adobe Acrobat for electronic documents, but I describe how to obtain missing plug-ins in the following section.

Finding plug-ins you might need

As you explore the Web, you might encounter content that requires plug-ins you don't already have, such as Flash for complex, animated Web sites. In such cases, Firefox displays a toolbar above the page to notify you that a plug-in is required. You also see an empty box on the page with a green puzzle piece inside, as shown in Figure 11-4.

Click the puzzle piece.

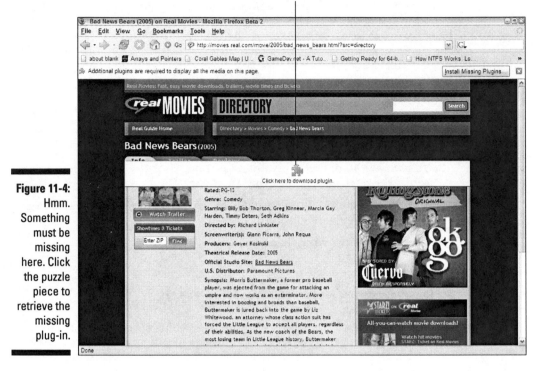

Figure 11-4:
Hmm.
Something
must be
missing
here. Click
the puzzle
piece to
retrieve the
missing
plug-in.

This box is where the plug-in content would load if the plug-in were available, and the puzzle piece represents the missing plug-in. Click the puzzle piece to have Firefox find the plug-in and walk you through the installation process as follows:

1. **Click the green puzzle piece to open the plug-in installation wizard, shown in Figure 11-5.**

   Firefox searches for available plug-ins. Any matches it finds are displayed in a list and installed by default. If multiple plug-ins are available, you can indicate which plug-ins you don't want to install by deselecting the check boxes next to their names.

2. **Click Next to continue.**

3. **Read through the license agreement for the plug-in you're installing.**

   This agreement outlines the terms and conditions under which you can use the plug-in, and explains the rules governing the plug-in's behavior.

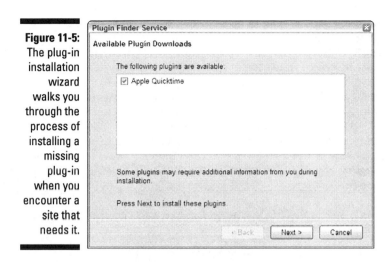

Figure 11-5:
The plug-in installation wizard walks you through the process of installing a missing plug-in when you encounter a site that needs it.

4. **Select I Agree and click Next to continue with installation.**

   Firefox downloads and automatically installs the plug-in. This process should take less than a minute, at which point the completion screen appears.

5. **Click Finish to close the wizard.**

Some plug-ins require you to restart Firefox before they work. Otherwise, Firefox automatically loads the content that required the plug-in in place of the empty box with the puzzle piece as soon as installation finishes.

 Although Firefox maintains a comprehensive plug-in database (located at `https://pfs.mozilla.org/plugins`), you might encounter a Web site that requires a rare plug-in that Firefox can't find. In that case, you need to find the plug-in yourself on the Internet or you will be unable to view the content that requires it.

Overriding default actions with Save Link

Sometimes, Firefox might act on your behalf in undesirable ways due to the automatic settings I discuss in "Bypassing the download decision window," earlier in this chapter. Perhaps you click a link with the intent to save the file to which it links, but Firefox opens the file automatically. Or perhaps Firefox saves the link automatically to a certain location, but you wanted to save it to a certain folder.

Earlier in the chapter, I explain how to prevent or disable all automatic behaviors, but you might find these behaviors to be convenient in *most* scenarios. For example, if you want to open a downloaded document in Word 99 percent of the time, it makes sense to have Firefox do that automatically. But what about those one or two documents you need to open in WordPerfect because Word can't handle them correctly? For these and other scenarios, Firefox offers a simple solution: the Save Link mechanism. Rather than clicking the link itself, you merely instruct Firefox that you wish to save the content to which the link *points*. This not only ensures that you can save a file without Firefox opening it, but also gives you the chance to save it to a location of your choosing. You can then open the file manually in whichever program you choose.

1. **Right-click the link to the file you want to save and choose Save Link As to open the Save window.**

   You can also hold down Alt (Windows) or Option (Mac) and click the link.

2. **Select the location to which you would like to save the file.**

   You can also provide a new filename if you don't like the default provided by the Web site.

3. **Click Save when you're finished.**

Although you can use the Save Link mechanism at any time, it is most useful for overriding default download behaviors.

Saving Web Sites

Downloading files from Web sites is something most people who browse the Internet are familiar with. But what about downloading the Web sites themselves? Firefox allows you to save a copy of any Web site to your computer, like a digital snapshot of the site as it exists at that time. This provides peace of mind that you'll always have a copy of the page even if it disappears from the Internet — for example, if you write an online newspaper article that will stay up only for two weeks and you want to keep a copy of it. It also comes in handy when you want to save a copy of a long document to read on a plane or in other offline environments.

1. **Visit the Web site you want to save.**

2. **Choose File⇨Save Page As.**

   Press Ctrl+S (or ⌘+S on a Mac) to open the Save window more quickly.

3. **Select the location to which you would like to save the file.**

   You can also provide a new filename if you don't like the default, which is provided by the Web site.

4. **From the Save as Type drop-down list at the bottom, select one of the following options:**

   - **Web Page, Complete:** Instructs Firefox to save the entire Web site, including all images, colors, and designs. This option is the default, and it's the best option if you want Firefox to save an exact replica of the page to your computer.

     Firefox saves the main Web page file to the directory of your choosing and places all subsidiary files to a new directory called `WebPageName_Files`. For example, suppose you choose to save the CNN home page to a file called `CNN.html` in your computer's My Documents folder. Firefox would save `CNN.html` to My Documents as instructed and create a new subfolder called `CNN_Files` to hold images and other files associated with the Web site. You don't have to worry about reconstructing the page in the future; when you load `CNN.html` in Firefox, Firefox automatically does that work for you.

   - **Web Page, HTML Only:** Instructs Firefox to save the Web site itself, but not the images and other associated media. If you're online when you view your saved copy later on, the media may or may not be available depending on the way the Web site is programmed. If you're offline, however, the media is unavailable because you haven't saved it to your computer.

   - **Text Files:** Instructs Firefox to save only the plain text of the Web site. No images or other multimedia will be included, and any text styling (for example, bold or italic) will be lost.

After you save the page, the Download Manager appears. To view your snapshot of the page, simply double-click it in the Download Manager. If you're comfortable with your computer's file system, you can also navigate to the folder where you saved the snapshot and open the file (which probably has an `.htm` or `.html` extension) in Firefox.

Using the Download Manager

The Firefox Download Manager provides a single, simple interface for tracking the progress of ongoing downloads and opening files that have finished downloading.

Opening the Download Manager

You can access the Download Manager at any time by choosing Tools⇨ Downloads or by pressing Ctrl+J (⌘+J on a Mac). Whenever you begin a download, the Download Manager opens automatically so you can track its progress. If the Download Manager is already open, it flashes briefly on your computer's taskbar to indicate that a new download has begun.

You can instruct Firefox not to open the Download Manager automatically if you find such behavior annoying. Alternatively, you can allow Firefox to open it automatically but close it as soon your files have finished downloading:

1. **Choose Tools⇨Options.**

2. **Click the Downloads icon at the top of the window to access the download options, as shown in Figure 11-6.**

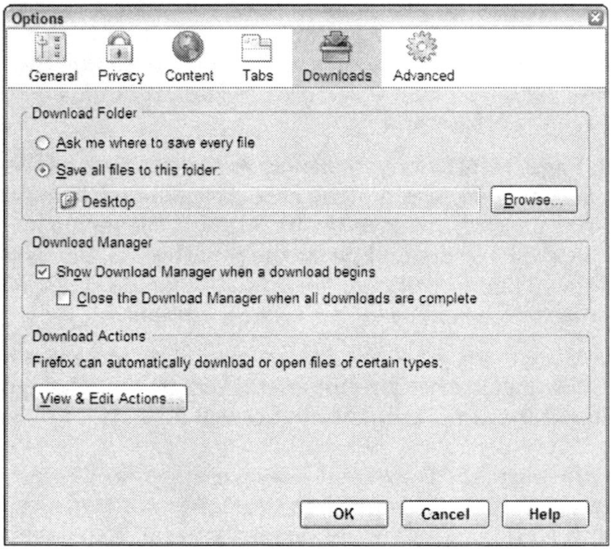

Figure 11-6:
You can tweak Firefox's downloading behavior or change when the Download Manager appears.

3. **Do one of the following:**

   • Deselect the Show Download Manager When a Download Begins check box to turn off the automatic opening feature.

   • Select the Close the Download Manager When All Downloads Are Complete check box to leave the automatic opening intact but force the manager to close as soon as all files finish downloading.

4. **Click OK to save your changes.**

Exploring the Download Manager

At the heart of the Download Manager is your downloads list, shown in Figure 11-7. This list contains both current and finished downloads, with most recent (or in-progress) downloads at the top and oldest downloads at the bottom. Each entry in the list displays the filename of the download as well as an icon representing the application that your computer will use to open it. For example, the symbol for Microsoft Word typically appears next to document files if you have Word installed on your computer.

A download in progress

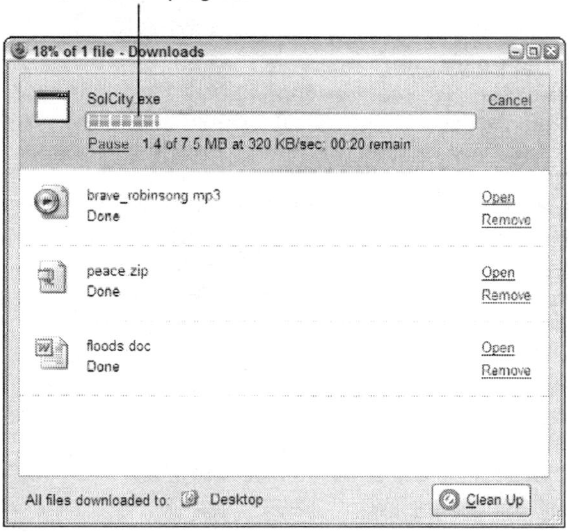

Figure 11-7: The Download Manager provides a simple interface for accessing both ongoing and finished downloads.

When a download is in progress, a progress meter indicates approximately how much of the file has been transferred and how much is still to come, as illustrated in Figure 11-7. The text beneath the progress meter reflects similar information in the technical language of kilobytes and megabytes, which represent digital file sizes. It also indicates your approximate download rate as well as an estimate of how much time is remaining before the download completes.

What you can do with a given download depends on its current status:

✔ **Ongoing downloads** (like the first download in Figure 11-7) can either be canceled or paused via the supplied links. You can resume a paused download at any time while Firefox remains open, but if you close Firefox while downloads remain paused, they are canceled entirely. In that case, Firefox asks you to confirm the shutdown before canceling your downloads.

✔ **Failed downloads** are downloads that were either canceled deliberately or terminated abruptly due to a connection error. You can restart these downloads by clicking the Retry link, or you can remove them from the list by clicking Remove.

✔ **Finished downloads** are downloads that completed successfully and exist on your computer. To open these files, click the Open link or simply double-click anywhere within the item. If the file is a program, such as an installer, Firefox asks you to confirm your decision to launch it due to security reasons. Before opening programs, make sure you trust the Web site that offered them for download. I also recommend using a professional virus scanner like Norton AntiVirus that automatically scans files you download and open.

If the file is a type of media (such as a graphic file or a document), and if you have a program on your computer that handles that media type, Firefox launches the program automatically. If Firefox is able to detect such a program, the icon to the left of a download is the program's logo. If not, Firefox asks you to select the program when you open the file.

Sometimes you don't want to open the file itself, but rather the folder that contains it. This is useful if you need to manage the file in a way that the Download Manager doesn't offer — such as renaming it or moving it — or if you just want to know where the file actually lives on your computer. To open the containing folder, simply right-click a download and choose Open Containing Folder from the menu that appears. If you're using a default download location, the Download Manager offers one-click access to it by clicking the button next to All Files Downloaded To at the bottom of the window. (Although it doesn't look like a button, the text is in fact clickable.) The default download location is the computer desktop, as I describe earlier in this chapter.

Firefox remembers the Web site from which you downloaded a file so you can return to it later. Simply right-click a download and choose Properties from the menu that appears. The Properties window opens and offers the address of the Web site that provided the download next to From. The Properties window also contains the path to the file on your computer, as well as the dates and times at which the download began and finished.

Of course, you can also remove a finished download from the list by clicking Remove. This does *not* remove the downloaded file from your computer; it simply removes the record that this download took place from the Download Manager.

Clearing your download history

By default, Firefox automatically retains a record of all your downloads — completed or canceled — but you control what remains in this history or even whether such a history is maintained at all. This section discusses various ways of managing and clearing your Firefox download history.

This history is merely a record of the downloads that took place and is in no way tied to the actual files downloaded to your computer. Removing records from your download history does not remove the files from your computer. However, you will no longer be able to access those files through the convenient Download Manager interface; you will need to access through your computer's standard file system. Chapter 14 covers clearing download history in more detail.

Removing individual download records

If you want to clean up the Download Manager without clearing all its records, you can delete records one by one with the following steps:

1. **Choose Tools⇨Downloads.**

2. **Find the download record you want to remove in the list and click the Remove link.**

Removing a record instructs Firefox to forget what it knows about that specific download only. If you download the same file again, Firefox creates a new record in your download history.

Removing all download records at once

If you're no longer using any of the records in the Download Manager, you can remove them with the following steps:

1. **Choose Tools⇨Downloads.**

2. **Click the Clean Up button in the bottom-right corner of the Download Manager.**

   Firefox won't ask you to confirm this process, which is irreversible.

Instructing Firefox to remove download records automatically

If you're concerned about privacy or overwhelmed by a long download history, you can instruct Firefox to remove download records automatically, either as soon as a download finishes or when Firefox exits:

1. **Choose Tools⇨Options.**

2. **Click the Privacy icon at the top of the window.**

3. **Click the Download History tab to view the download options.**

4. **Select one of the following options from the Remove Files from the Download Manager drop-down list:**

   - **Manually:** This is the default option. It means Firefox will never erase a download record until you tell it to do so.

   - **Upon Successful Download:** Removes a download record as soon as the file it represents is finished transferring.

   - **When Firefox Exits:** Removes all download records each time you close Firefox. Note that this setting affects existing records that have already accumulated. In other words, if you have 20 records in your history when you enable this setting and close Firefox, those 20 records will be erased.

5. **Click OK to save your changes.**

Chapter 12

Printing Web Pages

*W*ith the rise of e-mail and the Internet, some doomsayers predicted the death of the printed book. Business managers whispered the phrase "paperless office" to each other in excited tones. Some professors began accepting research papers electronically, and students groaned and moaned as usual. But has the Web replaced the printed page? Not at all.

For all the benefits of an online world, paper still has its days. Printed text and graphics are often sharper on the page than on the screen; reading long passages of text on-screen can still be awkward and uncomfortable. And the smallest and lightest laptops in the world still aren't as convenient to carry around as that rolled-up stack of paper.

Unlike many other browsers, Firefox recognizes the value of paper and makes the print experience as seamless as your online experience. In particular, Firefox offers a powerful Print Preview feature that lets you see exactly what a Web site will look like before you print it. This feature allows you to save paper by printing only the pages you need. You can even tweak the print format by changing the margins, header and footer text (the text that appears in the top and bottom margins of each page), and other features. This chapter shows you how.

All the page that's fit to print

Web sites and paper don't mix all that well. Web sites are dynamic, linkable, animated, and completely unconstrained by space. Paper is . . . well, paper. And when you try to print a Web site on it, bad things can and often do happen. Sometimes a seemingly brief article translates to a dozen sheets of paper. Other times, the printed version is too difficult to read because it's surrounded by silly ads that have lost their animated vigor and are no longer clickable. Designing content for the screen just isn't the same as designing it for paper.

To bridge the gap, many Web sites offer special print-friendly versions of their content that are more amenable to the paper format. These versions typically remove surrounding ads, enlarge text size, remove background colors and images, and format the content into columns to deliver a more magazine-like experience. Web sites offer print-friendly formats in different ways. Some link to a separate page from the original article, so you must click through to the page and print that one instead. Increasingly, however, Web sites are taking advantage of a new browser feature that allows them to specify a print format that automatically takes effect when you print the original article. In other words, you don't need to look for a special option — it just works.

A good rule is to use Print Preview to see how a particular Web site will look on paper. If you don't like what you see, examine the Web site to see whether it links to a print-friendly version.

Using Print Preview

How many times have you printed an interesting page only to discover that something was, shall we say, lost in translation? Maybe parts of an image are missing. Worse, maybe parts of the *story* are missing. This kind of thing happens frequently because many Web designers concentrate on designing the best possible on-screen experience. Because the screen and a sheet of paper have completely different dimensions, this focus often comes at the expense of the printed page. Now you just have a piece of paper to throw away.

You can use Print Preview to view a Web page as it will print *before* you print it and avoid wasting paper (and time). To open the Print Preview window (shown in Figure 12-1), navigate to the Web page you want to print, and choose File⇨Print Preview. Firefox offers a variety of correctional features you can use to improve the print layout if you don't like the preview. I discuss these in the following sections.

Macintoshes do not have the Print Preview feature. Furthermore, the Mac version of Firefox uses the default Page Setup and Print windows, but extends the Print window to offer Firefox-specific features. Most of the special formatting features discussed in this chapter, such as margin customization, are found in the Print window on the Mac.

You can access the Page Setup window from here.

Open the
Print
window
here.

Go back or forward
through the document
with these buttons.

Portrait/Landscape page orientation options

The Scale feature

Close the Print
Preview window here.

Figure 12-1:
The Print
Preview
window.

Changing the scale of the page

If a Web site is too wide to fit comfortably on paper (like the one in Figure 12-2), you can *scale* the page smaller, which is kind of like zooming out on a page for printing purposes. When you print wide pages, Firefox automatically wraps text so that it doesn't get cut off. However, wrapping text can add many pages, and you can avoid that by scaling the page smaller. Also, Firefox does not automatically prevent images that are close to the margins on wide pages from getting cut off. Scaling the page smaller can fix this as well.

If, on the other hand, a page has text too small to read comfortably on paper, you can scale the page larger — the paper equivalent of zooming in.

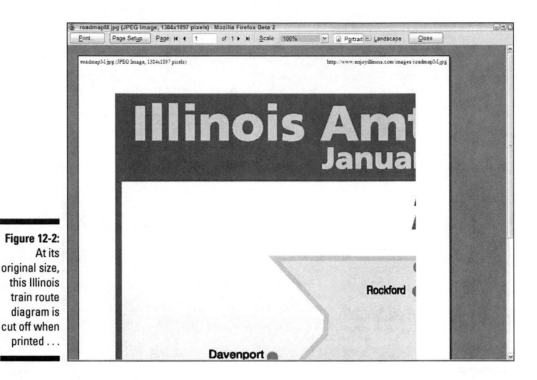

Figure 12-2:
At its
original size,
this Illinois
train route
diagram is
cut off when
printed . . .

Temporarily changing the text size of a Web page using the View⇨Text Size menu in the main Firefox window does not change the printed format of the page, so don't be surprised if Print Preview shows the page at its original text size. However, changing the text size of *all* Web sites, as I discuss in Chapter 19, does affect the printed page. If you don't want to enlarge or reduce the text size of all pages but want to change the text size of a particular page for printing purposes, Print Preview's scaling feature is the way to go.

To scale a page, simply open the Scale drop-down list in the Print Preview window and select one of the following settings:

✔ **A preset percentage:** Choose a percentage below 100% to scale a page smaller (I use 50% in Figure 12-3), above 100% to scale a page larger, or 100% to print the page at its current (original) size.

✔ **Shrink to Fit:** Select this option to automatically fit the page onto a standard 8½-x-11-inch sheet of paper.

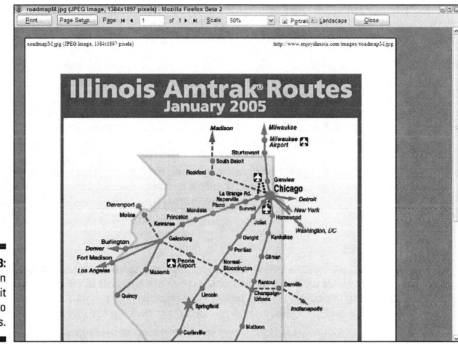

Figure 12-3:
. . . but when you scale it down to 50%, it fits.

If you decide to print on a nonstandard size of paper, such as a postcard or legal-size page, you have to set up your printer to accommodate this. The procedure for doing this varies depending on your printer, but typically you open the Firefox Print window, click the Properties button, and then navigate to a paper size option. Shrinking your page works well only if your printer knows the type of paper you're using.

✔ **Custom:** Select this option to specify your own scaling percentage. You can use any number, though anything over 200% usually makes the Web page look like a large-print book on steroids.

These options are also available from the Page Setup window, which you can access by clicking the Page Setup button in the Print Preview window. Some features of the Page Setup window aren't available directly from the Print Preview interface, as I discuss later in this chapter.

Changing the orientation of the page

Suppose you've just found that 14-column table listing all the stats of your favorite basketball team online, and you want to print it out for your own reference. The problem is every time you try to print the table, the right half of the table gets cut off. You try the Shrink to Fit feature I discuss earlier, but then it's too small to read. What do you do?

Sometimes the image you want to print is too wide for a standard 8½-x-11-inch piece of paper, but the image will print fine when you turn that piece of paper on its side. This is reorienting the page. The tall orientation, which is the default, is called Portrait, and the wide orientation is called Landscape. Figures 12-4 and 12-5 illustrate the difference between the Portrait and Landscape orientations.

To change the print orientation of a particular page, choose File➪Print Preview in the main Firefox window to open the Print Preview window, and then choose one of the following orientation buttons in the Print Preview toolbar.

Portrait

By default, Print Preview shows the page in Portrait mode, meaning the short side of the page (usually 8½ inches) is at the top and bottom. This is how most printing is done, as with a newspaper or newsletter. If you switch to Landscape mode, you can return to Portrait mode by clicking the Portrait button.

Figure 12-4: In Portrait mode, you see only half of this large auditorium...

Figure 12-5:
... but in Landscape mode, both halves of the room are visible.

Landscape

Sometimes you simply need to print something that's wider than the standard 8½ inches of a normal sheet of paper. To "turn" the page, click the Landscape button. Note that if you select Landscape mode, you'll wind up with many more printed pages because less content fits on each page. You can select which pages to print from the Print window.

You can also change the orientation setting from the Page Setup window, without having to open Print Preview. To open the Page Setup window, choose File➪Page Setup in the main Firefox window. However, changing this setting in the Print Preview window allows you to preview a Web site in each orientation.

The orientation setting affects all Web sites you print, not just the Web site you're currently viewing.

Printing background colors and images

By default, Firefox doesn't print background colors and Images because doing so can make pages more difficult to read, as well as using a tremendous amount of ink. You can change this behavior from the Page Setup window by following these steps:

1. **Choose File⇨Page Setup in the main Firefox window to open the Page Setup window.**

    The Page Setup window is also accessible via the Page Setup button in the upper-left corner of the Print Preview window.

2. **On the Format & Options tab, select the Print Background (Colors & Images) check box.**

3. **Click OK.**

This setting affects all Web sites you print, not just the Web site you're currently viewing.

Changing margins, headers, and footers

Firefox includes information about Web sites you print in the top and bottom margins (called the *header* and *footer,* respectively) of the printed page, such as the site title, page number, and date. To make more room for the page itself, you can shrink these margins. To include a more spacious border around the page, you can enlarge the margins. You also can customize the information that appears in the margins. Customization options include removing the title and changing where the date appears.

To get to the Margins & Header/Footer options, follow these steps:

1. **Choose File⇨Page Setup.**

2. **Click the Margins & Header/Footer tab.**

    The following two sections discuss the options on this tab, which are shown in Figure 12-6.

The Margins area

This area has four boxes that represent each of the margins on the page, as shown in Figure 12-6. The default value for each of the margins is 0.5 (half an inch), but you can change one or more of these. When you type in a new value, the preview image adjusts to the new margin.

Most printers require a minimum amount of margin space, since they can't print right along the edge of a page. This requirement varies among printers, and your printer's instructions may indicate its particular requirements. To be on the safe side, it's a good idea to ensure that you have at least 0.2 inches of margins on each side.

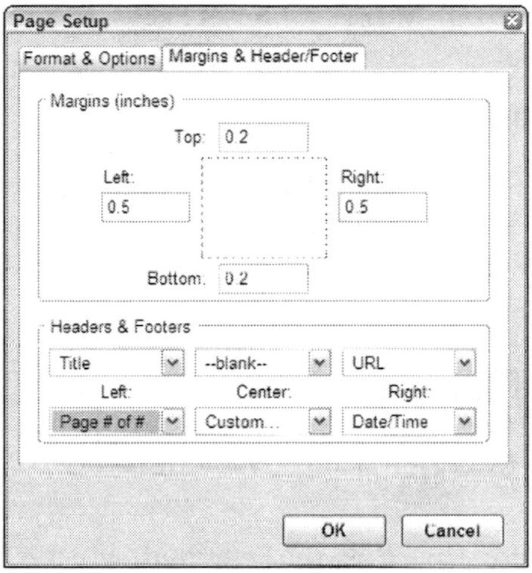

Figure 12-6:
The
Margins &
Header/
Footer tab
in the
Page Setup
window.

The Headers & Footers area

This area contains six drop-down lists that correspond to six positions on the printed page. You can use these drop-down lists to change what appears in each position. The first row of drop-down lists corresponds to the left, center, and right positions of the header (the top margin), and the second row corresponds to the left, center, and right positions of the footer (the bottom margin). You can select from the following options to include in each position:

- ✔ **–blank–:** Shows nothing in this part of the page.
- ✔ **Title:** Shows the title of the Web page. This is the title that appears in the main Firefox window's title bar when you visit the page.
- ✔ **URL:** Shows the Web page's address.
- ✔ **Date/Time:** Shows the date and time when the Web page was printed.
- ✔ **Page #:** Shows the page number of each page.
- ✔ **Page # of #:** Shows the page number along with the total number of pages in the print job. For example, on the fifth page of a 30-page print job, this area would show Page 5 of 30.
- ✔ **Custom:** Use this option when you want your own text to appear in the header or footer. You can type in any text you want. You can also include one or more of the following codes to substitute some of the preset pieces of information when you print:
  - **&D:** Date/Time
  - **&P:** Page Number

- **&PT:** Page Number with Total Number of Pages
- **&T:** Title
- **&U:** Web site address

For example, if a Web site's title is January Meeting Agenda, and you type **Work Documents: &T** into the left header position, the printed agenda shows **Work Documents: January Meeting Agenda** in the upper-left corner.

Configuring Print Options and Printing a Web Site

The Firefox Print window, accessible from the Print button in the Print Preview window, allows you to choose which parts of a page to print, and how many copies to print, as I discuss in the following section.

If you don't want to preview a page before you print it or if you're using a Mac, you can bypass the Print Preview window and open the Print window directly from the main Firefox window by choosing File➪Print. If you print frequently, you can also add a Print button to one of your Firefox toolbars. See Chapter 18 for more information about toolbar customization.

Unfortunately, Firefox doesn't currently allow you to use the Print Preview feature to preview changes you make in the Print window. For example, if you use the Print Range feature in the Print window to determine which pages to print, the Print Preview feature still shows you all the pages in the Web page. The team and I hope to offer this functionality in a future release.

Choosing which parts of a page to print

You can save plenty of time and paper by printing only the parts of a Web site that you need. Of course, Web sites aren't broken into traditional pages — they just scroll on endlessly — so there are a handful of ways to specify a part. Firefox allows you to specify which parts of a page to print in three ways: with a page range, with a selection, and by indicating a certain frame. I discuss each of these options in the following sections.

Printing by page range

The Print Preview feature, which I discuss at length earlier in this chapter, allows you to see how a Web site will break down into pages when you print it.

When you know which pages of a Web site you need, follow these steps to print them:

1. **Open the Print window.**

   I provide instructions for doing so a bit earlier in this part of the chapter.

2. **Under Print Range, select Pages and then enter the range of pages to print.**

   The default print range is All, which, of course, prints the entire Web page.

3. **Click Print to print the specified page range.**

This setting takes effect on a site-by-site basis. In other words, changing the page range for the site you're currently printing doesn't not affect pages you print in the future.

Printing by selection

If you find it easier to specify a print range by highlighting the part of the page you wish to print or if you want to print content that spans two pages on a single page, use the print-by-selection method as follows:

1. **Select (highlight) the portion of the page you want to print.**

2. **Open the Print window.**

   I provide instructions for doing so a bit earlier in this part of the chapter.

3. **Under Print Range, select Selection.**

4. **Click Print to print the selection.**

This setting takes effect on a site-by-site basis. In other words, choosing to print a selection on the current site does not affect pages you print in the future.

Printing by frame

Some Web sites are divided into box structures called *frames*. Each frame actually contains a separate Web site. Web sites use this when they need to aggregate two or more Web sites into a single presentation. For example, the online resource site About.com includes links to thousands of external Web sites (Web sites outside of the About.com network) about all sorts of topics. Rather than linking you directly to an external Web site, About.com loads the

Web site in a frame and inserts its own frame at the top of the page that links you back to About.com. This helps keep you in the About.com network, so you can move on to other topical pages discovered by About.com if the current page doesn't meet your needs.

Unfortunately, About.com also includes an advertisement in its top frame, as you can see in Figure 12-7. By default, Firefox prints all frames in a framed Web site, just as they're laid out on the screen. This means the printed page will have an ugly advertisement at the top. Luckily, Firefox allows you to print just a particular frame, or to print each frame separately.

Follow these steps to print a particular frame:

1. **Select the frame you want to print by clicking an empty space within it.**

   In other words, don't click a link. There's no visual identification of which frame is selected, but Firefox knows.

2. **Open the Print window.**

   I provided instructions for doing so a bit earlier in this part of the chapter.

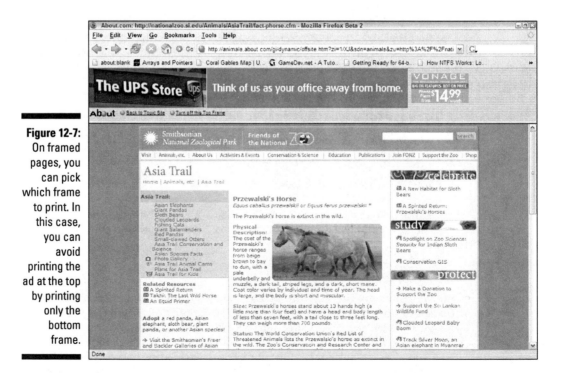

Figure 12-7:
On framed pages, you can pick which frame to print. In this case, you can avoid printing the ad at the top by printing only the bottom frame.

3. Under Print Frames, select The Selected Frame.

The default option is As Laid Out on the Screen, which prints the Web site just as it appears to you on the screen.

4. Click Print to print the selected frame.

Another way to print just a particular frame is to *isolate* the frame — in other words, load the Web site displayed in the frame by itself. You do this in Firefox by right-clicking the frame, selecting the This Frame submenu in the contextual menu that appears, and then choosing Show Only This Frame. The Web site in the frame loads separately, and then you can print the page normally, just like any other. This feature is also handy when you want to read the frame by itself on the screen.

If you'd rather print each frame individually, follow these steps:

1. Open the Print window.

I provide instructions for doing so a bit earlier in this part of the chapter.

2. Under Print Frames, choose Each Frame Separately.

The default option is As Laid Out on the Screen, which prints the Web site just as it appears to you on the screen.

3. Click Print to print each frame individually.

The Print Frames options are available only if the Web site you're trying to print is using frames. To quickly determine whether a page is using frames, and thus whether you can use the print by frame method, right-click anywhere on the page. If the contextual menu includes a This Frame option, as shown in Figure 12-8, the page is using frames.

New Web design techniques are making frames obsolete, so you will see fewer and fewer Web sites using them as time goes by. Some Web sites that appear to be using frames might actually be using a newer technique instead.

Printing multiple copies of a page

By default, Firefox prints a single copy of a Web site, but you can print as many copies as you need. This feature comes in handy if, for example, you need to pass out a copy of the Web site to everyone on your team at work.

To print multiple copies of a Web site, follow these steps:

1. Open the Print window.

I provide instructions for doing so a bit earlier in this part of the chapter.

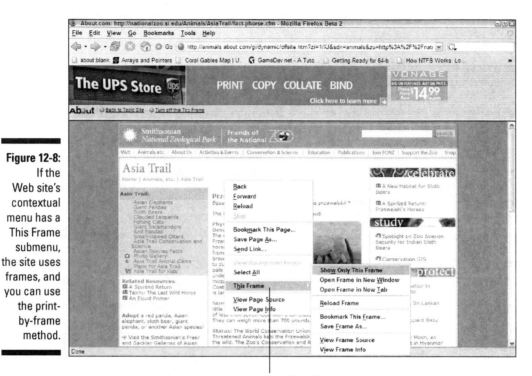

Figure 12-8:
If the
Web site's
contextual
menu has a
This Frame
submenu,
the site uses
frames, and
you can use
the print-
by-frame
method.

A contextual menu with a This Frame option

2. **Under Copies, enter the number of copies you want to print.**

3. **If you want to print the copies in a collated fashion, select the Collate check box.**

   Collation affects only multipaged print jobs. By default, Firefox prints all the copies of each page in a multipaged Web site in order. For example, if you're printing five copies of a three-paged Web site, Firefox prints five copies of page 1, then five copies of page 2, and finally five copies of page 3. If you collate the copies, Firefox prints entire copies of the Web site at a time. In this example, Firefox prints page 1, then page 2, then page 3, and repeats that five times. Figures 12-9 and 12-10 illustrate the difference between non-collated and collated printing. Collation is handy because when all copies finish printing, they're already in sets. Without collation, you have to reconstruct each copy of the Web site manually.

4. **Click Print to print the indicated number of copies.**

TIP

If you plan to print a lot of pages in black and white, you might want to consider buying a laser printer. Although they're more expensive than traditional ink jet printers, they print much more quickly.

Figure 12-9:
Without collated printing, Firefox prints all the copies of page 1, then all the copies of page 2, and so on . . .

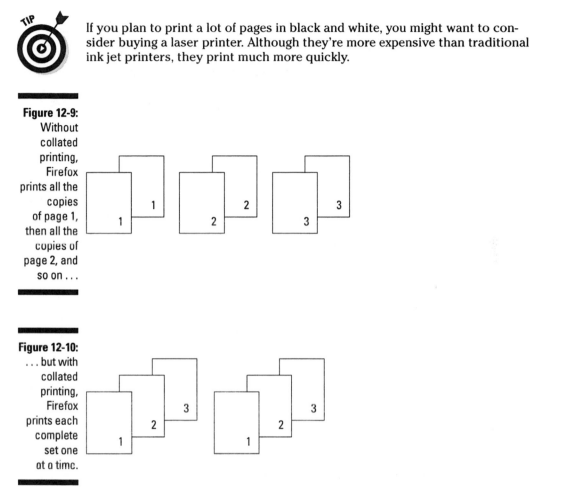

Figure 12-10:
. . . but with collated printing, Firefox prints each complete set one at a time.

Changing page size and other printer-specific options

Many printers offer additional formatting options beyond those offered by Firefox, which I discuss in this chapter. For example, certain printers allow you to specify different paper sizes or qualities and automatically optimize printing for those conditions.

The best way to determine what your printer supports is to consult its manual or simply to look in the Print window and see. (In Windows, you might need to click a Properties button in the window to access the printer-specific options.) I provide instructions for opening the Print window earlier in this chapter.

Chapter 13

Finding Additional Help

I've tried to make this book a comprehensive resource, but there are some things I just can't cover. I can't, for example, provide in-depth help on each of the hundreds of Firefox extensions (see Chapter 20). This chapter gives you some invaluable (and mostly free) resources you can turn to when you need additional help, not least of which is my own e-mail address.

Using the Help Window

The best place to start when you have a question I haven't answered in this book is Firefox's own built-in help feature. Although the feature is intended to offer quick-and-dirty answers rather than a comprehensive guide, it might have the answer you're searching for.

To open the Help Window, choose Help⇨Help Contents, or press F1 in Windows.

The Help window, as shown in Figure 13-1, opens to a welcome screen on the right side and an expandable list of help topics on the left. This list serves as the digital Table of Contents and is your primary means of navigation. The window also contains a Search text box in the upper-right corner that you can use to find a particular topic quickly. I discuss the Table of Contents and the search feature in the following two sections.

The globe icon

Figure 13-1:
Firefox
includes
built-in help
documen-
tation
written by
volunteers.

Browsing the Table of Contents

The Table of Contents contains a list of broad topics, such as Using the Download Manager and Customization. Most topics contain more specific subtopics, as indicated by a plus sign (+) next to the topic name. To see a topic's subtopics, click the plus sign. To view help on a particular topic, simply click it, and the help documentation appears on the right side of the window.

When you're reading the help documentation for a particular topic, you might encounter a link to a related topic. These links work just like regular Web site links; click them to go directly to the related topic's documentation. Then you can use the Back and Forward buttons in the help window to move among the two, just as you do with regular Web sites in the main Firefox window.

From time to time, help documents might also link you to real Web sites that open in a regular Firefox window. These links are marked with a globe icon.

See the Using the Help Window topic for more tips and tricks on using the help window. This is the first topic in the table of contents, and it's also linked from the help window's welcome screen, which appears by default when you open the help window. If you're switching from the Internet Explorer browser, I also recommend the For Internet Explorer Users topic to ease the transition. This topic is linked directly from Help⇨For Internet Explorer Users in the main Firefox window.

Searching for a particular topic

If you're looking for help with a particular topic, you'll probably find it faster to search for the topic directly rather than browsing the Table of Contents. Simply type part or all of the topic into the Search Box in the upper-right corner of the window. When you stop typing, Firefox searches for the topic and displays a list of matching results in a new Search Sidebar (on the left side of the window) that takes the place of the Table of Contents, as shown in Figure 13-2. Click a result topic to view the associated help documentation, just as you do with the Table of Contents.

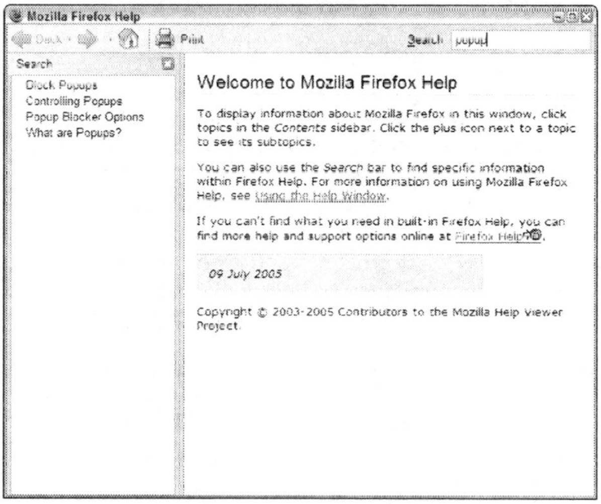

Figure 13-2:
The Search
Sidebar
contains a
list of topics
that match
your search
phrase.

When you find the help you need, click the red X in the corner of the Search Sidebar to close it. After you close the sidebar, the Table of Contents returns. You can also shrink or hide the sidebar temporarily by dragging the gray line — that separates the sidebar and the content — to the left. To reopen it, drag the gray line — which is now flush with the left edge of the window — back to the right.

The search feature isn't a full-text search, which means it doesn't search the help documentation itself. It searches only the help topics themselves. The best way to find help with a particular topic is to search for a succinct keyword that describes it. For more tips, see the Search Tips subtopic under the Using the Help Window topic, which is the first topic in the Table of Contents.

Getting Help on the Web

If you can't find the answer you need in Firefox's built-in help, the Web offers two types of resources you can try. The first is a collection of walkthroughs, Frequently Asked Questions (FAQs), and other documentation you can use to help yourself. The second is an online discussion forum where experienced Firefox users can usually walk you through the proper solution. I discuss both types of resources in the following sections.

Finding help documents online

Here are some of my favorite online resources:

- **The MozillaZine Knowledge Base:** Though not officially affiliated with the Mozilla Foundation, MozillaZine (www.mozillazine.org) is an excellent community news and support site. One of its best features is a so-called *knowledge base,* a community-edited and -maintained resource. The knowledge base contains a list of the most common trouble spots in Firefox (with solutions, of course!), a comprehensive Frequently Asked Questions (FAQs) page, and a bevy of tips and tricks. The knowledge base is available at http://kb.mozillazine.org/Mozilla_Firefox.

- **An Introduction to Mozilla Firefox:** A Web site called Open Source Articles offers a complete walkthrough of Firefox in a dozen different languages, complete with full-color screenshots. The walkthrough is available at http://opensourcearticles.com/introduction_to_firefox.

- **The Official Firefox Support Site:** The Mozilla Foundation maintains an official Firefox support page that contains useful links to external help sites (including the other two sites in this list), as well as some original content of its own. The official support page is available at www.mozilla.org/support/firefox.

Using the support forums

If you have a question that you can't solve yourself by examining Firefox's built-in help or the online resources I list in the preceding section, you can turn to the vibrant and growing Firefox user community for help. Before doing so, see the sidebar in this chapter, "A word on netiquette."

A word on netiquette

The Firefox user community is comprised of Firefox's most advanced users and serves as an invaluable help resource. These users are not paid for their efforts, and it's important to show them the same respect they are showing you in trying to answer your question. Aside from normal conventions of etiquette, you should abide by some additional *netiquette* rules when seeking help in the community.

✔ **Try not to ask a question that is already answered in Firefox's built-in help, in the online help sites, or most importantly, in the forums themselves.** Forum helpers get many of the same questions again and again, and understandably get frustrated at having to answer repeatedly. Use the forum search feature to see whether your question has already been addressed. Many years and hundreds of thousands of forum posts are archived, so there's a good chance it's been answered already. Still, don't kill yourself trying to find it. If a search doesn't uncover it within ten minutes or so, don't feel bad about asking the forum users.

✔ **If you do decide to create a new forum post with your question, make sure you create it in the right forum, which is the Mozilla Firefox Support forum under the User**

Support heading on MozillaZine. If you put your question in the wrong forum, users of that forum are going to be upset by the intrusion and will be less likely to help you or redirect you to the right place.

✔ **Don't post your question multiple times.** Because forum helpers are volunteering their free time, it might take a few days to get a response, though it usually doesn't. If you don't get a response, that probably just means the forum helpers don't know the answer; asking again isn't likely to help.

✔ **Don't use all capital letters when posting your question.** Doing so is the online equivalent of shouting, even if that was not your intent.

✔ **Consider registering for a MozillaZine account, which takes just a minute or two, if you intend to return to the forums in the future.** Although you can post to the support forums without a username, forum helpers are more likely to help when they can match a persona to a question. If you frequent the forums and follow these simple rules of netiquette, you'll quickly earn a positive reputation among forum helpers, and they'll be more willing to help you.

A Web site called MozillaZine serves as the online home of Firefox's user community. MozillaZine is not officially affiliated with the Mozilla Foundation and offers the latest Firefox news, a comprehensive knowledge base (as I mention in the preceding section), and a set of discussion forums where anyone can ask a Firefox question (like the one shown in Figure 13-3). If you've already checked the knowledge base and the other online resources I list in the preceding section, your best bet is to ask your question in the MozillaZine Mozilla Firefox Support forum.

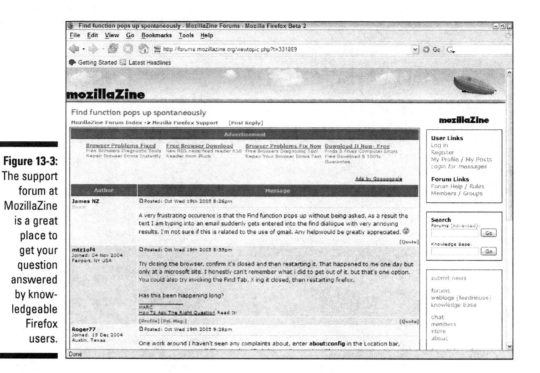

Figure 13-3:
The support forum at MozillaZine is a great place to get your question answered by knowledgeable Firefox users.

To get to the forum, go to `http://forums.mozillazine.org` and click Mozilla Firefox Support, the very first forum in the list. There, you can create a new discussion thread by clicking the Create New Topic link at the top of the screen. You don't need to create an account to post, although doing so might be a good idea, as I discuss in the sidebar, "A word on netiquette." I also discuss in that sidebar why you should search the forums for your question before posting.

E-mailing Blake

If you still can't find the answer you're looking for, please don't hesitate to e-mail me at `blake@firefox.com`. It takes me a little (okay, a lot of) time, but I do respond to every e-mail.

Part III
Outfoxing Hackers

The 5th Wave By Rich Tennant

"Oh, Arthur is very careful about security on the Web. He never goes online in the same room on consecutive days."

In this part . . .

Here's a scary thought: Every time you access the Internet, you expose yourself to millions of potential hackers. Here's a scarier thought: Most of them are 12 years old! Just think what they'll be able to do when they're older. What's a person to do?

This part outlines what you need to know and do to stay safe online, as well as how to secure personal information like browsing history from prying eyes. But Firefox wouldn't be much of a browser if it left you to fend for yourself, so I also tell you about the steps Firefox takes to protect you. Those 12-year-old twerps don't stand a chance.

Chapter 14

Clearing Your Tracks

*I*t's your tenth anniversary. Your spouse turns to you inquisitively and says, "I'm sorry, and you are?"

It wasn't all that long ago that computers were equally rude. So-called *dumb terminals* knew nothing about the person in front of them and had to keep asking the same question day in and day out: "I'm sorry, and you are?"

Thankfully, you live in the personal computing era. And what's the use in having a computer if there's nothing *personal* about it? Life is hard, and computers make it easier by remembering information about you so you don't have to keep entering it.

As possibly the most-used program on your computer, your Web browser in particular needs to keep track of all sorts of information: your usernames, passwords, where you downloaded stuff, and the complicated addresses of sites you visit frequently. Can you imagine if you had to remember everything on your own? Human brains just weren't designed to store the Internet (and the Firefox developers haven't yet acquired the licensing to redesign them).

Trustworthy technologies, of course, keep you in control of your private information at all times. Firefox gives you control over just how much information you want Firefox to remember about you and allows you to wipe the slate clean at any time. Also keep in mind that *none* of the information Firefox stores about you is accessible via the Internet; it all remains on your own computer.

Using the Clear Private Data Feature

Firefox stores a variety of information while you browse, such as your browsing history, your download history, and the online forms you fill out. Each piece of information is stored to make your browsing experience more convenient. Download history, for example, is maintained so that you can easily find and open the files you download. Although this kind of memory is convenient, you will probably want to clear it frequently if other people use your computer (such as family members or co-workers) so that no one can invade your privacy.

The easiest way to clear stored information in Firefox is by using the Clear Private Data mechanism. The feature is simple but powerful. First, you specify which kinds of information you want to clear regularly, such as browsing history and saved form entries. Then, every time you use the feature — which I discuss in the following steps — that type of information is cleared, but other types (such as download history, in this case) remain intact.

To configure and use the Clear Private Data feature, follow these steps:

1. **Choose Tools⇨Clear Private Data.**

   The Clear Private Data window appears, as shown in Figure 14-1. This window contains a list of information that Firefox stores (for example, "Saved Form Information"). See "Working One-on-One with Your Data" later in this chapter for specific coverage of each type of information.

   If you're on Windows, you can press Ctrl+Shift+Del to open the Clear Private Data window quickly. (There's no keyboard shortcut for Macintosh users.)

2. **Select each type of information you want to clear and make sure all other types are deselected.**

   If a particular option is grayed out (and thus not selectable), Firefox currently has no information of that type stored about you, and you don't need to clear it.

   I discuss the first six types of information listed in this window in the section "Working One-on-One with Your Data," later in this chapter. The seventh, Authenticated Sessions, is technical jargon that refers to information that Firefox remembers for a particular *session* (a session begins when you start Firefox and ends when you close it), such as your Amazon.com shopping cart items. Although Firefox automatically forgets this information when a Firefox session ends, you might want to clear it manually (without having to shut down Firefox) when you walk away from your computer (especially if others share your computer), which is why this option is available.

Figure 14-1:
The Clear
Private Data
window lets
you specify
any com-
bination of
information
to clear and
then wipes
it out on a
regular
basis.

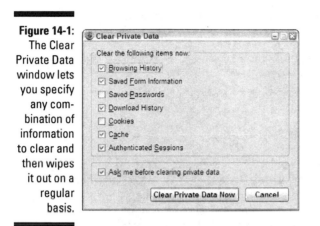

3. Click Clear Private Data Now to clear the information you indicated.

This action is permanent and irreversible, and you will not have a
chance to confirm the decision after you click the button.

The Clear Private Data feature clears only the information Firefox has already
stored. New information continues to accrue unless you tell Firefox to stop
storing it altogether. I outline how to do this for each type of information in
"Working One-on-One with Your Data" later in this chapter.

Bypassing the Clear Private Data window

At the bottom of the Clear Private Data window is a mysterious check box
that says Ask Me Before Clearing Private Data, and it is selected by default.
If you deselect this option, choosing Tools⇨Clear Private Data (or pressing
Ctrl+Shift+Del on Windows; there is no Mac shortcut) clears whichever types
of information you had previously selected immediately and silently. In other
words, you won't be offered the Clear Private Data window or any other confirmation. This option is intended for people who clear their information regularly and want to avoid the window every time.

The Clear Private Data window remembers your decision regarding the Ask
Me Before Clearing Private Data check box even if you press the Cancel
button. Thus, you should make sure the check box is selected or deselected,
depending on your preference, when you close the window.

If you decide to bypass the window and later want to turn it back on or
change exactly which tracks are cleared each time, you can still access the
Clear Private Data settings window from the Firefox Options window:

1. **Choose Tools➪Options to open the Options window.**

2. **Click the Privacy icon at the top of the window.**

3. **Click the Settings button at the bottom of the window to open the Clear Private Data settings window.**

4. **Select the Ask Me Before Clearing Private Data check box.**

5. **Click OK.**

6. **Click OK to close the Options window.**

Can't remember whether you set the preference to bypass the Clear Private Data window? Well, you certainly don't want to try the option and see whether or not the window appears — because if it doesn't, your information just got cleared! Instead, open the Tools menu and examine the Clear Private Data option. If it ends in an ellipsis, you have not bypassed the confirmation window, and it appears when you use the feature. If it doesn't . . . the window is bypassed. Figures 14-2 and 14-3 show the difference.

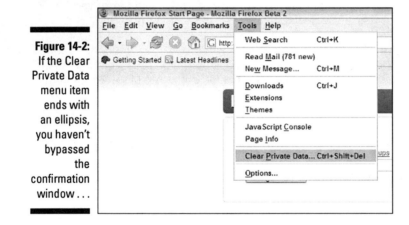

Figure 14-2:
If the Clear Private Data menu item ends with an ellipsis, you haven't bypassed the confirmation window . . .

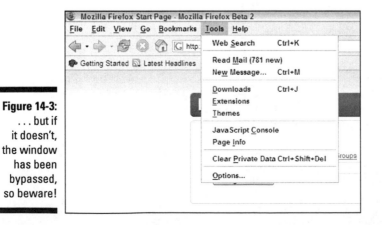

Figure 14-3:
. . . but if it doesn't, the window has been bypassed, so beware!

Clearing private data when Firefox closes

With the window-bypassing feature I describe in the preceding section, clearing your tracks in Firefox is as easy as choosing a menu item or (on Windows) pressing a few keys. But if you're very privacy-conscious, that might not be enough. After all, as easy as it is to clear your data, you still have to remember to do it. What if you forget?

If you want, you can tell Firefox to clear some or all of your private data each time it shuts down:

1. **Choose Tools⇨Options to open the Options window.**

2. **Click the Privacy icon at the top of the window.**

3. **Click the Settings button at the bottom of the window to open the Clear Private Data settings window.**

4. **Select the types of information that Firefox should clear on shutdown, and ensure that all other types are deselected.**

5. **Select the Clear Private Data When Closing Firefox check box.**

6. **Click OK.**

7. **Click OK to close the Options window.**

Working One-on-One with Your Data

The Clear Private Data feature is great for people who always find themselves clearing the same set of information — say, download history and browsing history, but not saved passwords or form information. But the feature just doesn't do the trick if your habits are irregular or if you need more specific control over each type of stored information (such as choosing how many days' worth of browsing history to maintain). In either case, the Options window provides more powerful tools for working closely with each kind of information that Firefox remembers:

1. **Choose Tools⇨Options to open the Options window.**

2. **Click the Privacy icon at the top of the window.**

3. **Click the tab that corresponds to the type of information you want to configure.**

   Figure 14-4 shows the six tabs that are available.

When you reach the tab pertaining to the kind of information you want to configure, refer to the appropriate section that follows for further help.

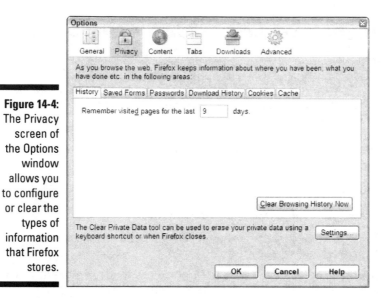

Figure 14-4:
The Privacy
screen of
the Options
window
allows you
to configure
or clear the
types of
information
that Firefox
stores.

Erasing your browsing history

As I discuss in Chapter 6, Firefox keeps a record of the Web sites you visit so you can find them later if you forget their addresses. This is called *browsing history,* and by default, Firefox stores records of all the Web sites you visited in the past nine days. To configure or clear browsing history, follow the directions in the preceding section, "Working One-on-One with Your Data," to get to the History tab of the Options window. From there, you can do any of the following:

- ✔ **Shorten or expand how many days' worth of Web sites Firefox remembers in browsing history** by replacing 9 with a new number.

- ✔ **Instruct Firefox not to remember browsing history anymore** by replacing 9 with 0. Firefox won't track any Web sites you visit in the future, but your current browsing history remains until you clear it.

- ✔ **Clear your current browsing history** by clicking the Clear Browsing History Now button. Firefox clears the history as soon as you click the button and the action is irreversible. Note that this doesn't *turn off* browsing history; it only clears your current history. New history accumulates when you resume surfing. If the Clear Browsing History button is unavailable, your browsing history is already empty.

More information about browsing history is available in Chapter 6.

Getting rid of old saved forms

As I discuss in Chapter 8, Firefox remembers information you enter into Web sites so you don't need to keep reentering it. For example, it can remember your username at a site you log in to frequently, or your ZIP code at a weather site. Firefox also remembers phrases you enter into the Firefox Search Box so you can use them again more quickly. Collectively, this is called *saved form information,* and by default, Firefox remembers it indefinitely. To configure or clear saved form information, follow the directions in the section "Working One-on-One with Your Data," earlier in this chapter, to get to the Saved Forms tab of the Options window. From there, you can do any of the following:

- ✔ **Instruct Firefox not to remember form information anymore** by deselecting the Save Information I Enter in Forms and the Search Bar check box. As the wording implies, if you choose this option, Firefox also stops remembering phrases you search for in the Search Box in the upper-right corner of the main Firefox window.

- ✔ **Clear your current Saved Form Information** by clicking the Clear Saved Form Data Now button. This takes place as soon as you click the button and is irreversible. Note that this doesn't *turn off* saved form information; it only clears the currently stored information. New form information accrues the next time you submit an online form or use the Search Box. If the Clear Saved Form Data Now button is unavailable, no form information is currently saved.

Saved form information doesn't include passwords you enter into online forms; those are stored separately, as I discuss in the next section.

More information about the automatic form-filling feature is available in Chapter 8.

Keeping your saved passwords safe

Firefox remembers passwords you use to log in to secure sites on the Internet (after asking you) so you don't need to enter them every time you log in. These are known as saved passwords, and by default, Firefox remembers them indefinitely. To configure or clear saved passwords, follow the directions in the section "Working One-on-One with Your Data," earlier in this chapter, to get to the Passwords tab of the Options window. From there, you can do any of the following:

- ✔ **Instruct Firefox not to remember passwords anymore,** by deselecting the Remember Passwords check box.

- ✔ **Set, change, or remove a Master Password.** If family members or co-workers share your computer, you might find it disconcerting that Firefox automatically prefills your passwords for them. On the other hand, the feature is convenient when you are at your computer. Firefox offers a feature called Master Password that lets you enjoy both security and convenience. See the section on using a Master Password in Chapter 8 for more information about this feature.

- ✔ **View the passwords Firefox has collected thus far,** by choosing the View Saved Passwords button. If Firefox has prefilled your password for so long you've actually forgotten it, this is a good way to retrieve it! The window that opens contains a table of Web sites and the usernames you use at each site, as shown in Figure 14-5. To see your passwords at all sites, click the Show Passwords button to add a new Password column. If you have a Master Password, you need to enter it before you can access the stored passwords even if you've entered it previously. Otherwise, Firefox asks you to confirm the decision. Make sure nobody is looking over your shoulder before you proceed. To hide your passwords again, click the Hide Passwords button. See the section on viewing and clearing saved login information in Chapter 8 for more in-depth help with this feature.

- ✔ **Clear some or all of the stored passwords.** Click the View Saved Passwords button, select the sites whose saved passwords you want to clear, and click Remove. Otherwise, to remove all saved passwords, click Remove All. These actions take effect immediately and are irreversible. Note that this doesn't *turn off* the password-saving feature; it only clears the current list of passwords.

- ✔ **Instruct Firefox that it's okay to prefill passwords** at a particular site where you previously indicated otherwise. When you enter a password at a Web site Firefox hasn't seen before, you can decide whether Firefox should remember the password and prefill it later. If you choose No, Firefox will continue to ask you each time you log in to the site. To minimize distractions, a third option, Never for This Site, allows you to tell Firefox that you *never* want it to remember passwords you enter on that particular Web site (which is useful if, for example, it's a banking site), and to stop asking you.

  To reverse this decision later on, click the View Saved Passwords button on the Privacy tab, and then click the Passwords Never Saved tab. Firefox displays a list of Web sites for which you have told it never to ask you about saving. To remove a particular site, select it and click Remove. To clear the entire list, click Remove All. After you remove a site from this list, Firefox will ask you again whether to save the password the next time you try to log in to the site.

More information about Saved Passwords is available in Chapter 8.

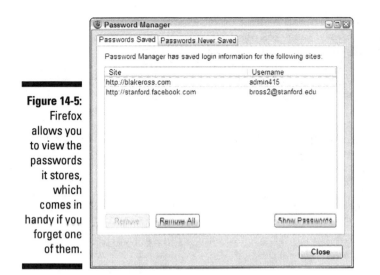

Figure 14-5:
Firefox
allows you
to view the
passwords
it stores,
which
comes in
handy if you
forget one
of them.

Tidying up your download history

As I discuss in Chapter 11, Firefox keeps a record of the files you download so you can access them easily. This is known as *download history*, and by default, Firefox keeps records of all your downloads until you clear them manually. Note that these are simply records of the download itself; clearing a download record doesn't affect the downloaded file that exists on your computer. To configure or clear download history, follow the directions in the earlier section, "Working One-on-One with Your Data," to get to the Download History tab of the Privacy category of the Options window. From there, you can do any of the following:

✔ **Specify when the download history is cleared** by using the Remove Files from the Download Manager drop-down list. By default, download records remain until you clear them manually, with the Download Manager, the Clear Private Data feature, or the Clear Download History Now button in the Options window. However, you can also instruct Firefox to clear a download record as soon as the corresponding download completes (by selecting Upon Successful Download), or each time you exit Firefox (by selecting When Firefox Exits). Note that if you choose the latter, the new policy begins immediately; in other words, your existing download history will be cleared as soon as you exit Firefox.

✔ **View your download history** in the Download Manager by clicking the View Download History button. The Download Manager is also accessible from the Tools menu in the main Firefox window.

✔ **Clear the entire download history** by clicking the Clear Download History Now button. This takes place as soon as you click the button and is irreversible. Note that this doesn't *turn off* download history; it only clears the currently stored records. New download records accrue as you start new downloads. If the Clear Download History Now button is unavailable, your download history is already empty.

You can clear individual download records from the Download Manager window. For more on the Download Manager as well as anything else related to how Firefox downloads anything off the Internet, turn to Chapter 11.

Sweeping up your cookie crumbs

Billions of different Web sites exist, each serving a different purpose. Although Firefox can help you remember aspects that are common to many of them — such as the concept of a username and password — it is impossible for Firefox to remember the information necessary for each Web site genre. For example, what about a shopping site that needs to remember what's in your shopping cart as you navigate the digital aisles? What about an online newspaper that wants to remember that you like the sports page? If the other Firefox developers and I spent our time designing a custom "memory" for anything a Web site might need to store, we wouldn't have time for anything else.

Clearly, then, Web sites need their own (generic) way to remember information about you, and the mechanism for doing this is called a cookie. A Web site can leave a *cookie* — a brief bit of information — on your computer, and your browser sends it back to the site when you return to that site. It's as if the Web site is temporarily storing a tiny memory on your computer.

To prevent your computer from getting cluttered up with these memories, most Web sites owners give their cookies expiration dates. By default, Firefox — like virtually all other browsers — allows all Web sites to set cookies and keeps them until they expire. But Firefox gives you extensive control over which cookies are set and for how long they are kept.

You can impose more restrictions on which sites are allowed to set cookies, with the understanding that certain Web sites might not function properly without them.

To configure or clear cookies, follow the directions in the section "Working One-on-One with Your Data," earlier in this chapter, to get to the Cookies tab of the Options window. From there, you can do any of the following:

✔ **To prevent all Web sites from setting a cookie,** deselect the Allow Sites
to Set Cookies check box. You can specify an exception to this rule by
clicking the Exceptions button, entering a Web address, and clicking
Allow. To undo this decision later, return to the Exceptions window,
select the Web site in the list, and click Remove. I cover the Exceptions
window in more detail in Chapter 16.

✔ **To prevent certain Web sites from setting a cookie,** leave the Allow
Sites to Set Cookies check box selected, but click the Exceptions button,
enter the address of a Web site, and then click the Block button. To undo
this decision later, return to the Exceptions window, select the Web site
in the list, and click Remove.

✔ **To prevent so-called affiliates from setting cookies,** select the For the
Originating Site Only check box. An *affiliate* is a Web site that lives
within another Web site but is not actually *part of it.* Though you don't
realize it, most of the Web sites you visit every day contain affiliates in
the form of advertising. Most of the banner ads you see, for example, are
not actually part of the Web site that contains them, but are generated
by a third-party advertising firm. Because these are another form of Web
sites, they can also set their own cookies, and most of these cookies are
used for undesirable purposes such as tracking your viewing habits as
you move among other Web sites in the ad's network.

Allowing *only* the originating site — and not affiliates — to set cookies is
a good way to ensure that Web sites continue to work while preventing
affiliate advertisers from storing cookies.

✔ **To prevent Web sites you've dealt with previously from setting more
cookies,** select the Unless I Have Removed Cookies Set by the Site check
box. In this context, *dealt with* means you've taken the trouble in the
past to manually delete cookies set by the Web site by using the Cookie
Manager. Such drastic and specific action probably means the Web site
did something untrustworthy in your eyes. This option allows you to
automatically block cookies from all such Web sites in the future so you
don't need to waste time doing so manually.

From the Cookies tab, you can also view, search, and remove stored cookies
by clicking the View Cookies button. The Cookie Manager opens to offer
information about the cookies on your computer, organized into groups by
the Web site who stored them, as shown in Figure 14-6. To find a cookie more
quickly, you can enter part of its name or originating site address into the
Search text box. To view information about a particular cookie, select it and
look at the bottom of the screen. Most of the supplied information is of a
highly technical and irrelevant nature, but you can also take a look at when
the cookie is set to expire. If you aren't happy with what you see, you can
manually remove the cookie by clicking Remove Cookie. You can also remove
all stored cookies by clicking Remove All Cookies. Note that both actions take
place as soon as you click their respective buttons, and you can't undo a
removal.

Figure 14-6:
The Cookie
Manager
displays info
about every
cookie
stored on
your
computer
and allows
you to
remove any
that you find
suspect.

Clearing your cache

You want to go to a new restaurant in town, so you call for directions. It's so good that you decide to go there every night. Are you going to call for the directions every night? Probably not. At some point, the head waiter is going to recognize your voice and ask why on earth you keep calling — the restaurant isn't moving!

You would, of course, write the directions down or commit them to memory. In the digital world, the idea that you can make copies of information instead of constantly returning to the source is known as *caching*. Technical details aside, caching allows Firefox to make copies of Web sites you visit frequently and store them on your computer so they load more quickly. When you instruct Firefox to visit a Web site, it simply compares the version stored on your computer with the current version. If they're the same, it saves time by loading the Web site directly off your computer.

By default, Firefox caches the last 50MB worth of Web sites that you visit onto your computer.

To configure or clear the cache, follow the directions in the section "Working One-on-One with Your Data," earlier in this chapter, to get to the Cache tab of the Options window. From there, you can do any of the following:

✔ **Increase or reduce the amount of hard drive space** Firefox uses to store cached Web sites on your computer by entering a new number in place of 50. Most computers these days have so much hard drive space that 50MB is but a tiny fraction, so you probably shouldn't worry about reducing this number. If you have available hard drive space, enlarging the number improves page-load performance because Firefox can cache more sites.

A *megabyte* (MB) is a technical unit of measurement used to describe how much space something uses on a computer. Many computers these days have at least 20 *gigabytes* (GB) of space, which — because a gigabyte roughly equals 1,000MB — is equivalent to about 20,000MB.

✔ **Clear the current cache** by clicking the Clear Cache Now button. This action takes place as soon as you click the button and is irreversible. Note that this doesn't *turn off* the cache; it clears only the currently cached sites. New cached Web sites accrue as soon as you begin surfing. If the Clear Cache Now button is unavailable, your cache is already empty.

Chapter 15

Staying Safe Online

Security alerts come and go with the tide, and even the most leisurely of activities is marred by new vigilance. Unfortunately, the Internet offers little escape. Every day, hackers determine new ways to relieve unwitting users of their passwords, credit card information, and other key credentials. Identity theft might seem hard to pull off to common folk like you and me, but the reality is that it usually begins with a single online password being guessed or stolen.

Firefox is determined to give you the smoothest possible online experience, and security is no exception. Still, your security online ultimately rests in your hands. This chapter outlines the safeguards Firefox includes and offers recommendations for how you can protect yourself best.

Phishing, Pharming, and Phriends

Perhaps more frustrating than the online attacks themselves is that each one has its own technical alias. You don't have to know the lingo to stay safe, but it's helpful to speak the same language as the security organizations that are working on your behalf.

Phishing: Don't get hooked!

One of the most popular types of attacks today falls under a category known as *phishing*. Phishers bait unsuspecting users into divulging their passwords by creating perfect replicas (known as *spoofs*) of popular Web sites. One of the most common victims of phishing, for example, is eBay (see Figures 15-1 and 15-2). Every year, hundreds of phishers set up fake versions of the renowned auction site and notify customers that, for whatever reason, they need to click a link (that loads a fake replica of eBay) and enter their eBay login information. As soon as a customer does, his username and password are sent to the owner of the fake eBay, who can then use it on the *real* eBay.

Phishing scams are prevalent because they're successful, and they're successful because they're nearly impossible to detect. Some phishers are plain lazy and create error-ridden pages that no professional company would churn out, but sophisticated phishers can create look-alikes that mimic legitimate Web sites down to the pixel. The e-mails they send appear to come from respected addresses such as `support@ebay.com` or `accounts@citibank.com`. There are, however, a few precious aspects of legitimate Web sites that fakes can't duplicate. Phishers aren't expecting you to recognize these aspects, but these so-called untouchables are your window to safety, as I outline in the next few sections.

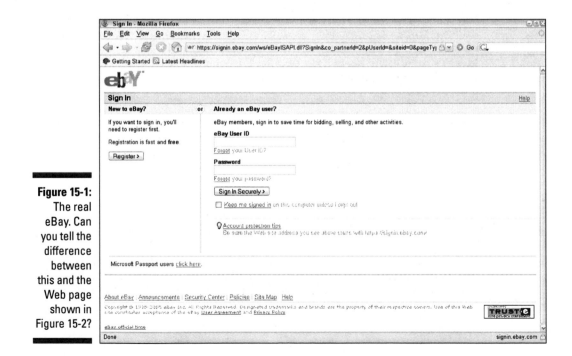

Figure 15-1:
The real eBay. Can you tell the difference between this and the Web page shown in Figure 15-2?

Figure 15-2:
A recent
phishing
eBay
replica.
Notice the
eBay logo,
the login
form, and
even the
Trust button
have been
faithfully
replicated.

Even the most experienced computer users fall prey to well-crafted phishing scams. Keep these tips in mind while surfing and be sure to review your bank statements regularly for unusual charges, just in case a hacker gets past your guard.

Don't believe what you read

Most identify thefts begin with a phishing scam, and most phishing scams begin with an e-mail or an instant message that appears to come from a reputable source (see Figure 15-3). These messages exist to convince you that you absolutely, positively *must* click a link and enter in your personal information immediately. Phishers have concocted a dizzying array of explanations: Your information was lost; you might have won a contest; you need to verify that your information is current; your account will be closed; and so on. Although the messages often look professional and seem to come from legitimate addresses, the links they contain take you to the hacker's replica.

Most legitimate Web sites never ask you for your personal information by e-mail or instant message. After all, why would they need to? They already have your information. Powerhouses like eBay don't take chances on losing user information: They back it up several times over in their own databases. And, I'm sorry, but you probably *didn't* win a contest. (Did you even enter one?)

Being anti-social isn't such a bad thing

I spend most of this chapter — and most of my programming career — examining the technical ways in which your online security can be violated. However, studies have shown that hackers often don't need complex algorithms and supercomputers; all they need is a telephone and a friendly voice. In an increasingly popular attack called *social engineering,* hackers call up their would-be victims and cajole the needed information out of them. Sometimes they say they're from your Internet Service Provider (ISP) and that they need your password or your Internet will be disconnected. Other times they claim they're calling on behalf of the bank or a popular site such as eBay. Whatever the guise, the end game is always the same: Convince you to divulge your personal information to a stranger who sounds friendly and authoritative.

What makes social engineering scary is that the best computer tools aren't going to protect you. What makes it scarier is that even if *you* are aware of this attack and know not to fall for it, your private information can still be socially engineered out of those you entrust to protect your information. That's because hackers don't just play the ISP or the bank in this sick charade; sometimes they call your ISP or bank and play *you.* In this scenario, the hacker doesn't play the friendly, authoritative company official. He plays the angry, exasperated user whose password is being rejected online. The hope is that if he acts frustrated enough, the company will divulge or reset your password even though the hacker can't properly verify his (your!) identity.

The best way to protect yourself against social engineering is to be aware of the scheme and to ensure that the companies who hold the keys to your identity, such as your ISP and your bank, are also aware. Confirm that your ISP's and bank's policies forbid employees from divulging your information over the phone or by e-mail to people who can't authenticate themselves, no matter how frustrated or angry they get.

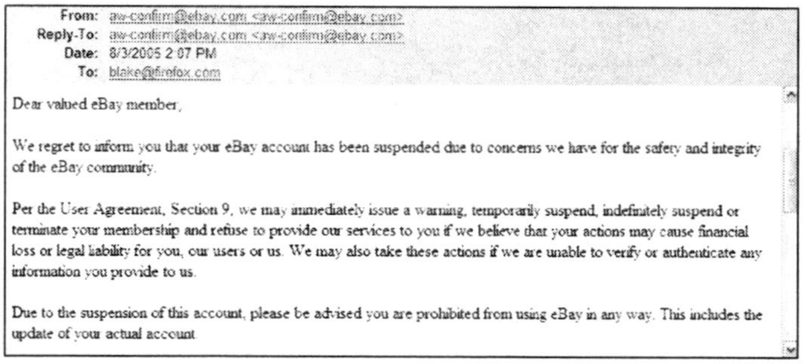

Figure 15-3:
A typical
phishing
e-mail.

From: aw-confirm@ebay.com <aw-confirm@ebay.com>
Reply-To: aw-confirm@ebay.com <aw-confirm@ebay.com>
Date: 8/3/2005 2:07 PM
To: blake@firefox.com

Dear valued eBay member,

We regret to inform you that your eBay account has been suspended due to concerns we have for the safety and integrity of the eBay community.

Per the User Agreement, Section 9, we may immediately issue a warning, temporarily suspend, indefinitely suspend or terminate your membership and refuse to provide our services to you if we believe that your actions may cause financial loss or legal liability for you, our users or us. We may also take these actions if we are unable to verify or authenticate any information you provide to us.

Due to the suspension of this account, please be advised you are prohibited from using eBay in any way. This includes the update of your actual account

If you get an e-mail asking for your personal information, delete it. If you want to be sure you're doing the right thing, contact the company by using the contact information you find in Table 15-1 or on its Web site. (And get there by typing in the company address, of course — don't click the e-mail link!)

Table 15-1	Companies Most Frequently Targeted by Phishers
Company Name	*Contact Info to Report a Scam*
America Online (AOL)	abuse@aol.com
Citibank	emailspoof@citigroup.com
eBay	spoof@ebay.com
PayPal	spoof@paypal.com
SunTrust	abuse@suntrust.com
U.S. Bank	fraud_help@usbank.com
Visa	phishing@visa.com
Washington Mutual	spoof@wamu.com
Yahoo!	abuse@yahoo.com

Don't worry: You aren't alone

When you read about all the devious schemes I describe in this chapter, it's easy to believe that it's you and your computer against a sea of brilliant hackers. The truth is that in the fight against hackers, you have some very powerful allies. The world's largest corporations — and not just those in the computer industry — have some very good reasons to win the war. First of all, these schemes cost some companies tens of millions of dollars every year. When a thief splurges with your credit card, for example, your bank typically foots the bill. And that's just the direct monetary cost. What about the harm done to a company's brand and reputation when a phisher posing as a company official steals your password?

Many companies have set up e-mail addresses or phone numbers you can use to report hacker solicitations. For example, if you receive an e-mail that appears to be from eBay and directs you to a Web site that asks for your password, forward it to spoof@ebay.com. Table 15-1 lists the companies that are most often targeted by phishers, as well as the e-mail address to use when you receive a phishing scam.

It's important (and comforting) to realize that companies like eBay aren't kidding around. If the company catches a hacker, it doesn't send him a warning notice; it sends him to jail, in collaboration with local authorities.

Know where you are

The links in phishing e-mails and instant messages rarely display an address such as http://www.ebay.com. Rather, they generally offer enticing text like Billing Information, or simply eBay. That's because the Web site address is the one fundamental aspect of a legitimate site that phishers *cannot copy*. There is exactly one www.ebay.com in the world, and it's the real eBay. The hope, then, is that when you click the link and Firefox opens it automatically, you'll forget to check the Location Bar. So that's an important step:

Always verify that you're really at the Web site you think you're at by checking the address in the Location Bar.

Unfortunately, protecting yourself isn't that simple. As you can tell by now, phishers are nothing if not persistent. They've devised a number of clever ways to disguise or obfuscate the addresses of their fake replicas so that even people who know to check are fooled! Here are some indicators to watch out for:

✔ **Most legitimate Web site addresses don't contain the at sign (@).** This symbol has special meaning when contained within a Web address: The phrase before it is considered to be login information, and the phrase after it is interpreted as the Web site to which you wish to login. For example, an address of http://www.ebay.com@blakeross.com, is interpreted as user www.ebay.com logging in to the Web site http://blakeross.com and will actually navigate to http://blakeross.com, even though it might appear to point to eBay at first glance. If all that didn't make much sense, that's okay — it's a technical detail you don't need to worry about. When you visit these kinds of addresses, Firefox automatically asks you to confirm the decision, as shown in Figure 15-4. (I use my Web site for demo purposes.)

Practically no legitimate Web sites use this kind of addressing scheme, so if you ever encounter a window like this, the right answer is almost certainly No.

✔ **Be wary of numerical addresses.** Reputable Web sites use words or phrases in their addresses so you can return to them easily. Malicious sites often sport numerical addresses, such as http://94.116.102.156, to make them more difficult to trace.

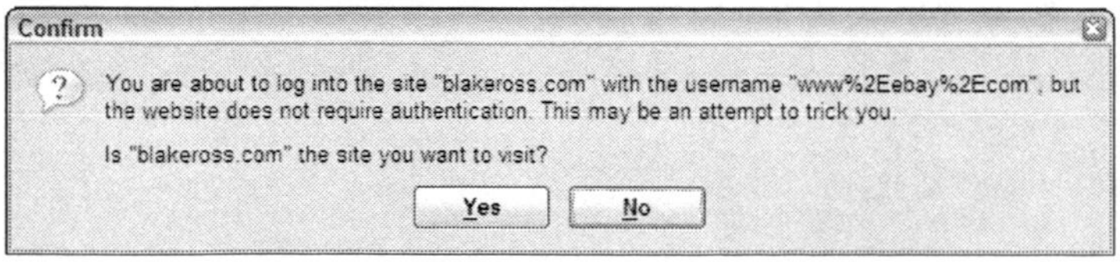

Figure 15-4:
Firefox asks you to confirm going to suspicious Web sites.

Confirm	☒
⚲ You are about to log into the site "blakeross.com" with the username "www%2Eebay%2Ecom", but the website does not require authentication. This may be an attempt to trick you.	
Is "blakeross.com" the site you want to visit?	
[Yes] [No]	

✔ **Follow the yellow brick road, er, Location Bar.** Legitimate Web sites that ask you for highly sensitive information, such as banks, always use a security technology such as SSL (Secure Sockets Layer). Firefox makes it easy to tell whether you are at a secure Web site: The entire Location Bar turns yellow and is punctuated by a lock icon, as shown in Figure 15-5. Note that if you aren't using the default theme, the Location Bar might be shaded with another color, such as green. Although the other developers and I don't encourage it, some themes change the color to better match their design. (See Chapter 17 for more information about the themes feature.)

If you ever find yourself entering critical information into a Web site whose address is not enshrouded in yellow, something is wrong. If you attempt to submit information at a non-secure Web site, Firefox displays the warning shown in Figure 15-6.

If you aren't entering sensitive information, you don't need to concern yourself with this warning. It isn't unusual for Web sites to transmit nonsensitive data in an unencrypted (non-secure) fashion. In fact, it's so common that by default, Firefox doesn't show this confirmation again unless you specifically request it by selecting the Alert Me check box. If you leave the confirmation off, you can continue to detect suspicious activity by observing the Location Bar, as I describe earlier in this section.

The lock icon indicates a secure Web site.

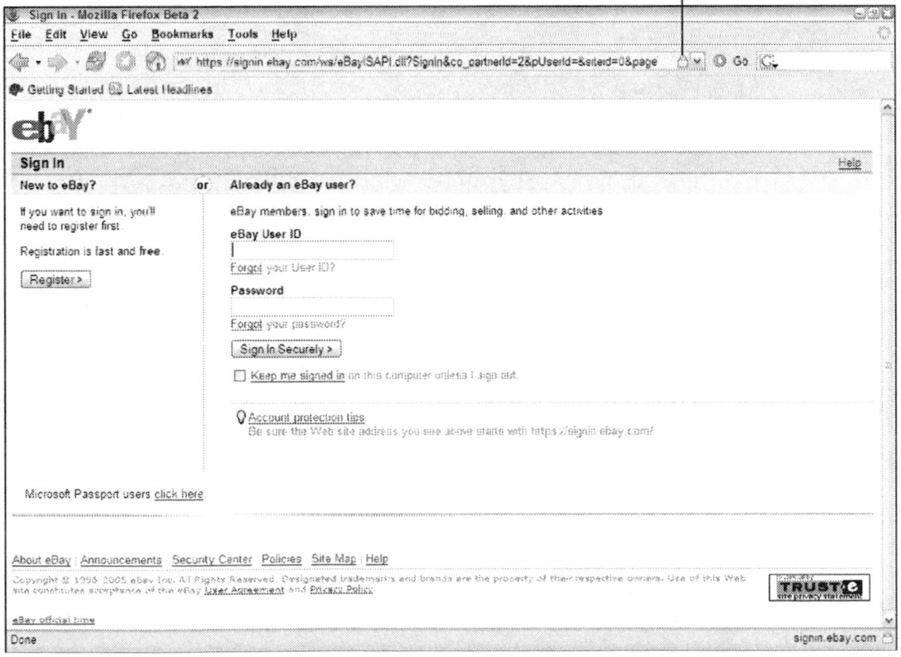

Figure 15-5:
The Location Bar turns yellow, and a lock appears at the end of it, when you view a secure Web site.

Figure 15-6:
If you attempt to submit information at a non-secure Web site, Firefox displays this warning.

Security Warning

ⓘ The information you have entered is to be sent over an unencrypted connection and could easily be read by a third party.

Are you sure you want to continue sending this information?

☐ Alert me whenever I submit information that's not encrypted.

[Continue]   [Cancel]

Likewise, when you leave a secure Web site through a link on its page, Firefox warns you that you're venturing back out into non-secure territory (see Figure 15-7). Again, this should be a concern only if you expected to remain in secure territory — that is to say, if you intended to enter sensitive information into the newly loaded Web site.

Figure 15-7:
Firefox warns you when you leave secure territory.

Security Warning

⚠ You are about to leave an encrypted page. Information you send or receive from now on could easily be read by a third party.

☐ Alert me whenever I leave an encrypted page for one that isn't encrypted.

[OK]

Firefox always displays the actual address of any secure Web site you view in the bottom-right corner of the window, regardless of whatever tricks a phisher uses to try to disguise it. Note that a *secure Web site* is simply one that transfers your information securely over the Internet; whether it's transferring that information to a reputable source is another matter. See the following section, "Phending off pharming," for more information.

Know where you're typing

Get in the habit of asking yourself "Where am I typing this?" each and every time you enter your password. Some phishers try to deceive you by opening browser windows that replicate not other Web sites, but other programs on your computer. For instance, a phisher might design a Web site that looks like an AOL Instant Messenger (AIM) window and asks you to verify your password. If you're an AIM user and are currently logged on to AIM, you might be fooled into thinking this is an AIM window.

Remember this simple rule: If the title bar of the window begins with "Mozilla Firefox," it is a Web site masquerading as a program, *not* another program, because another program on your computer would have its own name in its title bar or something even more descriptive. The AIM Buddy List window, for example, contains your instant messaging screen name (such as Johnny123's Buddy List Window). A phisher can't replicate that part of the window in his spoof Web site because he doesn't know your screen name, just as he can't prevent Mozilla Firefox from appearing in the title bar.

Phending off pharming

A new crop of attacks is on the horizon, and it's even more insidious than phishing — and more poorly named. Pharming is a new way of luring you to fake Web sites with the same old goal: stealing your identity. Instead of setting up a convincing replica of a popular site, hackers attack *the site itself* and set up a site redirect that takes effect when you and others try to visit it. In other words, even if you type the correct address yourself, you can still end up at a fraudulent Web site. Because the Location Bar actually reflects the correct address and because the scammer didn't interact with you in any other fashion, none of the phishing tests can help you detect pharmers!

Imagine that you have to call a friend for directions to his house. Now imagine that someone posing as your friend answers the phone and, with a voice just like your friend's, directs you to his house instead so he can rob you. Now you can begin to understand why pharming is so sinister.

The good news here is that pharming is a very difficult attack to pull off because hackers need to successfully break into the Web site itself. Technical details aside, they essentially need to update the table of information that says, "when the user types ebay.com, load the information off *this* computer." Furthermore, if a hacker does manage to successfully pharm a major Web site, the company that operates it can notice and correct the problem very quickly.

The rarity of pharming is a saving grace, but you should still take steps to prevent being pharmed. Doing so requires a little knowledge of *browser certificates.* These aren't gift certificates; instead, they're more like the documents certifying that your doctor is trained to perform an operation. Browser certificates help you verify that you're interacting with the desired site, which cuts to the very heart of pharming.

In the phishing section, I discuss the concept of secure Web sites that use SSL technology and mention that all reputable sites asking for sensitive information should use this technology. Certificates are the next layer of security. Whereas SSL technology ensures that your information is being securely transferred, certificates ensure that your information is being securely transferred to the organization you intend to entrust with it. Trusted third parties such as VeriSign issue certificates to consummate your transactions with secure Web sites, just as an independent public notary would preside over the dealings of two strangers. These companies issue certificates only to reputable companies.

Keep in mind that certificates are built atop the SSL technology. Therefore, if the malicious Web site the pharmer is secretly redirecting to doesn't support SSL (which it might want to do as a ruse), Firefox won't be expecting a certificate and therefore won't warn of a mismatch. This is intentional because SSL should be considered the first hurdle that any legitimate Web site should pass. In other words, if the Web site *doesn't* support SSL — if that Location Bar doesn't turn bright yellow — something is already suspect before you even begin worrying about certificates.

The bottom line is that it's impossible — as far as I know today — for any hacker to replicate the combination of SSL technology (which displays the bright yellow Location Bar!) and a legitimate, matching certificate.

Protecting your password

Your password is the prize most hackers are seeking. It is often the key to your credit card and Social Security numbers, to your home address and other private data, and you should guard it with the same vigilance as you do the key to your home.

Besides using tricks like fake e-mail and fake Web sites to steal your passwords, there are hackers working on an entirely different approach: Rather than persuade you to give us your password, they'll just guess it themselves! Yes, that's right: *guess it*.

How certificates defend you

When you go to a secure site today, Firefox asks the site for the certificate issued to it by VeriSign or another trusted third party. If it's a legitimate site, it can do so without concern. If the site has been pharmed and is thus secretly redirecting to a different site, the new, illegitimate site has no access to the authentic certificate. Firefox smells something fishy, and — here's the important part — warns you that the provided certificate does not match and asks whether you want to continue. You should say *no* in all cases. There are very few cases where legitimate sites would cause this error — usually when they forgot to renew their certificates — and in those rare instances, you should say no and wait for the company to get its act together.

The unfortunate fact of security is that it often comes at the expense of convenience. Although computing power isn't yet to the point where hackers can quickly guess *any* combination of letters and numbers, they can realistically try every password in the dictionary and then some. And if the idea of a hacker slaving away at home entering passwords gives you some consolation, think again: Hackers today use sophisticated networks of computers that work together to guess passwords automatically (see the "How they do it" sidebar). That means that using your favorite color or even your mother's maiden name as your password just isn't going to cut it anymore. Here are some tips for keeping your password safe from prying eyes:

- **Throw convenience to the wind.** If you're using a password that has any kind of recognizable personal significance (such as your mother's maiden name or your birth town), you're putting yourself at risk. Hackers have assembled vast collections of words far beyond those found in the dictionary, including slang and names of people, streets, and pets. The safest route is to choose a random combination of letters and numbers, such as y94pJ332k. Mix the letters and numbers together and use both upper- and lowercase. If the Web site allows it, include special characters such as ! or $.

- **Write your password down on paper until you remember it.** It's going to take you awhile to remember lw2ih4smpw as easily as you remember your mother's maiden name. However, saving passwords on your computer is a bad idea because if someone is able to gain access to your computer, she can retrieve it. Instead, write it down on paper and store it in a safe location in your home. Throw it out as soon as you're comfortable with your new password.

  You can also try using a mnemonic device to remember a seemingly nonsensical password. For example, lw2ih4smpw looks like complete gibberish, but I remember it as "*I w*ant to (2) *i*mprison *h*ackers for (4) *s*tealing *m*y *p*assword."

- **Never give your password or other private information to anyone. *Anyone.*** This tip is just common sense. Employees of reputable companies will never contact you out of the blue to request your password or other private information.

- **Make your password as long as possible.** Different sites allow different length ranges. The longer you make your password, the harder it is for hacking technology to guess it.

- **Use different passwords for different sites.** Yes, it's much more convenient to remember a single password. But using the same password at multiple places weakens your overall security because your security is only as strong as the weakest link. If a hacker steals your password at a low-security site, you can bet he's going to see whether it also works at your bank.

✔ **Be careful where you log in.** Sites you're liable to visit frequently — such as your Web mail site, if you use a Web-based e-mail service — often remember who you are automatically so you don't have to keep entering your login information (see Figure 15-8). This is great when you're at home, but it's dangerous at a public computer where the very next person might also use your Web mail provider. Many Web sites offer a check box that says something to the effect of Remember Me on This Computer. Select this check box only if you're on your home computer. Alternatively, some Web sites remember you by default and offer an I Am on a Public Computer check box to bypass it, and you should select this whenever you are *not* on your home computer. If you can't tell whether a particular Web site will remember you, I recommend using that site only on computers that belong to you.

✔ **Limit access to your computer.** The Firefox Password Manager remembers your login information for you so you don't have to keep entering it when you return to Web sites. Although this is convenient, it might be undesirable if you share a single computer with other people, such as family members or co-workers. Unless you trust the other people who have access to your computer, you might want to disable the Password Manager or use its Master Password feature, as I describe in Chapter 8.

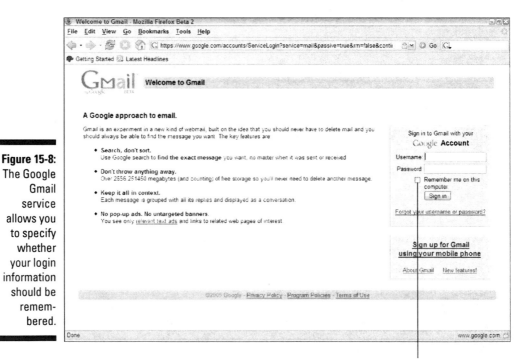

Figure 15-8:
The Google Gmail service allows you to specify whether your login information should be remembered.

Check this box if you want Gmail to remember your login info.

How they do it

While your computer takes its sweet time booting up, hackers are guessing thousands and thousands of letter combinations to crack a victim's password. How do they do it? And better yet, where can we common folk get such fast computers?

The truth is that hackers use the same kinds of computers that you and I use, but with a few differences. One is that hackers aren't actually using the computer interactively; they're using the computer only to try passwords endlessly until the correct one is found. This means they don't care to see a helpful error message or click an OK button when the wrong password is tried. Their programs run automatically and very quickly without any human interaction until the correct password is found.

The second and most important difference is that hackers aren't limited to a single computer. Instead, they can network multiple computers together and have them work in parallel to multiply the processing power and reduce the length of the operation. For example, while one computer is trying all the words beginning with *A,* another computer could try all the *B* words, and so forth.

The worst part comes when you ask that burning question: Where do those additional computers come from? Unfortunately, one way or another, the computer supplier is typically you or someone like you. Either the hacker purchases additional computers with the money he obtains by stealing a victim's banking information, or he is actually using a victim's computer directly because he stole the victim's password. Yes, you read that correctly: Many hackers take control of victims' computers and put them to work guessing other would-be victims' passwords. In this way, hacking is a viciously self-supporting endeavor.

Most modern Web sites try to counter or slow a hacker's ability to guess a user's password by pausing a second or two before revealing whether a guessed password is correct or not, or by preventing users who use an incorrect password three times from logging in. These measures have been fairly successful at staving off hackers.

Another silver lining is that the same networking technique (called distributed computing) used by hackers to guess passwords is also used by leading scientists and researchers worldwide for the benefit of mankind. Many researchers who require enormous amounts of computing power to solve the problem they're working on distribute a program you can download to "donate" your computer's processing power to the research effort. When you aren't using your computer, these programs use your computer to work on complex mathematical calculations and submit the results back to the researchers. Although your computer is only solving a miniscule portion of the overall problem, researchers can aggregate all the data they receive to figure out the larger picture. Two of the most famous projects to use this method are Stanford's Folding@Home (`http://folding.stanford.edu`), which seeks to understand protein folding and cure-related diseases such as Alzheimer's, and Berkeley's Seti@Home (`http://setiathome.ssl.berkeley.edu`), which analyzes radio telescope data in the hopes of discovering extraterrestrial communication.

Using the PwdHash Extension

Reading a chapter about all the work involved in keeping your identity secure can be a real downer. Firefox was created to make your life *easier* in every possible respect, and here I am giving you a laundry list of facts to keep in mind during everyday surfing. What a pain! You shouldn't have to worry about those details. With that in mind, I and a group of security experts at Stanford set out to create a browser extension called PwdHash, short for Password Hash. (See Chapter 20 for more information about Firefox extensions.) The goal of PwdHash is to afford users the convenience of remembering a single password with the security of using a different password on each Web site you visit. It does this by automatically and transparently generating a different version of your password for each Web site.

Discovering PwdHash

As convenient as it is, using a single password at every Web site you visit creates one huge problem: When someone gets your password from one Web site, all other sites you log in to are exposed.

Your password can fall into the wrong hands when

- Someone hacks one of the Web sites you log in to
- A phisher convinces you to enter your password at a replica site

PwdHash handles hacking scams and phishing scams slightly differently, but the good news is that it protects you from both. The following two sections tell you how.

Doing the password mash with PwdHash

If your password is the same at every other site in your network, one hack is no longer an isolated incident — it's a nightmare. It's also a hacker's dream because your security is only as strong as the weakest site you visit.

Suppose you visit two Web sites regularly. The first is a low-security, makeshift high school reunion page that an old classmate slapped together over the weekend. The second is Citibank, which houses your financial accounts. Both sites require a username and password. Citibank can implement the most expensive and cutting-edge password defenses in the world, but they'll be entirely useless if a hacker breaks into the reunion page and steals the password list. Do you think he wants to see how you and your classmates are celebrating your 25th? Of course not. He wants to take your password to the bank — literally.

Using different usernames at different Web sites makes it more difficult for a hacker to use the login information he obtains from hacking one Web site at another site you use because he still won't know your username at the other site. (This isn't always possible, though, because many sites ask for your e-mail address in lieu of a username.)

If you use PwdHash, you can continue to type the same password into both Citibank and the reunion site. The difference is that right before you submit the information to the sites, and without bothering you, PwdHash automatically generates a different version of your password for each site. (If you're using a computer without the PwdHash extension, you need to generate this version manually, as I discuss in "Using PwdHash from other computers" later in this chapter.) This process is called *hashing,* and in a non-technical sense, you can imagine the process works as follows. Say your password is 42family19. When you log in to Citibank, PwdHash adds the site's address — citibank.com — to the end of your password, yielding 42family19citibank.com. Then it scrambles up this new phrase in a random order. The same process is repeated at reunion.com with 42family19reunion.com. The scrambling technique is, of course, much more complicated, with the end result that it's impossible for a hacker to get from the scrambled version to the unscrambled version.

So how does this fix the problem? Well, even if a hacker does retrieve your reunion password, that password works *only* at the reunion site. It doesn't work at Citibank because Citibank is expecting the Citibank-specific "definition."

Giving the phishers a hook to swallow

If you use only one password, the moment a phisher tricks you into entering your password at a fake replica site, all other Web sites you log in to are now exposed. This scenario is related to the Citibank/reunion conundrum I describe in the preceding section, and PwdHash remedies it in a similar fashion. Suppose the replica phishing page is located at www.ebay.org instead of www.ebay.com. As soon as you type in your password (for this example, 42family19), and before the hacker has a chance to see it, PwdHash takes 42family19ebay.org, scrambles it, and then sends it to the hacker. What the hacker receives is a completely useless password because it works *only* at his fake site. It doesn't work at the real eBay.

Using PwdHash every day

PwdHash was designed with Firefox principles in mind — that is, it tries to stay out of your hair. The extension is available from www.pwdhash.com, and the installation process is the same as for all other Firefox extensions. I describe this simple procedure in Chapter 20.

Using the extension is easy. All you have to do is tell PwdHash whenever you're about to type in a password. You do this by typing two at signs (@@) before typing your password (for example, if your password is family, you would type **@@family**) or by pressing F2 before typing your password. You can then rest assured that PwdHash is safeguarding the password you type in next.

Configuring PwdHash

Before you can log in to your existing Web sites, however, you have to complete a little bit of configuration. This configuration needs to be done only once, and unfortunately it isn't something PwdHash could do for you. Basically, because PwdHash will be generating new, scrambled versions of your password for each Web site you visit, you need to tell these Web sites what your new password is. Even though you yourself continue remembering the old one, PwdHash will be generating new ones for you on your behalf, and you need to notify the sites of the change so they allow you to log in.

Luckily, this configuration is quick and painless, and you can do it on an as-needed basis. The first time you log in to a site after installing PwdHash, simply go to the Web site's Change Password page. These pages usually have three password fields: The first asks you to enter your current password for security reasons, and the latter two ask you to enter your new password. In the current password field, enter your password as usual. For the latter two fields, you must tell PwdHash to scramble the passwords you input. In other words, you want to notify the Web site of your new, scrambled password. To do this, click in the field and type @@ or press F2, and then type your current password into the field. (Follow the steps for both of the new password fields.)

This is the only time you have to worry about which fields to scramble and which to leave alone. Whenever you visit this Web site in the future, you should always scramble your password by typing @@ or pressing F2 before beginning.

Using PwdHash from other computers

PwdHash works automatically and silently when it's installed on your computer, but what happens when you're on a computer that doesn't have PwdHash installed? How can you obtain the scrambled versions of your password for each of the sites you need to access? The best solution, of course, is to install the PwdHash extension on the new computer — but in some environments, such as Internet cafes, that isn't permitted. To remedy this situation,

PwdHash offers a Web site accessible from anywhere that will generate your scrambled version for you. This Web site is located at www.pwdhash.com and is simple and intuitive to use: Just copy and paste the address of the Web site you need to log in to (such as http://www.ebay.com) and enter your password, and the PwdHash site automatically generates the scrambled version for you.

Be sure to note a couple important details here:

✔ Your scrambled password will be visible as soon as you click the Generate button. If someone is looking over your shoulder, she can see it, too. You should immediately cut and paste it from the PwdHash Web site to the Web site you're trying to log in to.

✔ Your unscrambled password (the one you remember) is not saved or transmitted anywhere when you enter it on www.pwdhash.com. A third party could never intercept it because it isn't sent over the Internet.

Preventing Spyware and Viruses

If phishing is the digital equivalent of someone stealing your credit card number, spyware and viruses are like having criminals living in your bedroom. (*Spyware* is software that monitors and records everything you do, and a *virus* is a program that deletes files or causes other damage.) Unlike phishing scams, both spyware and viruses actually live on your computer. These types of infections typically find their way onto your computer through a malicious file you download. The bottom line is this:

> **You should never, ever download a file unless you know exactly what it is, where it's coming from, and whether the person or company offering it is trustworthy.**

Avoiding malicious extensions

Unfortunately, many browsers make it easy to download files inadvertently in the form of extensions. In Internet Explorer, for example, a Web site can spit out a big, annoying confirmation window as soon as it loads. If you click Yes in a hurry to get to the page, a malicious extension is installed. Firefox does everything it can to prevent you from installing malicious files inadvertently. Instead of allowing Web sites to get in your face with extension downloads, Firefox displays the non-intrusive toolbar that you see in Figure 15-9. (This toolbar doesn't appear for the official Firefox site, though.)

Figure 15-9:
Firefox displays this toolbar at the top of Web sites that try to install a browser extension.

Note that the mere appearance of this toolbar doesn't necessarily suggest impropriety on the part of the Web site. The toolbar appears whenever a Web site other than the official, trusted Firefox Plugins Web site (`http://addons.mozilla.org`) tries to install an extension. If you trust the Web site you're viewing, go ahead and proceed, as I discuss in Chapter 20 in the section on installing from another site.

Acquiring additional software protection

Firefox does everything it can to keep you safe, but your computer has many borders to protect, and the browser is only one of them. You *must* install three additional tools to remain safe and sound on the Internet:

- ✔ **Antivirus software:** This tool monitors the files on your computer and checks newly downloaded files for viruses. If it finds one, it notifies you immediately and allows you to either delete the file or quarantine it so it can't harm your computer. It's critical that you **keep your antivirus software up-to-date** because new viruses are discovered regularly. *Recommendations:* Norton AntiVirus and McAfee VirusScan are available in stores.

- **Antispyware software:** Like antivirus software, this tool monitors the files on your computer as well as new downloads, but it's looking for spyware. If it finds any, it notifies you immediately and allows you to delete the file. You must also **keep your antispyware software up-to-date** because new spyware threats are discovered regularly. Plenty of high-quality antispyware tools are available free of charge, although many antivirus suites (which usually cost money) include them nowadays. *Recommendations:* Ad-Aware is freely available from Lavasoft (www.lavasoftusa.com/software/adaware), and Spybot-Search & Destroy is freely available from www.safer-networking.org/en/download.

- **Firewall:** A firewall monitors inbound and outbound Internet connections on your computer — that is to say, it checks when your computer tries to connect to the Internet, and when other computers try to connect to yours. The newest versions of Windows, XP and Vista, come with a built-in firewall that is on by default, so you don't have to do anything. *Recommendation:* If you have an older version, I recommend ZoneAlarm, available from www.zonelabs.com.

Additionally, you should install new security patches for your computer as soon as they're available. See http://microsoft.com/security for more information about the Windows patching process, or www.apple.com/support/downloads for the latest Macintosh security patches.

Staying Up-to-Date

Perhaps the most important fact to remember about your security online is that it's a never-ending battle. Phishers are devising new tricks on the hour, and new strains of computer viruses and spyware appear daily. In addition to keeping your software tools up-to-date, it's critical that you keep *yourself* up-to-date with new developments in the world of security so you know what kinds of new scams to look out for.

Updating Firefox

You need to keep your antivirus and antispyware software current. However, it's also important that you keep your version of Firefox up-to-date as well, because the Mozilla Foundation will release security patches from time to time. Firefox automatically checks for updates once a day. If any are available, it downloads and installs them and notifies you upon completion, providing that the update is compatible with your extensions and themes. Virtually all critical updates (such as those that fix security flaws) are compatible, but major Firefox updates (such as from version 1.5 to 2.0) might be incompatible.

If you're using an extension or theme that is incompatible with the updated version, Firefox presents a list of the incompatible extensions and themes and asks you to confirm the update. Click the Show List button to see the list of incompatibilities. If you proceed with the update, Firefox automatically disables the incompatible extensions and themes until their authors release compatible versions. When compatible versions are released, Firefox discovers and installs them the next time it checks for updates, and then Firefox re-enables the extension or theme. That's because the update feature checks for updates not just to Firefox itself, but also to your installed extensions, themes, and Search Box engines.

If you don't like the automatic update features, you can disable them and check for updates manually. Even if you leave automatic updating on, you can still check for updates manually at any time. I discuss these options in the following two sections.

Disabling automatic update checking or installation

You can disable automatic update checking or installation by following the steps in this section. If you don't like the idea of anything being installed without your permission, it's all right to disable automatic installation. However, I don't recommend disabling automatic checking because then you won't be notified when important updates are available.

To disable automatic update checking or installation, follow these steps:

1. **Choose Tools⇨Options to open the Options window.**

2. **Click the Advanced icon at the top of the window.**

3. **Click the Update tab.**

4. **Do one of the following:**

   • **To disable automatic update checking,** deselect the desired update types. For example, to disable automatic checking for updates to your installed themes and extensions, deselect the Installed Extensions & Themes check box.

   • **To disable automatic update installation,** under When Updates to Firefox are Found, select Ask Me What I Want to Do.

5. **Click OK.**

Checking for updates manually

If you decide to disable automatic update checking, or if you want to check for updates more frequently than the Firefox once-a-day check, you can check for Firefox updates manually at any time by following these steps:

1. Choose Help⇨Check For Updates in the main Firefox window.

If an update is available, the Update Wizard appears and walks you through the update process, as shown in Figure 15-10. Otherwise, Firefox tells you that no updates are available. If no updates are available, click Finish and skip the remaining steps.

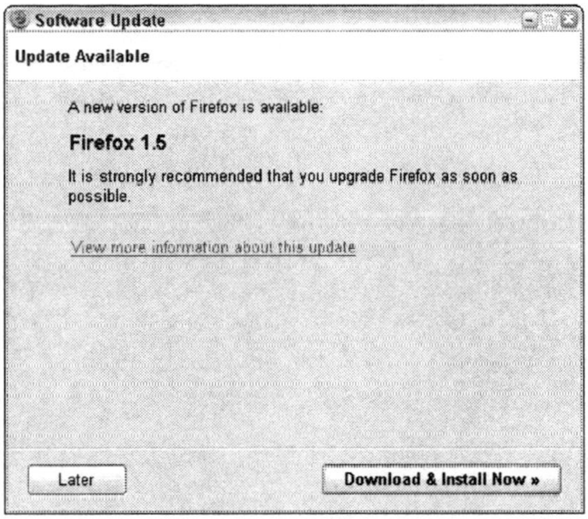

Figure 15-10:
If you choose to install updates manually, the Update Wizard walks you through the process.

2. Read about the available updates and decide whether you want to install them.

If an update is incompatible with one or more of your installed extensions or themes, Firefox warns you and offers a list of the incompatible extensions and themes, which you can access by clicking the Show List button. If you decide to proceed with the update, Firefox automatically disables the incompatible extensions and themes until their authors release updated versions. You can discover and install these updated versions by repeating these steps, or you can wait until Firefox automatically discovers and installs them, provided you have not disabled the automatic update features (as I discuss in the earlier section, "Disabling automatic update checking or installation").

3. To install the updates, click Download & Install Now.

Firefox displays a progress meter indicating the progress of the update.

4. Click Finish to close the Update Wizard.

When the update finishes, you might need to restart Firefox.

Monitoring new developments

Hundreds of new security exploits and attacks have been discovered between the time this book was published and the time you're reading it now. It's critical that you monitor the latest developments so you know how to protect yourself against new tricks. Plenty of online resources update daily. Here are a few of the top dogs of security:

- ✔ **Microsoft Security Home Page:** Offers one-click access to the latest Windows updates, new tips for protecting your computer, and the ongoing blog of the Microsoft Security Response Team.

  ```
  www.microsoft.com/security
  ```

- ✔ **CERT Coordination Center:** Run by the Software Engineering Institute at Carnegie Mellon University, CERT is one of the world's most renowned security response teams, and for good reason: It was also the first. At its Web site, the team posts information about critical security flaws in a wide array of software.

  ```
  www.cert.org/nav/index_red.html
  ```

- ✔ **US-CERT:** The United States Computer Emergency Response Team was formed in 2003 to protect the United States Internet infrastructure against emerging attacks. Its Web site maintains a list of flaws in popular software and is updated daily.

  ```
  www.us-cert.gov
  ```

- ✔ **Anti-Phishing Working Group:** The APWG is a global task force of industry leaders and law enforcement officials working to combat phishing. Its Web site offers a wealth of information about the plague and how you can defend against it.

  ```
  www.antiphishing.org
  ```

Part IV
Dressing Up
the Fox

The 5th Wave   By Rich Tennant

"Look at this, Mother! I customized the browser
so I can navigate the Web the way I want to."

In this part . . .

Because you probably use your browser more than
any other program on your computer, it would be
nothing short of criminal to make you use a browser you
didn't love. So think of the default Firefox setup as a mere
suggestion. It's the developers' best guess as to what a
Web browser should be, but it certainly isn't the only way
to go. Perhaps you want this button over there or that
menu gone entirely. Perhaps Firefox is missing a feature
you need, or maybe you just think it looks better in black.
Whatever your fancy, anything is possible thanks to the
extensive customization features I outline in this part.

Chapter 16

Setting Your Options

In This Chapter

▷ Finding your way around the Options window

▷ Understanding the Firefox options

*O*ptions are heresy among Firefox developers. We don't hate the idea of customization; we just want Firefox to cater to you automatically. It should fit your needs out of the box, so we consider every preference we add a personal failure.

That said, different people have different tastes. Just because I find reality better than reality TV doesn't mean the latter shouldn't be an option. The Firefox Options window helps you configure every aspect of your browsing experience, from home page to shutdown. This chapter provides a brief overview of the Options window and points you to additional information about each option.

The right choice

As strange as it sounds, one of our primary goals in developing Firefox is to *reduce* a user's choices. If you've ever used an application that buried one or two useful options in a sea of absurd ones — and I think that's most software applications these days — you can probably appreciate our intentions. We want to deliver the best possible experience out of the box, and then allow a level of customization that most people are likely to need. For those who really want to trick out Firefox, our community offers a sea of extensions.

So how do applications end up so bloated and, if I may invent an apt word, *featureful?* Having observed or participated in the development

processes of many applications, I can tell you the answer is simple: Developers are an indecisive bunch. Much of the time, the addition of a setting has little to do with what *you* might want; it's a compromise between two developers who disagree about how a feature should behave. Rather than discussing with users to figure out the right behavior, it's generally much faster just to make it an option.

In Firefox, we force ourselves to make decisions about feature behavior rather than adding an option and calling it a day. The only way an option makes it into the product is if the world at large disagrees about how the feature should behave — not two developers.

Using the Options Window

The first thing to do is navigate to the Options window. Choose Tools⇨ Options (Windows) or Firefox⇨Preferences (Mac) to open the Options window, as shown in Figure 16-1. The Options window is designed to be easy and straightforward. It contains six categories of settings in a horizontal bar along the top of the window. Click an icon to view its options. (Note that whichever category you're currently viewing has a highlighted background behind its icon, as the General icon does in Figure 16-1.) Firefox remembers the last category you viewed when you close the Options window and shows that category the next time you open it.

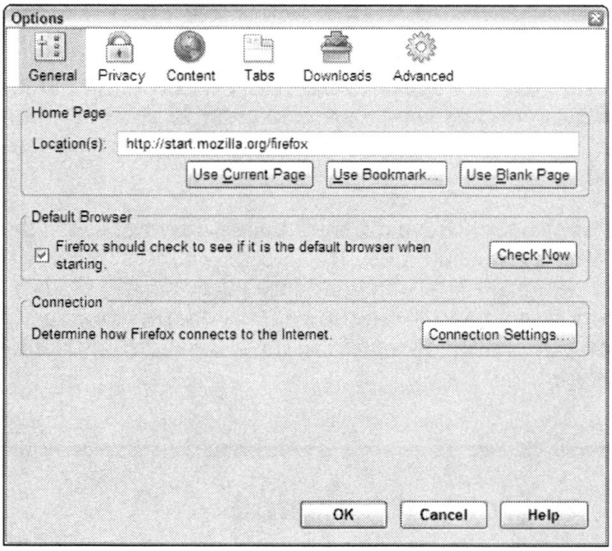

Figure 16-1:
The Options
window
helps you
configure
every aspect
of the
browsing
experience.

Each category is further divided into groups of options. For example, the General category contains three boxed groups: Home Page, Default Browser, and Connection.

You can switch freely between groups and categories and make as many changes as you need to before finalizing your decisions by clicking OK. In general, the changes you make in the Options window aren't saved until you click OK. For example, if you change your home page in General, turn off popup blocking in Content, and then click Cancel to exit the Options window, neither of those changes are saved. (Closing the Options window with the Close button in the corner is equivalent to clicking Cancel.)

However, the Options window contains a few action buttons — such as Clear Browsing History Now — that take effect immediately. Clicking Cancel doesn't undo them. I note these exceptions as they arise in the rest of this chapter.

The Options window demands your attention. In other words, you can't access any other part of the Firefox interface while the Options window is open. However, if you have more than one Firefox window open, you can continue to browse in other windows.

To keep the Options window simple, the developers occasionally move lesser-used settings to separate window. For example, the Colors button in the Content category opens a separate window with coloring options (see Figure 16-2). These secondary windows typically have OK and Cancel buttons. As you would expect, clicking Cancel tells Firefox to forget any changes you made to the options in the window. To save the changes, you must click OK in the secondary window *and* in the main Options window. I note exceptions to this rule in the rest of this chapter.

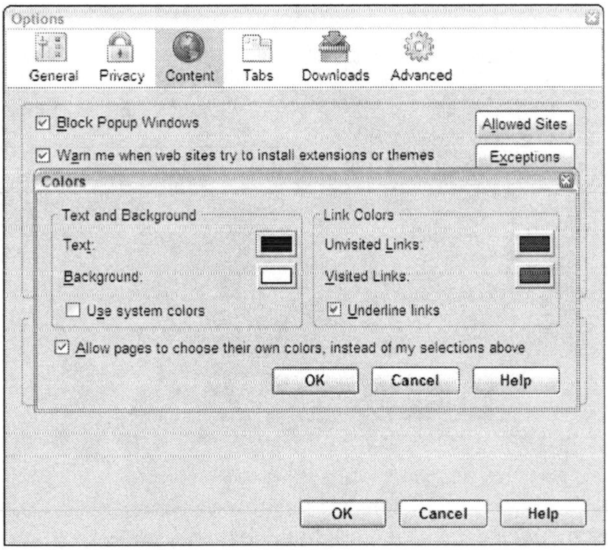

Figure 16-2:
After changing these settings, you must click OK in the secondary window *and* the main Options window.

Also notice the Help button in the bottom-right corner. This button knows which options you're looking at when you click it. For example, if you click it while viewing the Privacy category, it displays help on the Privacy options. See Chapter 13 for details on the Firefox built-in help system.

Oodles of Options

The following sections walk you through the available options by category. I cover most of these options more thoroughly in other chapters, so this section is best used as a starting point.

The General category

The General category (see Figure 16-3) contains options that don't fit well into any of the other categories.

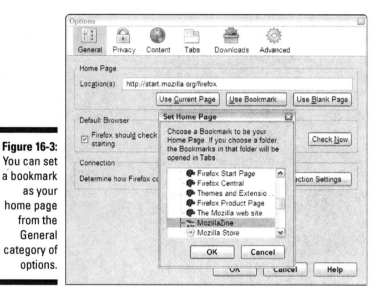

Figure 16-3:
You can set a bookmark as your home page from the General category of options.

Home Page

By default, Firefox uses a special Google page (www.google.com/firefox) as your home page, which is the first page you see each time you start Firefox. Here you can enter the address of a new home page.

If you can't remember the address of the site that you want as your home page, try the following tricks:

✔ **Type what you remember.** Firefox displays suggestions from your browsing history as you type. You can also leave the box empty and press the down arrow to see a list of addresses you've typed into the Location Bar recently.

✔ **Visit the page first.** Firefox can automatically set any Web site you visit as your home page. First, cancel out of the Options window (or click OK if you made other changes you want to save). Now return to the page by using any means, such as a search engine. When it's displayed, reopen the Options window and click the Use Current Page button.

You don't have to return to the Options window to set a page you're viewing as the home page. Just drag the tiny icon on the left end of the Location Bar onto the Home button. Firefox asks you to confirm the decision.

✔ **Find it in your bookmarks.** If you previously bookmarked your desired home page, click the Use Bookmark button to open your bookmarks list, as shown in Figure 16-3. Select the bookmark you want to use and click OK or select a bookmarks folder to set all the bookmarks it contains as your home pages. If you have more than one home page, Firefox opens them in tabs, a feature I discuss further in Chapter 7.

If you don't want any home page, click the Use Blank Page button. This option is useful if there's no one Web site you like to check every time you start Firefox, and don't want Firefox to waste time loading a home page.

You can also set multiple home pages that will open in tabs (see Chapter 7 for details).

Default Browser

When a program on your computer needs to display a Web site, it launches your default browser. If you would like to make Firefox the default browser, click Check Now. If Firefox isn't already the default, it offers to make the change. If you click Yes, Firefox becomes your default browser immediately, and clicking Cancel in the Options window won't unset it. To change your default to another browser in the future, use that browser's options.

Firefox never makes itself the default browser unless you allow it to. Unfortunately, certain ruder browsers do so automatically. To have Firefox ensure that it's the default each time it starts, select the check box in this area. Firefox prompts you at startup only if another browser has been set as the default.

Connection

Because Firefox accesses the Internet, you must have a working Internet connection, such as dial-up, DSL, or cable. Firefox usually detects your connection automatically. However, certain companies use so-called *proxies* (computers that forward Internet requests from one computer to another) that can obstruct the connection. Company administrators should click Connection Settings to open a window where they can configure these proxies. This isn't something you should have to worry about.

The Privacy category

Firefox remembers information for you while you browse, such as browsing history and passwords. The Privacy category, shown in Figure 16-4, allows you to configure how much information Firefox stores and when it gets cleared. It's broken down into six tabs, one for each type of information Firefox stores. I discuss the Privacy settings in depth in Chapter 15, so I just review them briefly here.

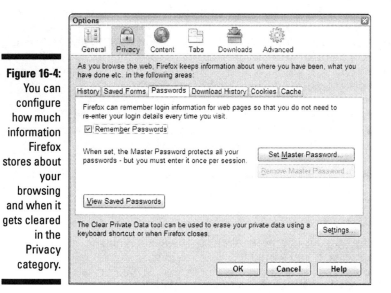

Figure 16-4:
You can configure how much information Firefox stores about your browsing and when it gets cleared in the Privacy category.

History

Firefox maintains a history of the Web sites you visit so you can return to them easily. By default, Firefox remembers the pages you visited in the last nine days. For more on browsing history, turn to Chapter 6.

Saved Forms

Firefox remembers information you enter into online forms, such as a ZIP code, so it can prefill them for you in the future. Likewise, Firefox remembers phrases you search for from the Search Box on the Navigation Toolbar so you can search for them again more quickly. For more on forms, check out Chapter 8.

Passwords

Firefox remembers your online passwords and prefills them for you so you can log in to Web sites more quickly. Chapter 8 covers passwords in depth.

Download History

Firefox keeps records of downloaded files in the Download Manager so you can find and open them easily. See Chapter 11 for more information about the Download Manager. Deleting a record of a download does not delete the downloaded file itself. By default, Firefox stores records forever — or at least until you delete them manually. Or until your computer explodes. And let's hope that doesn't happen.

Cookies

Web sites put tiny bits of information called *cookies* on your computer to improve your browsing experience. Amazon, for example, might store a cookie that contains the contents of your shopping cart, so you can browse the site just as you browse a supermarket. See Chapter 14 for more information about what cookies are and how to configure them.

Cache

Firefox archives the pages you visit in a cache so they load more quickly in the future. Unlike browsing history, you don't have direct access to the cache; Firefox accesses it behind the scenes to speed browsing.

Clear Private Data Settings

As I discuss in Chapter 14, Firefox includes a feature called Clear Private Data (Tools⇨Clear Private Data) to help you clear many kinds of private information quickly. The Settings button at the bottom of the Privacy tab opens the Clear Private Data settings window, where you can configure which kinds of information are cleared, and whether or not a confirmation window is shown, each time you use the Clear Private Data feature. From the settings window, you can also instruct Firefox to clear the specified information automatically each time it shuts down. See Chapter 14 for more information.

The Content category

The Content category (see Figure 16-5) configures the display of Web sites themselves.

Popup Blocking

Firefox blocks Web sites from opening popup windows without your consent, as I discuss in Chapter 9.

- ✓ **To turn off popup blocking,** deselect the Block Popup Windows check box.

- ✓ **To allow popups on certain Web sites,** click the Allowed Sites button to open the exceptions list. Some sites use popup windows legitimately and might not work properly without them. See Chapter 9 for more information about this feature.

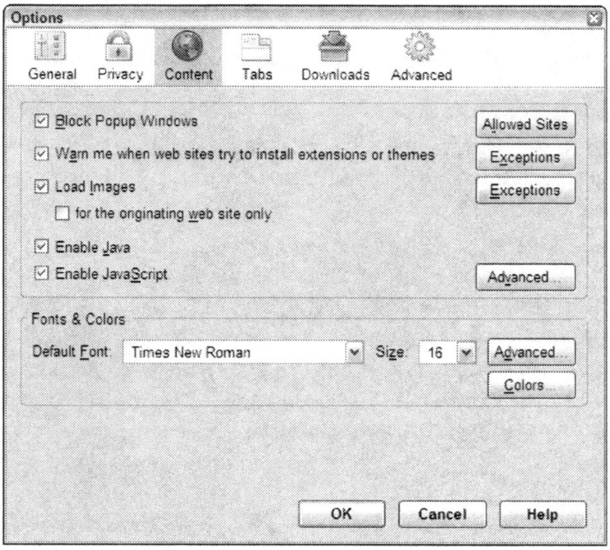

Figure 16-5:
You can customize fonts and colors, turn off images, and configure sites through the Content settings.

Extension and Theme Installation

As I discuss in Chapters 17 (for themes) and 20 (for extensions), only the official Firefox site is allowed to install extensions and themes by default. When you try to install an extension or theme from another Web site, Firefox displays a warning toolbar that you need to dismiss before the installation can proceed, as I discuss in those chapters.

✔ **To enable installation from certain trusted Web sites without a warning,** leave the Warn Me When Web Sites Try to Install Extensions or Themes check box selected, and click the Exceptions button to open the Exceptions window, where you can specify a list of Web sites you trust. When you try to install an extension or theme from one of these sites, Firefox allows the installation without requiring you to deal with the warning toolbar. When you add a site to the exceptions list, the change takes effect immediately. Although clicking Cancel in the main Options window doesn't undo it, you can return to the list and use the Remove buttons if necessary.

✔ **To enable installation from all sites,** deselect the Warn Me When Web Sites Try to Install Extensions or Themes check box. Make sure you trust the company or individual offering an extension before you install it because malicious extensions could carry viruses or have undesirable side effects.

Loading Images

By default, of course, Firefox loads images on all Web sites you visit. To speed browsing or cut down on visual distraction, you can set Firefox to load only certain images or you can turn off images entirely. See Chapter 19 for more information.

> ✔ **To prevent Web sites from loading images from other Web sites,** select the For the Originating Web Site Only check box. This is a reasonable way to block advertising, but it can also break many pages, so I don't recommend it. For a better way to block ads, see the section on the AdBlock extension in Chapter 22.
>
> ✔ **To turn off Web site images,** deselect the Load Images check box.
>
> ✔ **To block or allow images on certain Web sites,** click the Exceptions button to open the exceptions list. If you keep images on, you can use this list to block certain Web sites from loading images. Likewise, if you turn images off, you can allow certain Web sites to keep loading them. To add a Web site to the list, simply enter its address (for example, www. ebay.com) and click the Allow or Block button depending on whether the site should be allowed to display images. This is a highly advanced feature. If you just want to block advertisements, see the section on the AdBlock extension in Chapter 22.

Java and JavaScript

Advanced Web sites use technologies called Java and JavaScript to offer more interactive experiences. Why would you want to disable them? Well, Java sometimes loads slowly, and JavaScript effects are sometimes so interactive they're just annoying. However, if you disable either technology, many Web sites might stop working properly. These options are intended only for advanced users who understand the consequences.

Fortunately, you can prevent annoying JavaScript effects without turning off JavaScript entirely. See Chapter 21 for more information about this feature.

Fonts and Colors

Web site designers, like other artists, spend a great deal of time crafting their work. Nevertheless, you can override the fonts and colors used on Web sites to suit your tastes. See Chapter 19 for more information about these options.

The Tabs category

Use the settings in the Tabs category (see Figure 16-6) to configure the tabbed browsing experience. See Chapter 7 for more information about tabbed browsing, and the section on tweaking tabs in particular for help with each option.

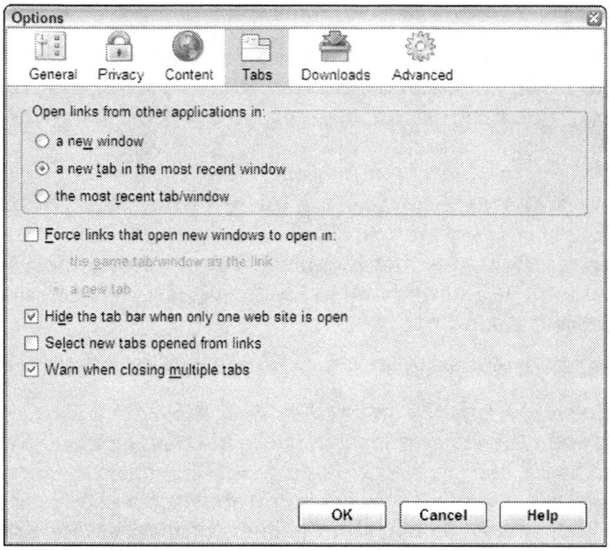

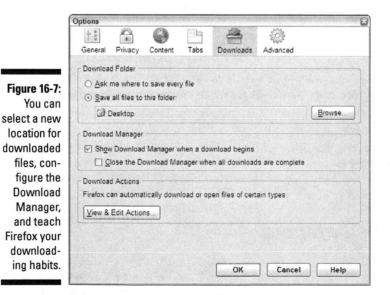

Figure 16-6:
The Tabs category gives you control of your tabbed browsing experience.

The Downloads category

The Downloads category, shown in Figure 16-7, allows you to change the default destination of downloaded files and configure the behavior of the Firefox Download Manager. See Chapter 11 for more information.

Figure 16-7:
You can select a new location for downloaded files, configure the Download Manager, and teach Firefox your downloading habits.

Download Folder

By default, Firefox saves files you download to your computer's desktop so you can find and open them easily. However, you can modify this behavior:

- ✔ **To be prompted for a destination each time you download,** select the Ask Me Where to Save Every File option.

- ✔ **To skip the prompt and save all files to the same location,** select the Save All Files to This Folder option and click Browse to choose a folder. By default, Firefox downloads all files to your computer's desktop.

If you specify a default download location (or leave it as the desktop), you can override the save destination for a specific file by right-clicking the link to the file and choosing Save Link As. You can also press Alt (Windows) or Option (Mac) while clicking the download link. I discuss this feature at length in Chapter 11.

Download Manager

By default, Firefox opens the Download Manager when you begin a download and leaves it open when the download finishes so you can open the new file. If the Download Manager is already open when a download begins, Firefox simply flashes the button for the window on your computer taskbar so you know.

Deselect the Show Download Manager check box in this category if you don't want the Download Manager to open when you start a download. Alternatively, you can leave it on but select the Close the Download Manager check box to have the Download Manager close automatically when all downloads finish. Even if you select this option, Firefox (Windows) briefly shows an animated message in the bottom-right corner of the window when your downloads finish. You can click this message before it disappears to open the Download Manager and access the finished downloads.

Download Actions

Most people pick up certain downloading habits over the years. Every time I download a document, for example, I immediately open it in Microsoft Word. Firefox can save you time by automatically taking a certain action whenever a download finishes. Clicking the View & Edit Actions button opens a window that helps you configure this behavior. See Chapter 11 for more information.

The Advanced category

The Advanced category (see Figure 16-8) contains options intended for experienced Internet users.

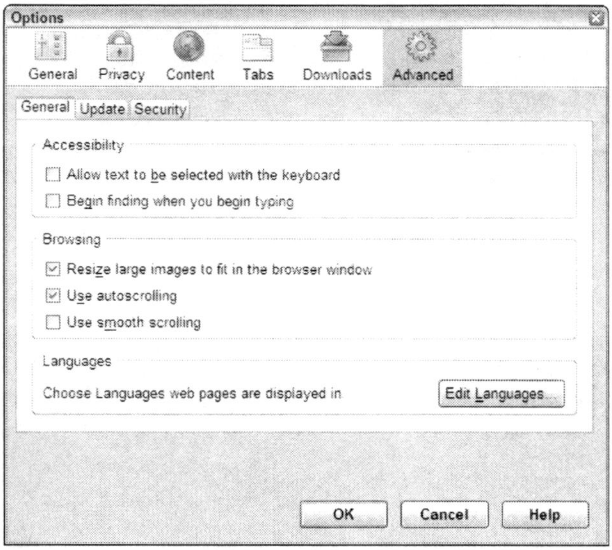

Figure 16-8:
The
Advanced
category
contains
some of the
more
complicated
settings.

These options are divided into the following three tabs.

The General tab

The General tab lets you configure Firefox's keyboard accessibility, some advanced browsing features, and how Web sites offered in multiple languages are displayed.

Accessibility

This area contains options that make Firefox more usable from the keyboard.

- ✔ **Allow text to be selected with the keyboard:** As you know, a flashing line in a text box indicates your typing position. Set this option to show a flashing line in Web sites you visit. Although you can't type into Web sites, you can select the text by using the keyboard, and the flashing line indicates where the selection will begin.

  To move the flashing line, click a spot on the page or use the keyboard arrows. Then, to select the text to the right of the flashing line, press Shift+→. Likewise, to select leftward, press Shift+→. The flashing line also indicates where on the page the Find Bar (which I discuss in Chapter 4) will begin searching.

- ✔ **Begin finding when you begin typing:** Set this preference to search for text on a page just by starting to type, without having to open the Find Bar first. See Chapter 21 for more information about this feature.

Browsing

This area lets you configure certain advanced features of the browsing experience, such as whether large images are automatically resized to fit in the Content area.

✔ **Resize large images to fit in the browser window:** By default, Firefox automatically shrinks large images so you can view them without scrolling. This feature kicks in only when you're viewing a large image on its own (for example, by right-clicking an image in a page and choosing View Image from the contextual menu). Large images within a Web page are not resized. When Firefox resizes an image, the mouse pointer becomes a magnifying glass as you move it over the image. You can restore a shrunken image to its original size by clicking it. Deselect this option to turn off this feature.

✔ **Use autoscrolling:** If your mouse has a middle button, you can use autoscrolling to scroll a page quickly and automatically. See Chapter 21 for more information about this feature. Deselect this option to turn off autoscrolling.

✔ **Use smooth scrolling:** By default, Firefox scrolls a page in notches — that is, it bumps the page up or down a certain amount each time you scroll. Some people might find this behavior jerky when reading a document line by line. Turn on smooth scrolling to have Firefox slide pages up or down more smoothly each time you scroll. If you previously browsed in Internet Explorer, you might feel more comfortable with smooth scrolling because Internet Explorer uses it.

Languages

Firefox automatically detects the language of Web sites you visit so it can display them properly, but some sites are offered in multiple languages. Click the Edit Languages button to open the Languages window. Use the drop-down list and the Add button at the bottom of the window to add languages you understand to the language list, and then use the Move Up and Move Down buttons to organize the list according to your language preferences. When Firefox encounters one of these Web sites, it chooses the highest language on your list that the page supports.

The Update tab

We developers occasionally update Firefox to fix defects and add features. Likewise, extension developers, theme designers, and search engine companies that offer Search Box add-ons are working hard to improve their products. By default, Firefox checks for updates to itself and to each of these other components once a day and automatically installs any that are available.

To configure this automatic behavior or to see a complete history of the updates installed, do any of the following on the Update tab:

- ✓ **To prevent Firefox from automatically checking for updates,** deselect the check boxes for the components for which Firefox should stop checking. You can deselect any of the following:

  - **Firefox:** Updates to the Firefox product itself. I don't recommend disabling automatic checking for Firefox because then you won't be aware of critical Firefox updates that fix security flaws and other important bugs.

  - **Installed Extensions and Themes:** Updates to any of the extensions or themes you have installed.

  - **Search Engines:** Updates to any search engines you added to the Search Box in the upper-right corner of the main Firefox window, as I discuss in Chapter 4.

- ✓ **To prevent automatic installation of available updates,** select Ask Me What I Want to Do to have Firefox display the Update Wizard whenever an update is available. By default, Firefox automatically installs most available updates to Firefox itself as well as to your installed extensions, themes and Search Box engines. However, if a Firefox update is incompatible with at least one of your installed extensions or themes, Firefox warns you before installing the update. If you leave automatic updating enabled, you can turn off this warning by deselecting the Warn Me If This Will Disable Extensions or Themes check box. For more information about extension and theme compatibility, see the section on updating Firefox in Chapter 15, and check out Chapters 17 (on themes) and 20 (on extensions).

- ✓ **To see a list of installed updates,** click the Show Update History button to open the Update History window.

See Chapter 15 for help with Firefox updates, Chapter 17 for help with theme updates, and Chapter 20 for help with extension updates.

The Security tab

Firefox is built to keep you secure, which means you shouldn't touch the security options unless you're an advanced systems administrator. See Chapter 15 for things you can do to stay safe online.

Chapter 17

Finding Your Dream Theme

My living room has a mahogany coffee table, a handsome grand piano finished in jet black, and a big gray box that whirs. Why are computers so *drab?* And what can anyone do about it?

Although we developers don't have the time to build computers, we're doing what we can on the Firefox front. Firefox supports *themes* that completely change the look and feel of the browsing interface while leaving all your features intact. An elegant glass finish, a wooden feel, something bright and silly for your inner child, even a scene from a movie — whatever your tastes, you're sure to find something you like among the hundreds of available Firefox themes.

Going to the Theme Park

The Mozilla Foundation maintains an official list of the best themes at a site called Mozilla Update (`http://themes.mozilla.org`). You don't need to remember that address because it's linked from the Theme Manager, which I talk about momentarily. Millions of people use the themes on this site, but because we don't create them ourselves, we can't guarantee your satisfaction.

Like extensions (see Chapter 20), most themes are created not by the core Firefox team but by volunteer developers during their spare time. Therefore, some themes might not work properly, and others might have undesirable side effects, such as slowing down Firefox. Some, of course, might just be ugly!

Mozilla Update organizes themes into categories, as shown in Figure 17-1. Some of these categories indicate theme content, such as Nature and Sports, and others indicate the approximate size of a theme's buttons, like Compact and Large. Click a category to see its description and a list of its themes. Most themes offer a small preview that gives you a taste of what to expect.

I include a sampling of my favorite themes in Figures 17-2 and 17-3. If you're feeling overwhelmed, try the Popular or Top Rated categories to see what other Firefox users enjoy. You can also click a particular theme to read reviews from people who tried it, as shown in Figure 17-1.

Mozilla Update isn't the only place to find themes. Many designers offer their themes on their own home pages, and even Hollywood is getting into the act. For example, on the Warner Bros' Web site, the Batman Begins movie offered a Batman theme. Search Google (www.google.com) for *Firefox Themes,* and be sure to regularly check the Newest category of Mozilla Update.

When you find an interesting theme, don't spend a lot of time deciding whether to try it. You can install and remove themes so quickly that it's worth your while to experiment. First, however, make sure you read the following section on theme compatibility.

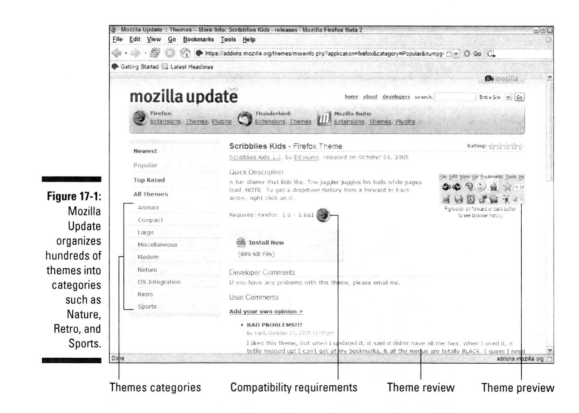

Figure 17-1:
Mozilla Update organizes hundreds of themes into categories such as Nature, Retro, and Sports.

Themes categories   Compatibility requirements   Theme review   Theme preview

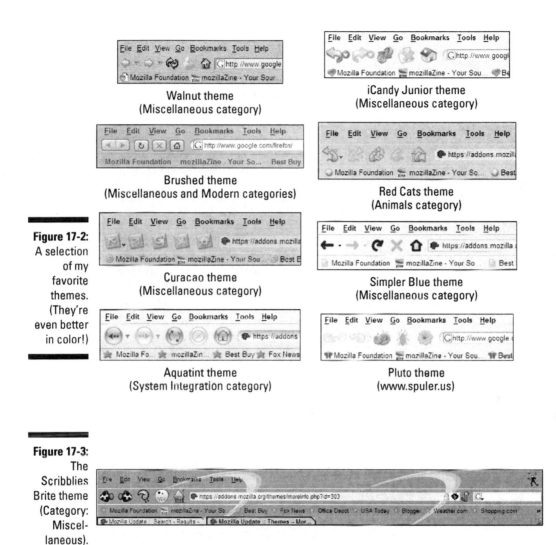

Walnut theme
(Miscellaneous category)

iCandy Junior theme
(Miscellaneous category)

Brushed theme
(Miscellaneous and Modern categories)

Red Cats theme
(Animals category)

Figure 17-2:
A selection of my favorite themes. (They're even better in color!)

Curacao theme
(Miscellaneous category)

Simpler Blue theme
(Miscellaneous category)

Aquatint theme
(System Integration category)

Pluto theme
(www.spuler.us)

Figure 17-3:
The Scribblies Brite theme (Category: Miscellaneous).

Ensuring Theme Compatibility

Each theme is designed to work with a particular version of Firefox or a range of versions. This seems strange at first, but makes more sense when you consider that each version of Firefox adds some new features. A designer has trouble theming a feature that hasn't been invented yet, just as a painter can't paint a room that hasn't been built.

Firefox prevents you from installing an incompatible theme, but you can save yourself some trouble by ensuring a theme's compatibility before installing it.

Mozilla Update provides a theme's compatibility information below its Install link in the form of a range of Firefox versions that it supports (for example, Firefox 1.0–1.5). If a theme supports only one version, the endpoints of the range are identical (for example, Firefox 1.0–1.0). Make sure that your version of Firefox, which you can find out by choosing Help⇨About Mozilla Firefox), falls within the listed range.

Even if you use a theme that's compatible with your version of Firefox, problems can occur if you're using an extension that changes or extends the Firefox interface. (See Chapter 20 for information about extensions.) Firefox does the best it can to apply your theme to installed extensions, but some things might look funny or stop working. In such cases, you will need to switch back to the default Firefox theme or disable the problematic extension.

Whenever you update Firefox to a new version, it checks to make sure that your installed themes remain compatible. If it finds any that aren't, Firefox notifies you and disables the incompatible themes until their designers release updated versions. Firefox checks for updates about once a day, but you can check manually at any time, as I explain in "Updating Themes," later in this chapter.

Installing and Applying Themes

After you've found a theme you like at Mozilla Update or elsewhere (see "Going to the Theme Park" at the beginning of this chapter), installing it is quick and easy. Follow these steps:

1. **Click the Install link.**

   Firefox displays a confirmation window, as shown in Figure 17-4.

2. **Click Install to continue with the installation.**

   The Theme Manager opens so you can track the installation progress, as shown in Figure 17-5.

3. **When the installation finishes, select the new theme in the Theme Manager list and click the Use Theme button at the bottom of the window.**

4. **Restart Firefox if you want to apply the new theme immediately. If not, you can now close the Theme Manager.**

   You must restart Firefox before the theme change takes effect, although you don't have to do it now.

To return to the Theme Manager later on, choose Tools⇨Themes.

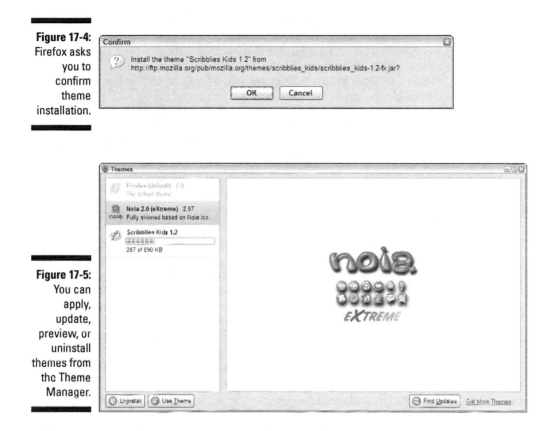

Figure 17-4:
Firefox asks
you to
confirm
theme
installation.

Figure 17-5:
You can
apply,
update,
preview, or
uninstall
themes from
the Theme
Manager.

Updating Themes

Firefox automatically checks for updates to (new versions of) your installed
themes about once a day and installs any that are available. If you don't want
Firefox to check or install updates automatically, you can disable this functionality, as I discuss in the section on updating Firefox in Chapter 15. You
can check for updates manually at any time by clicking the Find Updates
button at the bottom of the Theme Manager (choose Tools➪Themes).

Some theme authors update their themes to improve the look and feel of the
design, but most of the time, designers update their themes to be compatible
with a new version of Firefox, which is necessary for the reasons I discuss in
"Ensuring Theme Compatibility," earlier in this chapter.

When a new version of Firefox is made available, most theme authors update
their themes to be compatible with the new version, although it might take
them two or more weeks. Although Firefox checks for updates to itself each

day at the same time it checks for theme updates, Firefox asks you before installing an update that is incompatible with any of your installed themes. If you proceed with the update, Firefox disables the incompatible themes but continues to check for updates to them each day. When an update is available, Firefox installs it automatically and allows you to switch back to the now-compatible theme.

Each theme has a version number. The designer uses this number to keep track of the themes. You don't need to worry about it; just remember that the higher the number, the newer the theme.

Troubleshooting Themes

If you experience a problem in Firefox after installing a theme, you can launch Firefox in a special Safe Mode that temporarily disables the current theme and resorts to the default. Safe Mode also disables your current extensions (see Chapter 20 for more information about extensions). If the problem isn't present in Safe Mode, either your theme or one of your extensions is causing it. Try disabling the theme or your extensions one by one (from the Theme Manager and the Extension Manager, respectively) until the problem disappears.

To open Firefox in Safe Mode in Windows, shut down Firefox if it is currently open, and then choose Start➪Programs➪Mozilla Firefox➪Mozilla Firefox (Safe Mode).

To open Firefox in Safe Mode on a Mac, you need to enter a special command into the Macintosh Terminal. First, open the Terminal from Applications➪Utilities➪Terminal. Then type the following and press Enter:

```
/Applications/Firefox.app/Contents/MacOS/firefox –safe-mode
```

If you installed Firefox to a different location, you need to modify the path accordingly.

Uninstalling Themes

If things just aren't working out between you and a particular theme, you can uninstall it from the Theme Manager (Tools➪Themes). Simply select it in the list and click the Uninstall button at the bottom, and then click OK when Firefox asks you to confirm. It's okay to uninstall the theme you're currently using — Firefox falls back to the default theme, and the uninstalled theme cries on a friend's shoulder — but you need to restart Firefox before the change takes effect. Just remember you can't uninstall the default theme.

Chapter 18

Tailoring Your Toolbars

*I*f you've ever struggled to set the clock in your car — just turn off the AC and press Eject while going 61.5 mph, of course! — you'll appreciate the toolbar customization features in Firefox. The toolbars are those collections of buttons and text boxes that sit at the top of every Firefox window. Like your car's dashboard, the toolbars offer quick access to features you might use hundreds of times a day — such as going back to the previous page. Unlike your car's dashboard, Firefox toolbars are completely configurable. This chapter shows you how you can add, remove, and rearrange the toolbar items and even create new toolbars to ensure that the things you do regularly are always within reach and easy to use . . . unlike your car clock.

Changing the Items on Your Toolbars

Firefox is designed to be simple, and to that end, its toolbars offer access only to those features that nearly everyone needs every day — features such as Back, Forward, and Search. However, Firefox is also designed to be simple to *customize*. If you can drag and drop, you can give your toolbars a makeover by adding buttons that offer new functionality and by sprucing up the toolbar layout. The following sections look at the powerful Customize Toolbar window that makes all this possible.

 You can't customize the menu bar (the topmost bar, with File, Edit, and so on) in the Mac version of Firefox.

Adding items to the toolbar

By default, Firefox offers only a limited set of buttons on its toolbars. However, Firefox has a large collection of buttons from which you can choose to customize your toolbars as you like.

Many extensions, such as the Google Toolbar (http://toolbar.google. com), add items to the Customize Toolbar window when you install them. You can add these items to your toolbars in the same way you add the default items, by following the instructions in this section. See Chapter 20 for more information about extensions.

Follow these steps to add an item to the toolbar:

1. **Choose View⇨Toolbars⇨Customize.**

   The Customize Toolbar window appears, as shown in Figure 18-1.

   You can access this window more quickly by right-clicking on the Home, Reload, Stop, or Go buttons (or anywhere on the menu bar if you're using Windows), and then choosing Customize from the contextual menu that appears.

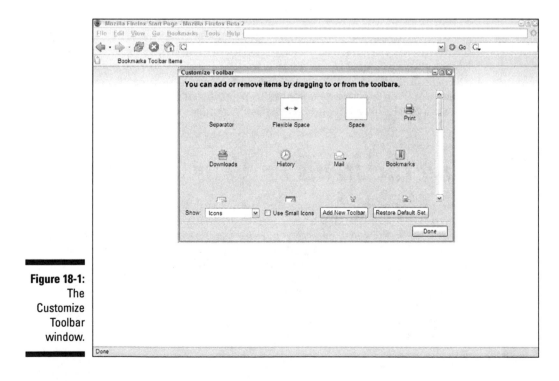

Figure 18-1:
The
Customize
Toolbar
window.

2. **Drag the item you want to add from the Customize Toolbar window and drop it onto the desired spot on a toolbar.**

   A black line indicates where the item will be inserted when you drop it, as shown in Figure 18-2.

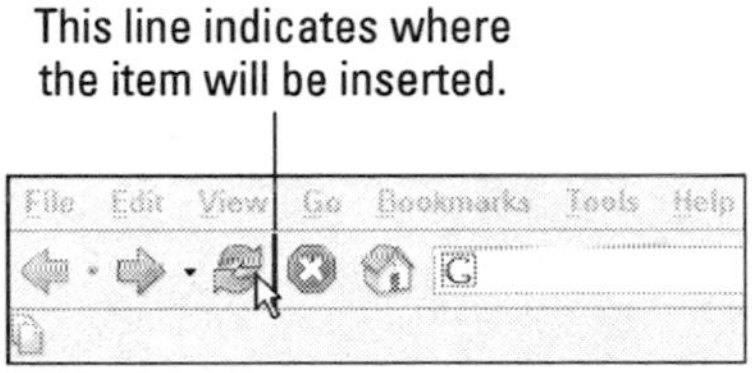

Figure 18-2:
Add an item
by dragging
it from the
Customize
window to
the desired
location.

This line indicates where
the item will be inserted.

3. **When you're done adding buttons, click Done to close the Customize Toolbar window.**

At any given time, the Customize Toolbar window displays only those items that aren't already on one of the toolbars.

You might want to enlarge the Customize Toolbar window by dragging the window border so you can view its entire collection of buttons in one screen without having to scroll.

Rearranging toolbar items

Firefox makes it easy to rearrange toolbar items if, for example, you want to move a button you click frequently to a more prominent location.

To move an item, follow these steps:

1. **Choose View➪Toolbars➪Customize to open the Customize Toolbar window and enter toolbar customization mode.**

   You can access this window more quickly by right-clicking on the Home, Reload, Stop, or Go buttons (or anywhere on the menu bar if you're using Windows), and then choosing Customize from the contextual menu that appears.

2. **Drag the toolbar item you want to move to its desired spot.**

   A black line indicates the position where the item will appear after you drop it.

For example, suppose you want the Stop and Reload buttons (as shown in Figure 18-3) to change places. Simply drag the Reload button and drop it to the right of the Stop button, as illustrated in Figure 18-4.

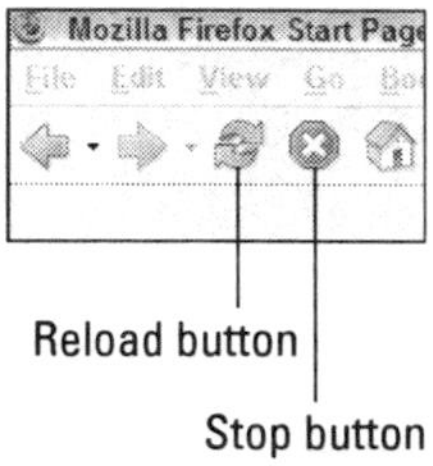

Figure 18-3:
By default, the Reload button is to the left of the Stop button . . .

Reload button

Stop button

Figure 18-4:
. . . but if you just drag the Reload button one position over, then . . .

As soon as you release the mouse button, the Reload button appears in its new location. Rather than leaving an empty space in the toolbar, Firefox automatically shifts the Stop button over to where the Reload button used to be, as shown in Figure 18-5.

Figure 18-5:
. . . voilá! The Stop and Reload buttons change places.

3. Click Done to close the Customize Toolbar window.

Removing toolbar items

First, make sure you have the Customize Toolbar window open by choosing View⇨Toolbars⇨Customize. Then, to remove an item, drag the item you want to remove from the toolbar to the Customize Toolbar window. Surrounding toolbar items shift over automatically. Firefox tries to make efficient use of toolbar space wherever possible. For example, if you remove the Go button, Firefox automatically extends the Location Bar instead of leaving an empty space on the toolbar.

Using special items: Spacing out

Many people squish all their toolbar items into as little space as possible in order to increase the screen space for Web viewing. Some people, however, prefer having empty space on their toolbars, either to reduce clutter or to visually group related items together. Firefox offers several special items from the Customize Toolbar window for managing space:

- **Separator:** A Separator is a thin vertical line frequently used to divide toolbar items into related groups. Figure 18-6 illustrates using a Separator to distinguish a group of Cut, Copy, and Paste buttons from the standard navigational group.

- **Space:** A Space is — as the name suggests — a small bit of horizontal space you can use to separate two adjacent items. Some people like to use Spaces like Separators to delineate a group of related toolbar items; others just find aesthetic appeal in having more spacious and less cluttered toolbars. Figure 18-7 illustrates using a space rather than a separator to distinguish the group of Cut, Copy, and Paste buttons. Notice that the bottom part of Figure 18-7 shows how the space fades into the toolbar color when you close the Customize Toolbar window.

Figure 18-6:
This Separator separates navigation and clipboard buttons.

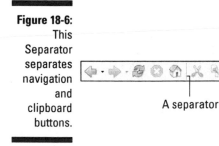

A separator

Figure 18-7:
Like
Separators,
Spaces help
you divide
up your
toolbars
logically.

The space in customize mode

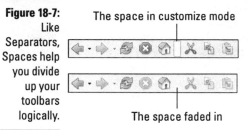

The space faded in

✔ **Flexible Space:** A Flexible Space is very similar to a Space, except that instead of offering a fixed amount of space, a Flexible Space stretches to fill all the unused space in the toolbar to which you add it.

The toolbar design in the Windows version of Firefox contains a Flexible Space by default. Look in the top-right corner of the Firefox window, and you see a small image called the Activity Indicator, which animates when a Web site is loading. This image is separated from the Firefox menus with a Flexible Space, which is revealed when you open the Customize Toolbar window, as shown in Figure 18-8. If you'd like, you can remove this Flexible Space by dragging it back into the Customize Toolbar window, just as you remove other toolbar items.

The Flexible Space revealed

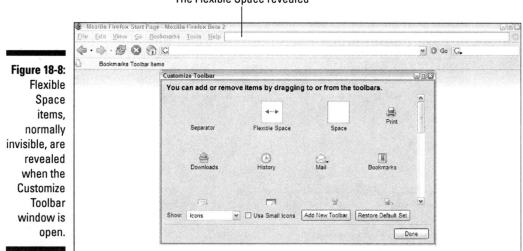

Figure 18-8:
Flexible
Space
items,
normally
invisible, are
revealed
when the
Customize
Toolbar
window is
open.

What's the best toolbar design?

Most people tend to think of software development as a technical discipline with little creative outlet. Sometimes the other Firefox team members and I wish that were true, because the debate over what constitutes the best toolbar design turned out to be one of the most divisive and heated in our development history. This wasn't a question of code. It was a question of, quite frankly, what *feels* right. Of the thousands of possible toolbar arrangements, which one offers the best balance of ease-of-use and aesthetics? Which is spacious without stealing precious screen real estate from Web sites? Which will adequately distinguish Firefox from other browsers without being so inconsistent that it's impossible to figure out?

To understand why the toolbar is such a big deal, consider how many times a day you click that Back button. Serious Internet surfers use the Firefox toolbars for hours at a time every day. An ugly, distracting, or nonintuitive toolbar design would be a deal-breaker for most people, even if they didn't consciously understand what it was that didn't feel right about Firefox. Even though we intended to offer customization tools, we knew that the overwhelming majority of our target audience would lack the time or technical literacy to fix our toolbar mistakes. And we couldn't just fix the toolbars in a subsequent release because that would be a jarring change to people who had grown accustomed to them. We had one shot at toolbar perfection.

One of the major points of contention during what we now call the Toolbar Wars was whether Firefox should follow other browsers in giving the Location Bar its own toolbar or try something new by merging the navigation buttons and the Location Bar into a single toolbar.

The first route was tried and true. Even if it wasn't the greatest design in the world, people expected it, which made it the safer route. Because it devoted an entire toolbar to buttons, the design would also allow us to include a variety of buttons to access features like Bookmarks and History, just as the popular Internet Explorer does.

The second route was much riskier. No browser had ever done it before. And it had very little space for buttons beyond the core set (Back, Forward, Stop, Reload, and Home) because we needed to keep the Location Bar a reasonable size so you could read its contents. But as we talked with people, a funny thing happened: We realized that the "disadvantages" were actually benefits. People didn't want a toolbar that offered access to everything under the sun. They wanted to go back, forward, and home. They wanted to stop and reload a page. And that was it. When we gave them trial versions of the new design for testing, hardly anyone missed the Bookmarks or Print buttons — they lauded the simplicity. Firefox 1.0 launched with the new design and nearly all of its competitors have since changed their designs. Of course, this chapter tells you everything you need to know to revert to the old-style layout if you prefer it.

The Firefox Location Bar is designed to be flexible in that it also stretches to fill unused space on whatever toolbar it resides on to give you plenty of space to view the current address. If you place a Flexible Space in the same toolbar as the Location Bar, the Location Bar wins out and takes up the unused space, and the Flexible Space is reduced to a thin black line (since, sadly, it has no space to take up).

These special items are for cosmetic purposes only and don't do anything when you click them.

Unlike the other items in the Customize Toolbar window, these special layout items don't disappear from that window after you drag them to a toolbar. You can drag as many Separators, Spaces, and Flexible Spaces onto the toolbars as you want.

Using the special Bookmarks Toolbar Items item

As I discuss in Chapter 5, Firefox allows you to add your most frequently accessed bookmarks to the Bookmarks Toolbar (the bottom toolbar) for quick access. The Bookmarks Toolbar Items item represents this set of bookmarks, enabling you to move all the bookmarks to a different toolbar by dragging a single item. Note that, by default, this item exists on the Bookmarks Toolbar instead of in the Customize Toolbar window, but it appears only when the Customize Toolbar window is open.

Adding, Hiding, and Removing Toolbars

As I discuss in the "What's the best toolbar design?" sidebar, Firefox developers have done plenty of brainstorming about toolbar design. That doesn't mean we got it right. Fortunately, you can create your own masterpiece toolbars, then hide or remove ours (sniffle). This section shows you how.

Creating new toolbars

If you're a power user with a penchant for buttons or just someone who prefers a more spacious arrangement, you might find yourself wishing that Firefox had more toolbars. No matter: Firefox allows you to add as many toolbars as you need.

1. **Choose View⊅Toolbars⊅Customize to open the Customize Toolbar window.**

   You can access this window more quickly by right-clicking the Home, Reload, Stop, or Go buttons (or by right-clicking anywhere on the menu bar if you're using Windows), and then choosing Customize from the contextual menu that appears.

2. **In the Customize Toolbar window, click the Add New Toolbar button.**

3. **When prompted (see Figure 18-9), enter a name for the new toolbar and click OK.**

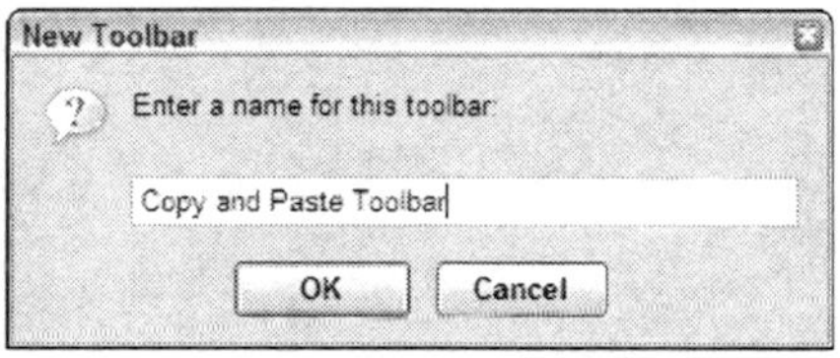

Figure 18-9:
Before you
can design
your toolbar,
you must
name it.

New Toolbar
(?) Enter a name for this toolbar:
Copy and Paste Toolbar
OK   Cancel

This is the name that will appear in the list when you choose View⇨ Toolbars. By default, Firefox comes with two toolbars, the Navigation Toolbar and the Bookmarks Toolbar, so you can't use those names.

Firefox creates and displays the new toolbar when you click OK.

4. **Drag items onto the new toolbar as desired.**

You can drag items either from existing toolbars or from the Customize Toolbar window.

You must add at least one item to the new toolbar immediately, before closing the Customize Toolbar window. If you leave the toolbar blank, Firefox assumes you don't want it and automatically deletes it.

5. **Click Done to close the Customize Toolbar window.**

Many developers have created toolbars with special functionality and offer them as Firefox extensions, which I discuss in Chapter 20, that you can install quickly. Two of the most popular are the Google Toolbar (http://toolbar. google.com) and the Yahoo! Toolbar (http://toolbar.yahoo.com), which make searching the Web easier, spell-check your online forms, translate Web sites you visit to a language of your choosing, and provide a number of other useful utilities.

Hiding toolbars temporarily

You can hide a Firefox toolbar at any time. For example, you might want to do so to make more room for a Web site you're viewing. Hidden toolbars stay hidden until you decide to show them again, even if you close and then reopen Firefox.

To hide a toolbar, choose View⇨Toolbars, and then select the name of the toolbar you want to hide. To show the toolbar later, return to the menu and choose the toolbar's name again. The list displays a check mark next to each toolbar that is being shown.

You can quickly access this list by right-clicking the Home, Reload, Stop, or Go buttons (or by right-clicking anywhere on the menu bar if you're using Windows).

Removing toolbars

Firefox allows you to remove all toolbars — even the built-in toolbars (except the top one on Windows, because it contains the menus).

Although you can recreate it with some effort, removing a toolbar is a permanent action. Don't do it unless you really don't want a toolbar anymore. If you remove a built-in toolbar, you can restore it by following the directions in "Restoring the Default Configuration" later in this chapter, but doing so restores *all* of the default toolbars and wipes out any toolbars you create. If you just want to hide a toolbar temporarily (perhaps to make more room for a Web site you're viewing), see the preceding section.

To remove a toolbar:

1. **Choose View⇨Toolbars⇨Customize to open the Customize Toolbar window.**

2. **Drag all of the doomed toolbar's items elsewhere — either to another toolbar or into the Customize Toolbar window — and then click Done in the Customize Toolbar window.**

   Firefox automatically deletes the empty toolbar.

Changing the Appearance of Your Toolbar Buttons

By default, the buttons on Firefox's toolbars are comprised solely of images that represent their respective functions. The Back button, for example, is symbolized by a green arrow pointing left. Firefox lets you change the appearance of buttons in a number of ways.

For example, what if a mere image isn't enough? You might find that you have trouble remembering what a particular button does, especially if you add a host of new buttons as I describe in the beginning of this chapter. To remedy this problem, you can instruct Firefox to display explanatory text beneath each button's image (for example, Bookmarks or New Window) or even indicate that you want buttons to consist of only text and no images at all.

To change the appearance of your toolbar buttons, follow these steps:

1. **Choose View⇨Toolbars⇨Customize to open the Customize Toolbar window.**

2. **From the Show drop-down list, select one of the following options:**

   • **Icons and Text:** Indicates that toolbar buttons should consist of an image followed by explanatory text underneath, as shown in the top of Figure 18-10.

   • **Icons:** Indicates that toolbar buttons should consist only of images. This is the default.

   • **Text:** Indicates that toolbar buttons should consist only of text and no images.

   If you select the Icons and Text option or the Icons option, you can also specify whether the images that appear in toolbar buttons should be large (the default) or small by using the Use Small Icons check box. This isn't just a cosmetic choice. Small icons conserve space and provide more room for viewing Web sites, but they're more difficult to click. The top of Figure 18-10 shows Icons and Text mode with large icons, and the bottom of Figure 18-10 shows Icons mode with large icons.

3. **Click Done to close the Customize Toolbar window.**

Figure 18-10:
If you have trouble identifying buttons by their pictures alone, add descriptive text.

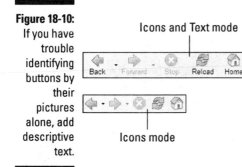

Icons and Text mode

Icons mode

Restoring the Default Configuration

Suppose you play around with the toolbars for a few hours and decide the original way was the best after all. Now, how did that look again? And how long will it take to get back there? Luckily, Firefox offers one-click access to restore the default configuration at any time.

The restoration process really is as easy as a single click. There's no confirmation window and no Undo button, so make sure you want to revert to the original configuration before proceeding. You will lose all the changes you have made to your toolbars — both built-in toolbars and extension toolbars such as Google Toolbar — and any toolbars you created will be deleted.

1. **Choose View⇨Toolbars⇨Customize to open the Customize Toolbar window.**

2. **Click the Restore Default Set button to revert to the original Firefox toolbars immediately.**

   There is no confirmation process and no way to undo this action.

Quicker clicking just for you

Not all of our decisions had such highly visible ramifications as the Location Bar debate I describe in the "What's the best toolbar design?" sidebar in this chapter. In fact, another one revolved around a single pixel! Think about that Back button again. Suppose it takes you 1 second to navigate to and click it, and you do that 60 times a day. That's a minute a day, or 365 minutes — over 6 hours — per year! Isn't there some way we could speed that up just a little bit and save you some time?

Yup. Think about when you click the X button in the top-right corner of the window. Not very strenuous, is it? That's because you don't need to spend any time at all locating the button. Because it's located in the rightmost and upper-most part of the screen, all you have to do is jam your mouse into the corner as far as it will go and click. If the button were shifted just one pixel down or left, you would have to spend an additional half-second every time ensuring that the cursor is in the right place before clicking.

The same is true of the Back button. Although we can't put it in a screen corner, we can ensure that it's aligned properly with the left edge of the screen so you only have to find the button vertically. The Firefox toolbar used to have a thin border that prevented the toolbar from butting up against the screen edge, and we removed it for exactly this reason.

You can rest assured that every aspect of Firefox has received this kind of careful scrutiny. We're worried about you down to the pixel.

Chapter 19

Controlling the Way
Web Sites Look

*I*f you went over to a friend's house and started redecorating, he probably wouldn't be too thrilled. But in Firefox, you're free to tweak the sites you visit to be more comfortable. This includes changing colors and text size, turning off images, and enlarging the viewing area. Of course, none of your changes affect other visitors.

Enlarging and Shrinking Text

If you've ever squinted at tiny text or grumbled at enormous headlines, you'll appreciate Firefox's resizing features. If you just need to tweak a particular site, you can change the text size in the current tab or window. However, you can also resize the text of all Web sites you visit.

Resizing text for the current tab or window

To resize the text on only the Web sites you visit in the current tab or window, choose View⇨Text Size and then choose Increase or Decrease accordingly. If the text still isn't as large or small as you'd like, you can continue resizing. Figure 19-1 shows Memeorandum (a great Web site for keeping up on what bloggers are talking about) at normal size, and Figure 19-2 shows the page after using the Increase command twice.

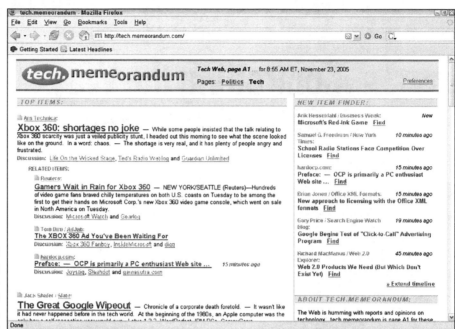

Figure 19-1: Meme-orandum at normal size.

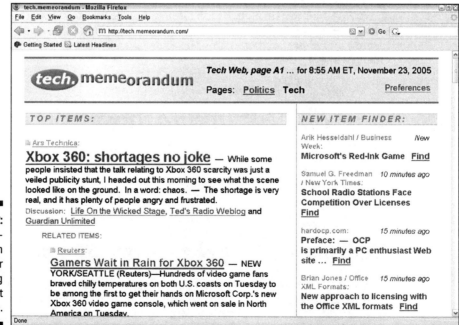

Figure 19-2: Meme-orandum after increasing the text size twice.

On Windows, press Ctrl++ (that's Ctrl and the plus sign) to enlarge text and Ctrl+- (the minus sign) to shrink it. The Macintosh shortcuts are ⌘++ and ⌘+-, respectively.

Any Web sites you visit in the current tab or window use the new text size. To return to normal size, choose View⇨Text Size⇨Normal or press Ctrl+0 (⌘+0 on Macintosh). Of course, you could also just start browsing in a new tab or window.

Resizing text permanently

Resizing the text on all Web sites you visit involves more steps than resizing for a single window, but it's also permanent, so you only have to do it once:

1. **Choose Tools⇨Options.**

2. **Click the Content icon at the top of the Options window.**

3. **In the Fonts & Colors section at the bottom, ignore the Default Font settings and click Advanced to open the Fonts window. Default Font is just a subset of the options in the Fonts window, and you should set the options in the Fonts window to affect all sites.**

   The Fonts window offers a variety of complicated options, but you don't need to worry about all of them right now. Basically, many different styles of text exist (such as Serif and Monospace), and the Web site designer picks a style. Firefox lets you control which font and size are used for each style.

4. **(Optional) Use any of the following techniques to resize text as needed:**

   • *To override the font size on all pages,* choose the new size from the Size drop-down lists next to Proportional and Monospace. Figure 19-3 illustrates the proper settings to use if you want Web sites to display text at size 18.

   • *To set a minimum size,* use the Minimum Font Size drop-down list. This is a good option if you're concerned about readability but don't need everything to be one particular size.

5. **(Optional) To override all Web page fonts, choose the new font from the Serif, Sans-Serif, and Monospace drop-down lists, and then deselect the Allow Pages to Choose Their Own Fonts check box.**

   Because designers go to great trouble to design pixel-perfect Web sites, it's probably best to leave Web site fonts alone. Changing them could affect the readability or the attractiveness of pages you visit.

6. **Click OK to close the Fonts window.**

7. **Click OK to save your changes and close the Options window.**

Preventing annoying tricks

Most sites on the Net are well-behaved, but as with anything, a few bad apples crop up. You've probably run into a couple during your online travels. Sometimes they use flashy tricks that distract you while you read the page. Certain Web sites, for example, scroll text in the Firefox Status Bar like those stock tickers in Times Square, or blink text to catch your eye again . . . and again . . . and again.

One of the most devious things a site can do is disable the contextual menu. If you've ever right-clicked a page only to see a message about copyright, or simply nothing at all, you can appreciate just how annoying this is. Usually,

sites block the contextual menu to prevent you from accessing the Save Image As command if they don't want you to take copyrighted images. It's an exceedingly arrogant move: after all, they're also preventing you access to all the other commands in the menu, not to mention that it's *your* menu. And it's a futile effort, anyway: You could retrieve the image via copy and paste, by saving the entire Web site, or through a number of other methods.

Whatever devious tricks a Web site decides to use, Firefox has you covered. See Chapter 21 for instructions on keeping the bad apples in line.

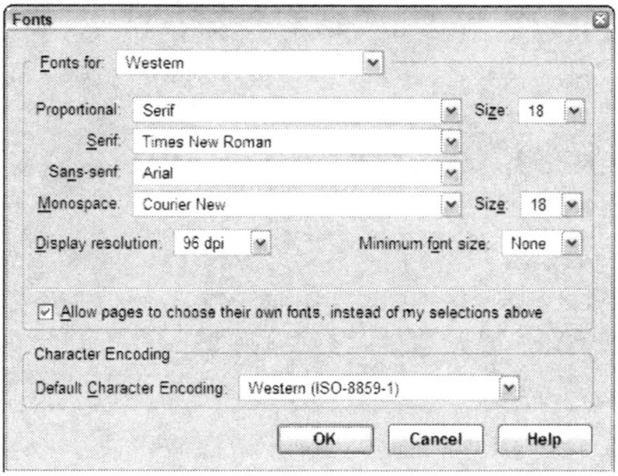

Figure 19-3: To override text size, select a new size for both Proportional and Mono-space. Here I use size 18.

Changing Web Site Colors

For all its virtues, the Web makes some things a little too easy. Now that you've become used to reading *black* text on a *white* background, for example, many Web sites have started to reverse the trend. As far as I'm concerned, these white-on-black designs are an eyesore. Firefox allows you to override the text, background, and link color of every site so you can view the Web the way you want:

Designers go to great lengths to design pixel-perfect Web sites, so forcing Web sites to use your own color scheme could lead to unreadable or awk-ward-looking pages. Feel free to experiment with these features (since it's easy to undo your changes), but be aware of this consequence.

1. **Choose Tools⇨Options.**

2. **Click the Content icon at the top of the Options window.**

3. **In the Fonts & Colors section at the bottom, click the Colors button.**

   The Colors window appears. The boxes next to Text, Background, Visited Links, and Unvisited Links indicate the current color of each element.

4. **Click the color boxes to select new colors, as shown in Figure 19-4.**

   Under Text and Background, you can select Use System Colors to have Firefox use your computer's default window background and text colors. These colors are specified in your system's control panel.

   You can also determine whether Firefox underlines links with the Underline Links check box in the Link Colors boxed group. By default, links are underlined so you can spot them more quickly.

   As the name suggests, a Visited link is a link to a Web site you've seen before. It's a good idea to select different colors for Visited and Unvisited under Link Colors so you can tell at a glance which links you've already followed.

5. **Deselect the Allow Pages to Choose Their Own Colors check box at the bottom.**

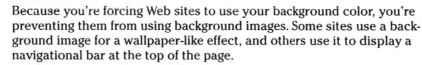

   Because you're forcing Web sites to use your background color, you're preventing them from using background images. Some sites use a back-ground image for a wallpaper-like effect, and others use it to display a navigational bar at the top of the page.

6. **Click OK to close the Colors window.**

7. **Click OK to save your changes and close the Options window.**

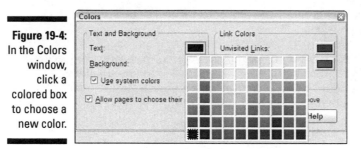

Figure 19-4: In the Colors window, click a colored box to choose a new color.

Changing How Firefox Displays Images

It's hard to believe, but when the Internet first launched over a decade ago, it had no images — just lots and lots of text. In a world of information overload, however, there's some charm to this austerity. There are two ways to control how Firefox displays images: You can change which images are loaded, and you can have Firefox automatically shrink images that are too large to fit on-screen. I discuss these options in the following sections.

Disabling image loading

If you want to return to simpler times and enjoy a faster surfing experience, you can turn off Web images:

1. **Choose Tools⇨Options.**

2. **Click the Content icon at the top of the Options window.**

3. **Deselect the Load Images check box.**

You can also choose to load images only for the originating Web site by leaving the Load Images check box selected and instead selecting the For the Originating Web Site Only check box beneath it. This option prevents a Web site from displaying images that are part of another Web site. It's a reasonable way to block advertising on the Web, but it can also break many pages, so I don't recommend it. For a better way to block ads, see the section on AdBlock in Chapter 22.

4. **Click OK to save your changes and close the Options window.**

Some Web designers associate brief textual descriptions with each of the images on their page. This is useful both to display placeholder text when an image isn't loaded, and for screen-reading software that needs to describe on-screen elements to users with vision problems. When Firefox doesn't load an image, it puts the textual description in its place if one is available, as shown in Figure 19-5. Otherwise, the space is left empty.

The "reading bird" text

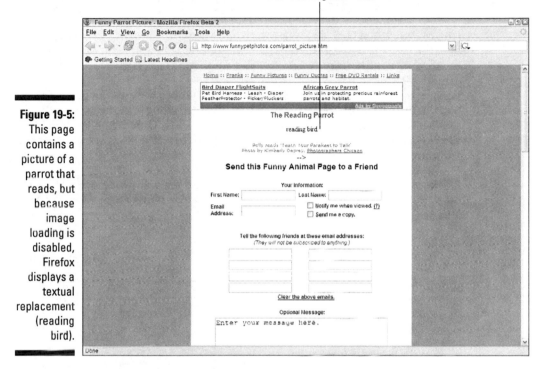

Figure 19-5:
This page
contains a
picture of a
parrot that
reads, but
because
image
loading is
disabled,
Firefox
displays a
textual
replacement
(reading
bird).

Turning off image autoshrinking

If you like *most* images but can't stand the enormous ones that dominate your screen, Firefox has you covered. Firefox automatically shrinks large images (images that can't be displayed entirely in the Content area without scrolling) to fit inside the browser window. When this happens, the mouse pointer becomes a magnifying glass as you move it over the image. To restore the image to its original size, simply click it.

You can turn off this autoshrinking behavior from the Options window if it bothers you:

1. **Choose Tools⇨Options.**

2. **Click the Advanced icon at the top of the Options window.**

3. **On the General tab, under Browsing, deselect the Resize Large Images to Fit in the Browser Window check box.**

4. **Click OK to save your changes and close the Options window.**

Viewing Web Sites in Full Screen Mode

One of the design goals in Firefox is to maximize the amount of space available for viewing Web sites. Still, the other developers and I can do only so much. You always need a menu bar and some toolbars, right?

Well, not necessarily. Full Screen mode allows you to hide all the clutter and use the entire screen to view a Web site. If you're using Windows, even the taskbar at the bottom is hidden in Full Screen mode. Only a thin version of the Navigation Toolbar remains, as shown in Figure 19-6, so you can access common commands or exit Full Screen mode.

Full Screen mode is especially useful for viewing slideshows or presentations or playing games within the browser, since it offers much more viewing space and less surrounding clutter.

Navigation Toolbar

Figure 19-6:
It's much easier to enjoy this scenic country shot in Full Screen mode.

Although Full Screen mode hides the menu bar, keyboard shortcuts still work. For example, you can still open the Bookmarks Sidebar by pressing Ctrl+B. Full Screen mode is not available in Firefox for the Mac.

To enter Full Screen mode, choose View⟳Full Screen or press F11. Firefox stays in Full Screen mode until you exit it, which you can do by clicking the Restore button in the top-right corner or by pressing F11 again.

Don't click the X button to exit Full Screen mode, since doing so closes the window as usual.

Chapter 20

Extending Firefox

Software is a compromise. Some parts are fantastic; others are lousy. The features you don't need are front and center, and the ones you're crying out for are nowhere to be found. You wish that button were a menu and that menu a button. It isn't perfect, but it's the best tool out there, quirks and all.

Firefox is built to be extensible so you don't have to settle. Unlike most software, Firefox isn't etched in stone. It's more like a collection of building blocks. We developers made the best design we could, but we invite you to move blocks around, remove them altogether, and even add your own. This flexibility is made possible through tiny applications called *extensions,* which you can install into Firefox.

The great thing about extensions is that they don't *feel* like extensions. Their features are integrated into the main Firefox interface as if they'd been there all along. Likewise, they can alter features that are already built in to Firefox. Extensions don't create a new, separate design; they work with the very blocks that Firefox is made of.

Of course, you don't have to make the extensions yourself. The Firefox development community has already created hundreds of them for you, and developers release new ones each day. (I describe ten of the best extensions in Chapter 22, so check it out for a more vivid sense of what extensions can do.) All you have to do is decide what your perfect browser looks like, and then mix and match the extensions that you want. What could be easier? This chapter shows you where to find great extensions, and how to start using them.

Finding Great Extensions

Before you dash off to find these magnificent beauties, here's a brief list of some of the wonderful things extensions can do:

- ✔ Integrate other applications — such as your music player — into Firefox.
- ✔ Bring you content that other Web surfers find interesting.
- ✔ Introduce wacky new ways of surfing the Web, such as by making mouse gestures.
- ✔ Remember the last Web sites you visited and restore them when you restart Firefox.
- ✔ Expand Firefox's built-in bookmarking tools to make your bookmarks accessible when you're on other computers.
- ✔ Show the latest news, weather, and other information within Firefox.

I list some of my favorite extensions in Chapter 22.

We maintain a list of the highest-quality extensions at a site called Mozilla Update (`http://addons.mozilla.org`). You don't need to remember that address because it's linked from the Extension Manager (see "Managing Your Extensions" later in this chapter). Millions of people use the extensions on this site, so you can be reasonably assured they work as advertised. However, because we don't create them ourselves, we can't guarantee your satisfaction.

Mozilla Update organizes extensions into categories that typically cover a specific area of Firefox, as shown in Figure 20-1. In the Download Tools category, for example, you can find a download toolbar that completely replaces the built-in Download Manager. Some categories, however, are broad and unusual. For example, if you're looking for an integrated egg timer, you can find it in Humor. (Hey, nobody said extensions had to make sense.)

Figure 20-1:
Mozilla
Update
neatly
organizes
over 500
extensions
into
categories
such as
Download
Tools.

Extension categories   Compatibility requirements   Extension preview

Extension review

If you're feeling overwhelmed, I list ten excellent extensions in Chapter 22. The front page of Mozilla Update also offers some great starting points. The Most Popular section lists the most-downloaded extensions of the past week, and Top Rated shows you the extensions with the highest overall ratings. I strongly encourage you to rate extensions after you try them, and you can also write reviews. Click an extension to see its reviews and other information that might help you decide whether to try it, such as screenshots, a description, and the Firefox versions it supports. Ensure that the extension works in your version of Firefox, which is listed in Help⇨About Mozilla Firefox.

When you find an intriguing extension, don't spend a lot of time deciding whether to install it. You can install and remove extensions so quickly that experimenting is worth your while.

Because the Firefox team is busy working on the core product, most extensions are developed by volunteers during their spare time. This means that some extensions might not work and others might have undesirable side effects.

Ensuring Extension Compatibility

Each extension is designed to work with a particular version of Firefox or a range of versions. Firefox prevents you from installing an extension that is incompatible with your current version of Firefox. However, you can save yourself some trouble by ensuring an extension's compatibility before you try installing it. Mozilla Update provides an extension's compatibility information below its Install link in the form of a range of Firefox versions that it supports (for example, Firefox 1.0–1.5). Simply make sure that your version of Firefox, which is displayed in the About Mozilla Firefox window (Help⇨About Mozilla Firefox), falls within the listed range.

Whenever you update Firefox to a new version, it checks to make sure that your installed extensions remain compatible. If it finds any that aren't, Firefox notifies you and disables the incompatible extensions until their developers release updated versions. Firefox checks for updates about once a day, but you can check manually at any time, as I explain in "Updating Extensions," later in this chapter.

Installing Extensions

In the earlier sections of this chapter, I talk only about extensions available through Mozilla Update. However, many volunteers choose to offer extensions through their own Web sites. Although these might work well, remember that we Firefox developers can verify the quality only of the extensions on Mozilla Update, so you should install extensions only from other sites you trust. In case you forget, Firefox makes it slightly more difficult to install extensions from sources other than Mozilla Update. I discuss both procedures here.

Installing from Mozilla Update

Installing an extension from Mozilla Update couldn't be easier. When you find an extension you like, click the Install Now link. Firefox asks you to confirm the decision, as shown in Figure 20-2. Click Install Now to continue.

You might notice that the Install Now button is unavailable for about two seconds. This is to prevent you from inadvertently clicking it.

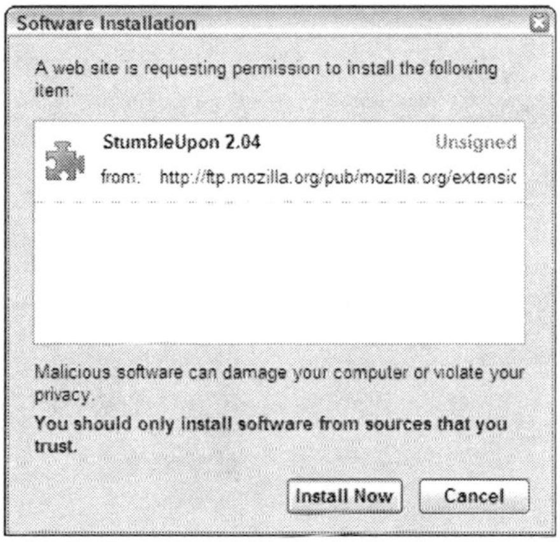

Figure 20-2:
Firefox asks
you to
confirm all
extension
installations.
Just click
Install Now;
Firefox does
the rest.

> **Software Installation**
>
> A web site is requesting permission to install the following item.
>
> StumbleUpon 2.04   Unsigned
> from: http://ftp.mozilla.org/pub/mozilla.org/extensic
>
> Malicious software can damage your computer or violate your privacy.
> **You should only install software from sources that you trust.**
>
> [Install Now]   [Cancel]

Firefox opens the Extension Manager to display the installation progress. Installation is typically very fast, and when it finishes, you need to restart Firefox before the extension will take effect. After restarting, see "Using Extensions" later in this chapter for more information.

Installing from another site

Mozilla Update is not the only place to find great extensions. Many developers offer their extensions on their own Web sites, and you can find these by searching the Web for *Firefox extensions*. There are also some sites that aggregate high-quality extensions, just like Mozilla Update, including the following:

- ✔ **The Extension Room** at `http://extensionroom.mozdev.org`
- ✔ **The Extensions Mirror** at `www.extensionsmirror.nl`

Firefox blocks the installation of extensions from other Web sites because they might be broken or unsafe. When this happens, a toolbar appears at the top of the Web site, as shown in Figure 20-3.

This toolbar alerts you when Firefox blocks an extension installation.

Figure 20-3:
By default,
Firefox
prevents
any site
other than
Mozilla
Update from
installing an
extension,
but displays
this toolbar
so you can
override
the policy.

To continue with installation, you need to verify that you trust the site:

1. **Click the Edit Options button at the right end of the toolbar to open the Allowed Sites window.**

   This window contains a list of sites that are allowed to install extensions. By default, only Mozilla Update's two sites are included on this list.

   Firefox prefills the address of your current site.

2. **If you're sure the site is trustworthy, click Allow to add it to the list.**

3. **Click Close to close the Allowed Sites window.**

Now that the site is in the trusted list, the installation process is the same as on Mozilla Update. Click the install link again and follow the directions in the earlier section, "Installing from Mozilla Update."

Using Extensions

Describing the use of an extension can be as hard as describing the plot of a book. Hundreds of different extensions exist, and each has its own way of doing things. Some extensions add entire sidebar panels or toolbars, as shown in Figure 20-4, and others stick to a single button or menu item. Extensions that modify existing Firefox features, rather than adding new ones, might leave no trace at all.

Many extensions quietly add buttons that offer fast access to their features to the Customize Toolbar window. You can drag these buttons to your toolbar, as I discuss in Chapter 18. I recommend checking the Customize Toolbar window after installing an extension.

Figure 20-4:
Some extensions, such as Scrapbook, install new sidebars into Firefox.

Some extensions include built-in help systems, but the best source of help usually is the Web site of the extension's developer. You can access the developer's site from the Extension Manager, which I describe in the next section:

1. **Choose Tools⇨Extensions.**

2. **Right-click the extension you need help with and choose Visit Home Page from the menu that appears.**

A new Firefox window opens and loads the page.

If this option is unavailable, either the developer has no Web site, or he forgot to list it. You can check for the latter by searching Google for the extension name to see whether it comes up.

Managing Your Extensions

After you install an extension, you can use the Extension Manager (shown in Figure 20-5) to configure, update, or remove it. To open the manager, choose Tools⇨Extensions.

Figure 20-5:
You can customize, upgrade, or remove installed extensions from the Extension Manager.

Configuring extensions

Most extensions are highly configurable and like to flaunt it by adding their own Options buttons or menu items. Some, however, are shyer and offer no obvious access. Regardless of how an extension exposes its settings in the main Firefox interface, you can always access its Options window through the Extension Manager. Just select the extension you want to configure and click the Options button at the bottom. If this button is unavailable, the extension isn't configurable.

Because each extension offers different options, it's impossible to provide more specific instructions here. The earlier section, "Using Extensions," explains how to get extension-specific help.

Updating extensions

Firefox automatically checks for updates to (new versions of) your installed extensions about once a day and installs any that are available. If you don't want Firefox to check for or install updates automatically, you can disable this functionality as I discuss in the section on updating Firefox in Chapter 15. You can check for updates manually at any time by clicking the Find Updates button at the bottom of the Extension Manager.

Developers update their extensions to add features, to fix bugs, or to make them compatible with a new version of Firefox, which is necessary for the reasons I discuss in "Ensuring Extension Compatibility" earlier in this chapter.

When a new version of Firefox is made available, most developers update their extensions to be compatible with the new version, although it may take them two or more weeks. Although Firefox checks for updates to itself each day at the same time it checks for extension updates, Firefox asks you before installing an update that is incompatible with any of your installed extensions. If you proceed with the update, Firefox disables the incompatible extensions, but continues to check for updates to them each day. When an update is available, Firefox installs it automatically and re-enables the now-compatible extension.

Each extension has a version number. The developer uses this number to keep track of his extensions. You don't need to worry about it; just remember that the higher the number, the newer the extension.

Removing extensions

Firefox offers three ways to turn off an extension depending on what you want to do.

A quick complaint about version numbers

You're probably already familiar with the concept of software versioning — the higher the number, the newer the software. You're probably also aware — perhaps painfully so — that software companies can't agree on a standard and therefore tend to version things however they please. For example, Microsoft went from Windows 98 to Windows ME to Windows 2000 to Windows XP to the forthcoming Windows Vista.

Unfortunately, the situation isn't much better in extension land. Although virtually all developers stick to numeric versions, they use varying levels of complexity. Don't be surprised if one extension's version is 0.4.7.241 and another's is 7.2. My advice is to ignore the numbers entirely and just remember that "higher is newer, and newer is better."

Uninstalling an extension

If you just want to get rid of an extension permanently, you can uninstall it from the Extension Manager. Simply select it in the list and click the Uninstall button at the bottom. You must restart Firefox to complete the process.

Disabling an extension

If you suspect that an extension is causing a problem in Firefox and want to find out, you can disable it temporarily by right-clicking it in the Extension Manager and choosing Disable. Like uninstalling, disabling requires a restart. However, if it turns out that the extension was *not* the source of the problem, you can re-enable it without having to reinstall it. Right-click it, choose Enable, and then restart Firefox.

Disabling all extensions with Safe Mode

Disabling is a good way to test a single extension, but what if you have a bunch? You would have to disable each extension one at a time to see whether it's the cause of the problem. That grows old fast, especially if it turns out that none of the extensions is behind the problem. Even worse: What if the problem you're experiencing is that Firefox won't start? Now you can't even get to the Extension Manager to turn off extensions. Safe Mode is the answer to both problems.

If you experience a problem in Firefox after installing an extension, you can launch Firefox in a special Safe Mode that temporarily disables all installed extensions. If you are not using the default Firefox theme, Safe Mode also disables your current theme (see Chapter 17 for more information about themes). If the problem isn't present in Safe Mode, either your theme or one of your extensions is causing it. If you're using a special theme, first try reverting to the default theme in Regular Mode and see if the problem persists. If it does, follow the directions in the preceding two sections to disable or uninstall your extensions until you fix the problem in Regular Mode.

To open Firefox in Safe Mode in Windows, shut down Firefox if it is currently open, and then choose Start⇨Programs⇨Mozilla Firefox⇨Mozilla Firefox (Safe Mode).

To open Firefox in Safe Mode on a Mac, you need to enter a special command into the Macintosh Terminal. First, open the Terminal by choosing Applications⇨Utilities⇨Terminal. Then type the following and press Enter:

```
/Applications/Firefox.app/Contents/MacOS/
        firefox -safe-mode
```

If you installed Firefox to a different location, you need to modify the path accordingly.

Part V
The Part of Tens

The 5th Wave

By Rich Tennant

"So, you want to work for the best browser company in the world? Well, let me get you a job application. Let's see...where are they? Shoot! I can never find anything around here!"

In this part . . .

What's a *For Dummies* book without The Part of Tens? Sad, that's what. This final part cuts to the chase with 20 features you can't leave the home (page) without. The first ten are built right into Firefox, and the rest are available through extensions (which you read about in Chapter 20, earlier in the book). Read on to get your fox fix!

Chapter 21

Ten Secrets to a Foxier Web

- -

- -

*T*he Firefox interface is designed to be simple and intuitive. The goal is to remove browser clutter so you can focus on the Web site, not on Firefox itself. However, underneath its simple exterior, Firefox includes a handful of little features to make your life easier, and we developers don't want you to miss them. Enjoy!

The Find Bar Can Read Your Mind

Chapter 4 introduces Firefox's innovative Find Bar for searching within a Web page. The Find Bar is built for speed: Rather than waiting until you finish typing, it searches *as you type*. You can also open and close the Find Bar by using keyboard shortcuts (Ctrl+F to open, or ⌘+F on a Mac, and Esc/Escape to close on both systems), meaning you never need to reach for the mouse.

In spite of all that, searching can get even faster. What if you didn't have to worry about the Find Bar at all? If you turn on a mode called Fast Find, you can tell Firefox to start searching a page whenever you begin typing. Firefox automatically opens the Find Bar so you can keep track of what you type.

After you finish typing, Firefox automatically hides the Find Bar so it doesn't get in the way. To turn Fast Find mode on:

1. **Choose Tools⇨Options.**

2. **Select the Advanced icon at the top of the Options window.**

3. **On the General tab, under Accessibility, select the Begin Finding When You Begin Typing check box.**

4. **Click OK to save your changes.**

To try out the new behavior, load `www.mozilla.org` and begin typing **Firefox**. Firefox opens the Find Bar and highlights in green the first occurrence of the word on the page. A few seconds after you stop typing, Firefox automatically closes the Find Bar.

For this feature to work, the Web site itself — not the Location Bar, or any other part of Firefox — must be focused. (The only way to tell whether a Web site is focused is to press the up- and down-arrow keys and see if the Web site scrolls.) The focus typically isn't an issue because Firefox sets focus to the Web site when you navigate to it. However, if Firefox doesn't open the Find Bar when you begin typing, try focusing the Web page first by clicking on a *dead* space within the page (that is, text or empty space, but not a link). The next search you conduct begins wherever you click.

Another nice thing about Fast Find mode is that it's optimized for links. To continue the earlier example, the first result for *Firefox* is actually a link to the Firefox Web site. Fast Find lets you follow this link by using only the keyboard. One side effect of this feature is that keyboard shortcuts on the Find Bar behave differently in Fast Find mode than they do in standard Find mode, and I summarize the differences in Table 21-1.

Table 21-1	Shortcuts in Standard and Fast Find Modes	
Shortcut	*Standard Find Mode*	*Fast Find Mode*
Enter	Selects next occurrence.	If the highlighted result is a link, the link is loaded. Otherwise, nothing happens.
Shift+Enter	Selects previous occurrence.	If the highlighted result is a link, the link is loaded in a new window. Otherwise, nothing happens.
Ctrl+Enter (⌘+Enter on a Mac)	Highlights all occurrences.	If highlighted result is a link, the link is loaded in a new tab. Otherwise, nothing happens.

Shortcut	Standard Find Mode	Fast Find Mode
Ctrl+G (⌘+G on a Mac)	Selects next occurrence (same as Enter).	Highlights next occurrence.
Crtl+Shift+G (⌘+Shift+G on a Mac)	Selects previous occurrence (same as Shift+Enter).	Highlights previous occurrence.

Stopping Annoying Web Sites in Their Tracks

The Internet is a great resource, but the truth is that some Web sites are just plain annoying. Perhaps they scroll text in the Firefox Status Bar when you're trying to read the page or disable the right-click menu so you can't save an image. Whatever the case, Firefox gives you complete control over your Web experience by letting you prevent these and other annoying habits:

1. **Choose Tools⇨Options.**

2. **Select the Content icon at the top of the Options window.**

3. **Next to the Enable JavaScript check box, click Advanced.**

   JavaScript is a general-purpose technology that some sites abuse to achieve these annoying effects.

4. **In the window that appears, you can determine what a Web site can and cannot do:**

   • **Move or resize existing windows:** This setting controls whether a Web site can move or resize your current Firefox window. By default, Firefox allows Web sites to do this.

   • **Raise or lower windows:** This setting controls whether a Web site can focus and defocus Firefox windows. For example, if you loaded Web sites simultaneously in two separate windows, one of the Web sites could steal focus, and that window would be brought to your attention. Firefox allows Web sites to do this by default.

   • **Disable or replace context menus:** This setting controls whether a Web site is able to disable the menu that appears when you right-click or replace it with something else. By default, Web sites are allowed to do this in Firefox. Some Web site owners use this to stop you from accessing the Save Image As command so you can't take their images. This is an illegitimate use, because there are many other commands on the contextual menu that the Web site is also preventing you from accessing, and because there's nothing unethical or illegal about saving an image for personal use. Other owners, however, use it for legitimate reasons. For example, if you were playing a game of Minesweeper online, you wouldn't want the contextual menu to appear each time you right-click.

• **Hide the Status Bar:** This setting controls whether a Web site can hide the Status Bar in any windows it opens. Malicious Web site authors might try to hide the Status Bar to obscure the crucial information it offers about a page's location and security status. Thus, by default, Web sites aren't allowed to hide the Status Bar.

• **Change Status Bar text:** This setting controls whether a Web site can change the text that appears in the Status Bar. By default, Firefox prevents Web sites from doing this. Firefox uses the Status Bar to display progress while a page loads, and to display a link's destination when you move the mouse over it. Some Web sites change the Status Bar text for legitimate reasons, such as to provide helpful information. Others do so to display distracting welcome messages or marquees or to obscure the true destinations of malicious links so they appear to lead somewhere benign.

5. **Click OK to close the Advanced JavaScript Settings window.**

6. **Click OK to save your changes and close the Options window.**

Making Your Privacy a One-Button Affair

Firefox compiles a variety of records about your travels on the Internet. Firefox doesn't transmit these records anywhere; they exist only for your convenience. For example, Firefox maintains a list of the Web sites you visit so you can return to them later. Chapter 14 describes the records Firefox keeps and shows you how to handle them if you're concerned about privacy.

However, if you turn off these records, you'll probably miss them later on. Instead of turning them off, you can permit Firefox to keep records, but use its Clear Private Data feature to clear them regularly. Ordinarily, Firefox asks you which records to clear each time you use the feature. However, if you clear private data frequently, you might want to tell Firefox to stop asking that question:

1. **Choose Tools⇨Options.**

2. **Click the Privacy icon at the top of the Options window.**

3. **Click the Settings button at the bottom of the window to open the Clear Private Data settings window.**

4. **Select the types of records you want to clear regularly and ensure that all other records are deselected.**

   If a type of record isn't selectable, Firefox currently has no records of the type.

5. **Deselect the Ask Me Before Clearing Private Data check box.**

   To turn the window back on later, just return to the Clear Private Data settings window and select this check box.

6. **Click OK to close the Clear Private Data settings window.**

7. **Click OK to save your changes and close the Options window.**

Now Firefox stops prompting you each time you use the Clear Private Data feature, which you access by choosing Tools➪Clear Private Data. On Windows, this feature also has a keyboard shortcut, so clearing your records is as simple as pressing Ctrl+Shift+Del whenever you're using Firefox.

Put It on My Tab!

Firefox is very humble about its tabbed browsing feature, which I explain in depth in Chapter 7. In fact, many tab fanatics say they had no idea it existed even weeks into using Firefox. We developers intentionally hid the feature so people who were accustomed to the old way of surfing wouldn't be overwhelmed when they switched to Firefox. However, tabs are seamlessly woven throughout the browser, just waiting for you to discover them.

Here are some easy ways to open tabs in Firefox:

✔ **Using the middle mouse button:** If your mouse has a middle button — or a scroll wheel that doubles as a button — you're in luck. At Firefox headquarters, we call this the tab button because it offers access to a new tab from virtually anywhere. Naturally, it works on links within Web sites, but it also works throughout the Firefox interface. Want to open a bookmark in a new tab? Just middle-click it, whether you're opening it from the Bookmarks Sidebar, the Manager, the Toolbar or (in Windows) the Bookmarks menu. The same goes for Web page history, whether you're using the Go menu or the History Sidebar. The basic rule is that you can middle-click anything that would normally load a Web site in your current tab to open it in a new tab: Back and Forward buttons, Home, you name it!

- **Ctrl+clicking items:** Don't have a middle mouse button? No problem. You can Ctrl+click (or ⌘+click on a Mac) Web page links and entries in your bookmarks and history lists to open them in new tabs. In other words, hold the Ctrl (or ⌘) key while left-clicking items.

- **Using the contextual menus:** So, you don't have a middle mouse button *and* you don't want to reach for the keyboard. In the case of bookmarks, history and Web site links, Firefox still has you covered in most cases. Simply right-click them and choose to open a new tab from the contextual menu that appears. If you're using a Mac and you use a mouse without a right button, you can hold the left mouse button for a second or two, and the context menu appears.

- **Using Alt+Enter (Option+Enter on a Mac):** This is a handy keyboard shortcut when you don't feel like reaching for the mouse. You primarily use this shortcut in the Location Bar: Simply type an address and hold Alt (or Option on a Mac) while pressing Enter to open it in a new tab.

- **Double-clicking the tab bar:** You can open a new tab at any time by double-clicking empty space in the tab bar (in other words, anywhere but on an existing tab).

- **Dragging a link onto the tab bar:** To open a link in a new tab, simply drag it to the tab bar. If you drop it on an existing tab, the link loads in that tab. Otherwise, it loads in a new tab.

- **Using the Add a New Tab button:** Tab aficionados can add a New Tab button to any of the Firefox toolbars via the Customize Toolbar window. See Chapter 18 for help with toolbar customization.

Bookmarklets: The Baby Extensions

Firefox is designed to be simple but extensible. If you want a feature that isn't included, odds are you can install it in under five minutes. Usually, you would do this by installing an extension and restarting Firefox, as I outline in Chapter 20. However, some smaller features are available as *bookmarklets,* which require no installation and no restart. These mini-extensions are so named because you access them just like you would a bookmark.

Bookmarklets are easy to use but difficult to explain, so the best method is to dive right in. You can use the following steps to obtain a bookmarklet that zooms in on a Web site's images:

1. **If your Bookmarks Toolbar isn't already open, open it by choosing View⇨Toolbars⇨Bookmarks Toolbar in the main Firefox window.**

   The Bookmarks Toolbar is visible by default.

2. **Navigate to Jesse Ruderman's Web site at** `www.squarefree.com/bookmarklets.`

   Jesse is a tester on the Firefox team who has compiled a large assortment of bookmarklets. Jesse's bookmarklets are divided into categories based on function.

3. **Click the Text and Data Bookmarklets link.**

   The page that loads contains a list of bookmarklets (in the leftmost column) and a description of each (in the middle column).

4. **Drag the Zoom Images In bookmarklet out of the page and onto your Bookmarks Toolbar.**

5. **Click the newly created Zoom Images In button on the Bookmarks Toolbar.**

When you click the button, the images on Jesse's Web site grow. If you click it again, they grow even larger. This isn't a permanent change. When you reload the page or visit a new page, the images are restored to normal size. Indeed, one reason bookmarklets are considered mini-extensions is that their effects are only temporary. This is also why they're so much easier to install than extensions: they can't have any long-term effects, so the risk of using them is much lower.

If you don't want to keep this zoom bookmarklet, you can delete it from your Bookmarks Toolbar just as you would delete a regular bookmark: Right-click it and choose Delete. Note that bookmarklets can reside in a regular bookmarks folder instead of on the Bookmarks Toolbar, but they're easier to access from the toolbar. Also, if you put a bookmarklet in a folder, Firefox tries to load the bookmarklet in a tab when you choose the Open in Tabs option (see Chapter 5), which can lead to some funky (but generally unharmful) results. This is a bug we developers hope to fix in a future release.

Be sure to explore the rest of Jesse's bookmarklets. You can test a bookmarklet before deciding to drag it to your Bookmarks Toolbar just by clicking it, and reloading the page always undoes its effects. Some of the bookmarklets are fairly technical in nature, but none are permanent — so feel free to experiment!

A Home for Every Occasion

The Internet holds billions of Web sites, and most browsers ask you to choose *one* to set as your home page. That doesn't seem fair. Firefox lets you have as many home pages as you want, and each one appears in its own tab whenever you start a new Firefox window.

You can specify multiple home pages in a few different ways. Here's the easiest way:

1. **Load the Web pages you want to use as your home pages into one window, each in its own tab.**

2. **Choose Tools⇨Options.**

3. **Click the General icon at the top of the Options window.**

4. **Under the Home Page boxed group, click the Use Current Pages button.**

   Alternatively, you can tell Firefox to set all the Web sites in one of your bookmark folders as the home pages by clicking the Use Bookmark button, selecting a folder, and clicking OK. This action will set as home pages only the bookmarks that already exist in that folder. In other words, any bookmarks you add to the folder in the future won't be home pages unless you return to this window and select the folder again.

   Although Firefox offers a number of ways to choose Web sites as your home pages, the end result is always the same: Firefox includes a list of the site addresses in the Location(s) text box, separated by a | (shift+ Backslash on most keyboards). (Firefox can't use more common separators like commas or spaces because those can be part of a site address.) Knowing this technical detail is quite useful because it allows you to remove a Web site from your home pages list by simply deleting its address from the text box and leaving the others intact. For example, if your home pages are Addicting Games, Kitten War, and The Onion, Firefox displays www. addictinggames.com | www.kittenwar.com | www.theonion.com in your Location(s) text box. To remove Kitten War as a home page, simply delete it, leaving www.addictinggames.com | www.theonion.com.

5. **Click OK to save your changes.**

Name That Bookmark!

Bookmarks are supposed to save you time, but when you accumulate too many, they might actually slow you down. No worries: You can skip all that pointing and clicking, and instead just assign keywords to your bookmarks. For example, you could give the bookmark to your sister's blog (Web log) the keyword *sis*. To go to her page later, simply enter **sis** into the Location Bar.

Assigning a keyword to a bookmark is easy:

1. **Right-click the bookmark and choose Properties.**

   The Properties window appears.

2. **Enter the keyword you want to use into the Keyword text box.**

   Because you'll be typing this word to access the bookmark, shorter words are better. Keywords are not case sensitive, so *sis* is the same as *SIS*.

3. **Click OK to save your changes.**

4. **To test the new keyword, enter it into the Location Bar and press Enter.**

Enjoying a Speedier Search

In the preceding section, you assign a keyword to a bookmark to return to it quickly. That's a great timesaver if the bookmarked page is your final destination, but what if it's just one stop on your route? For example, suppose you need fast access to Google News (news.google.com), Google's online news aggregator. You could bookmark the site and give it the keyword *mw*. But every time the front page loads, you still have to type in a word and wait for the definition to load.

Firefox lets you bypass this middle step by sending a word or phrase directly to a page from the Location Bar. For example, in the case of Google News, if *news* is your keyword for that site, you could type **news Super Bowl** into the Location Bar to go straight to a page of recent stories about the Super Bowl. In this case, *news* is a search keyword rather than a bookmark keyword. Naturally, search keywords work only with Web sites that accept search phrases, such as Google, Amazon, and so forth.

To set up this feature, you must tell Firefox what kind of search to conduct when you enter the search keyword and search phrase:

1. **Navigate to the search Web site.**

2. **Right-click the search box you would normally use to search.**

   For example, at Google News, you would right-click the search field at the top.

3. **Choose Add a Keyword for this Search from the menu that appears.**

   The Add Bookmark window appears.

4. **Enter a name for the bookmark.**

   This name will appear in the Bookmarks menu.

Assigning a search keyword is a little bit different than assigning a bookmark keyword. Whereas you can access a regular bookmark by using either the Bookmarks menu or its keyword, search bookmarks require a search phrase and thus can be accessed only by using their keywords (for example, *news Super Bowl*). They still show up in the Bookmarks menu and have a name, but you shouldn't access them this way. If that's confusing, the takeaway is this: Don't worry about the Name field here. The keyword is all that matters.

5. **Enter the keyword you want to use.**

   This is the word you will type into the Location Bar before the search phrase. In my Google News example, I use *news*.

6. **Click OK.**

7. **To test your new search keyword, type it into the Location Bar followed by a search phrase and then press Enter.**

Firefox includes a set of search keywords by default, and I list them in Table 21-2.

Table 21-2	Default Firefox Search Keywords	
Keyword	*Description*	*Example (Enter into the Location Bar)*
google	Searches for a word or phrase on Google	google ladybugs
wp	Searches for a word or phrase on Wikipedia, a community-edited encyclopedia	wp war of 1812
quote	Retrieves trading information for a stock ticker	quote GOOG
dict	Retrieves the definition and synonyms of a word or phrase	dict facetious

Feng Shui for Your Toolbars

Chapter 18 shows you how to go to town with your Firefox toolbars. Most people use this powerful capability to create new toolbars and load them up with buttons, but there's a certain Zen-like satisfaction to be had by compacting your toolbars to the bare essentials and reducing the amount of clutter that's in your face while browsing. Not to mention that you're also freeing up more space for Web sites.

Figure 21-1 shows my favorite layout. Unfortunately, this layout is possible only on Windows, because you can't customize the menu bar on the Macintosh. However, Mac users should head over to Chapter 18 to read about what else is possible with toolbar customization.

Below, I explain how I achieved my layout on Windows, and then I answer some of the questions you're probably asking (like, "how does he reload a page?"). The following directions assume that you're beginning from the default Firefox layout:

1. **Choose View➪Toolbars➪Customize.**

   The Customize Toolbar window appears, and the toolbars all go into customize mode (meaning elements such as Spaces become visible, as I discuss in Chapter 18).

2. **Drag the Back and Forward buttons from the Navigation Toolbar (the middle toolbar) to the menu bar (the top toolbar) and drop them to the left of the main menus (File, Edit, and so on).**

   You can drag only one button at a time.

3. **Drag a Separator from the Customize Toolbar window to the spot between the Forward button and the File menu.**

4. **Drag another Separator from the Customize Toolbar window to the spot after the Help menu.**

5. **Drag the Location Bar from the Navigation Toolbar to the menu bar and drop it to the right of the Separator you just added.**

6. **Drag one more Separator from the Customize Toolbar window to the menu bar and drop it after the Location Bar.**

7. **Drag the Search Box from the Navigation Toolbar to the menu bar and drop it after the Separator you just added.**

8. **Click Done to exit the Customize Toolbar window and get out of customize mode.**

9. **From the View➪Toolbars menu, hide the Navigation Toolbar.**

But the big question is, how do you access features such as Stop and Reload if those buttons are gone? The key is, well, the keyboard: Do you really need Stop and Reload buttons when the Escape and Ctrl+R (⌘+R on a Mac) keyboard shortcuts accomplish the same tasks, respectively? Do you need the Home button when you could press Alt+Home (Option+Home on a Mac)? Do you need the Go button when you could just press Enter/Return after typing an address?

If you're really keyboard-savvy, you don't even need the Location Bar. The Ctrl+L shortcut (⌘+L on a Mac) focuses and selects the Location Bar. However, if the bar isn't on one of your toolbars, Firefox opens it in a tiny window temporarily. You can remove the Location Bar from the toolbar, drag the Bookmarks Toolbar Items into its place, hide the now-empty Bookmarks Toolbar, and achieve the slim form factor shown in Figure 21-2.

Customized toolbars

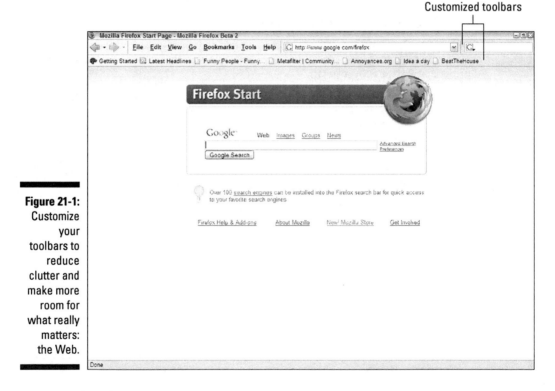

Figure 21-1: Customize your toolbars to reduce clutter and make more room for what really matters: the Web.

The slim-form-factor toolbar

Figure 21-2:
This slim
form factor
is possible
thanks to
Firefox's
toolbar
customiz-
ation
features.

The Scroll Wheel: Not Just for Scrolling

To accommodate the surge in scrolling in an Internet world, most mice now include a scroll wheel (or something similar) so you don't have to use the scroll bar. You can use this wheel in Firefox to scroll pages, but it also does so much more:

The mouse pointer must be over the Web site for each of the tricks below to work.

✔ **Going back and forth:** To navigate backward and forward through recent browsing history, hold Shift while scrolling the wheel down (to go back) or up (to go forward). Each tick of the wheel takes you backward or forward one page.

✔ **Enlarging or shrinking text:** To enlarge or shrink text on a page, hold Ctrl (or ⌘ on a Mac) while scrolling the wheel down (to enlarge) or up (to shrink). Each tick of the wheel enlarges or shrinks the size of the text by about 20 percent.

This change will affect future Web sites you visit in the same tab or window. To reset the text size to normal, go to View➪Text Size➪Normal, press Ctrl+0 (or ⌘+0 on a Mac), or just browse in a different tab or window.

✔ **Scrolling one line at a time:** By default, Firefox respects your system settings and usually scrolls about four lines at a time. If you want to focus on a document line by line, you can hold down Alt (or Option on a Mac) while scrolling the wheel.

✔ **Scrolling pages more smoothly with Smooth Scrolling:** By default, Firefox scrolls a page in notches — that is, it bumps the page up or down a certain amount each time you scroll. Some people might find this behavior jerky when reading a document line by line. You can turn on smooth scrolling in the Advanced category of the Options window, as I describe in Chapter 16, to have Firefox slide pages up or down more smoothly each time you scroll. If you previously browsed in Internet Explorer, you might feel more comfortable with smooth scrolling because Internet Explorer uses it.

✔ **Scrolling up and down a page quickly with autoscrolling:** If your scroll wheel doubles as a button, you can use it to scroll a page quickly and even automatically. Move the mouse pointer to a *dead* part of the page (somewhere that isn't a link) and hold down the wheel button. An icon overlays the spot you clicked. Now, still pressing the wheel button, move your mouse up and down to scroll the page much faster than usually. Alternatively, you can release the wheel button as soon as you see the icon, move the mouse up or down, and leave it there. Firefox scrolls the page automatically. If you don't like autoscrolling and find yourself activating it frequently, you can disable it in the Advanced category of the Options window, as I describe in Chapter 16.

Some mice don't support this feature even if they have a scroll wheel that acts as a button.

Chapter 22

The Ten Best Firefox Extensions

*F*irefox is completely *extensible,* which means you can literally build your dream browser by installing any of over 700 extensions (and counting!). Installation is a piece of cake, and you can find instructions in Chapter 20. After you install an extension, you can access the features it offers through the main Firefox interface as if they'd always been there.

This chapter outlines *la crème de la crème* of the Firefox extensions. Because developers can update their extensions at any time, specific directions would soon be obsolete, so in this chapter I try to provide a general overview. Most extensions are very simple to use and offer their own help systems. Have fun!

Before Getting Started

Extensions are created by the extended community, not by the Firefox team itself. I don't tell you this to frighten you; the extensions available on the official Firefox Web site are used by plenty of people every day. My point is that the Firefox developers don't decide when to upgrade or stop distributing a given extension. This means that by the time you read this, some of the extensions I discuss here might have changed drastically, and others might not even be available anymore. I hope that isn't the case and will do my best to prevent that, but it's a possibility.

I have three other notes before you get started:

- Check out Chapter 20 to familiarize yourself with the Firefox extension system before proceeding. That chapter explains where to find the extensions I discuss here, as well as how to install them. Remember that you need to restart Firefox after installing an extension!

- You can configure many extensions from the Options windows that you access through the Options button in the Extension Manager (Tools⇨ Extensions), as I describe in Chapter 20. Some extensions also put shortcuts to their options on the Tools menu.

- Many extensions quietly add buttons to the Customize Toolbar window. You can drag these buttons to your Firefox toolbars, as I explain in Chapter 18, to access the extension's features quickly.

Gaining Peace of Mind with SessionSaver

Extension: SessionSaver

Categories: Navigation, Tabbed Browsing

Wash the dog, feed the kids, wash the kids, feed the kids to the dog — think about all the stuff you keep track of every day. Wouldn't it be great if you could just download your brain to a disk, enjoy some worry-free downtime, and reload it later?

Technology still has a little ways to go, but the SessionSaver extension is the next best thing. As the name implies, SessionSaver remembers the state of Firefox from one browsing session to the next. For instance, if you open seven Web sites and then carelessly close Firefox, you see the same seven sites the next time you open it. The Web sites reopen in whatever form they were in when you closed Firefox. In other words, Web sites that were open in windows will reopen in windows, and Web sites that were open in tabs will reopen in tabs. SessionSaver even remembers information you've typed into Web forms but haven't yet saved or submitted. And the best part? You don't have to do *anything* to make this work.

SessionSaver restores exactly what you had open in your previous session, so unless your home page was open last time, it won't load the next time you start Firefox.

Thanks to SessionSaver, you no longer have to lose your open Web sites when your laptop battery dies or your spouse wants to go online. It also saves you from creating temporary bookmarks just to hold onto them. And even in the (rare!) case that Firefox crashes, SessionSaver protects your data.

How it works: SessionSaver automatically begins remembering your information across browser sessions as soon as you install it. You can configure SessionSaver by choosing Tools⇨SessionSaver⇨Settings to open its settings window. By default, the window displays in Simple Mode and contains a single setting to turn SessionSaver on and off. However, if you click the Simple toggle in the upper-right corner, the window changes to Expert Mode and makes a number of additional options available, as shown in Figure 22-1. For example, you can have SessionSaver ask you before it restores your last session by selecting the But Ask Me First check box.

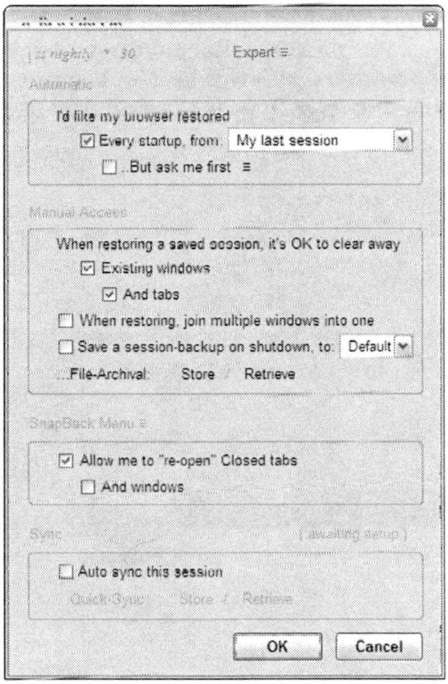

Figure 22-1:
SessionSaver works as soon as you install it, but you can customize it extensively by using its settings window in Expert Mode.

StumbleUpon the Web's Best Secrets

Extension: StumbleUpon

Categories: Navigation, Search Tools

The Internet holds over 10 billion pages, and quite frankly, many of them are boring. StumbleUpon is designed to separate the flowers from the weeds by helping you "stumble upon" Web sites that friends and people who share your interests recommend. Although StumbleUpon uses complicated algorithms to decide which Web sites will interest you, finding new and interesting content is as easy as clicking a button. Of course, you should also add good sites you find to the mix so others can have the pleasure of stumbling upon them. This, too, is as easy as clicking.

How it works: StumbleUpon adds its own toolbar (see Figure 22-2) under the Bookmarks Toolbar. After installation, click the Welcome to StumbleUpon button on the toolbar to create your account and indicate what kinds of sites you want to stumble upon. Then you're ready to go with the toolbar as your guide. To find a new site, just click Stumble. The results get more interesting when friends join your network; you can invite them by clicking the friend button to load the StumbleUpon invite form and filling out your friends' e-mail addresses, along with a short message. Recommend sites you visit with the I Like It! button or warn others with Not for Me. You can also see what others thought by clicking the Page Reviews button (the one with the speech bubble).

Additional help is available at www.stumbleupon.com.

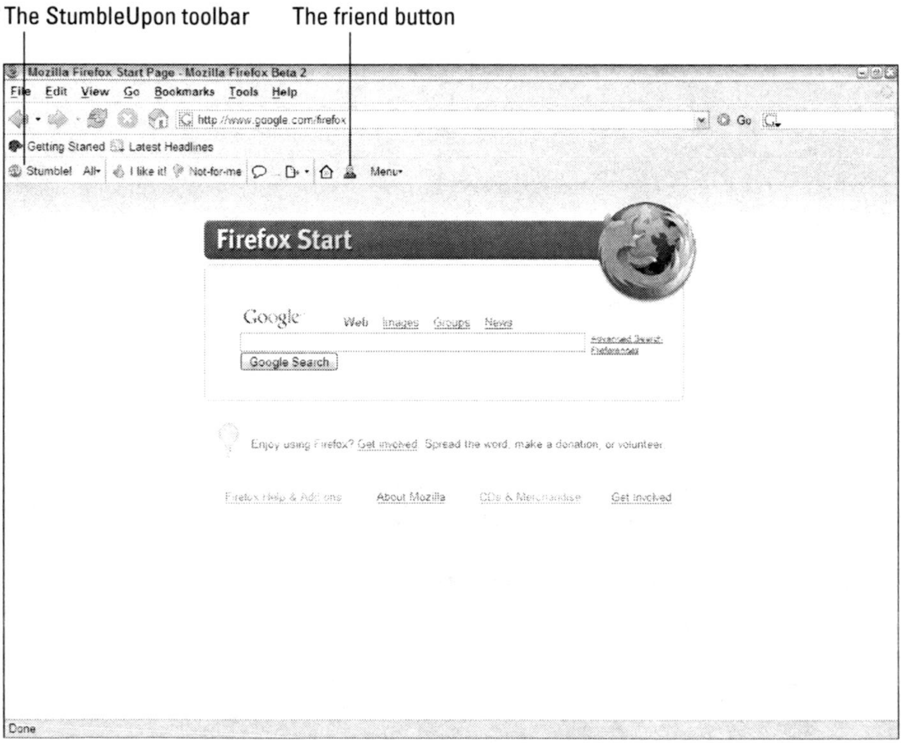

The StumbleUpon toolbar   The friend button

Figure 22-2:
Click the Stumble button on the StumbleUpon toolbar to visit a rec-ommended page.

Kissing Ads Goodbye with AdBlock

Extensions: AdBlock, AdBlock Filterset.G Updater

Category: Miscellaneous

Firefox blocks pop-up ads for you right out of the box. But as you're painfully aware, many other forms of online advertising are equally annoying. Enter AdBlock, an extension that can block anything you encounter with a click of the mouse.

Of course, blocking one ad a time could take you awhile. Even a single Web site might cycle through a network of tens of thousands of ads. But unless you block one ad at a time, how does AdBlock tell an ad from a legitimate image? AdBlock lets you block ads using filters that recognize content that comes from the same network as an ad you previously blocked. Rather than blocking one ad a time, AdBlock blocks advertising networks. Because most of the Internet's ads are served up by a small conglomerate of advertising networks, most ads disappear as soon as you've built up a small set of filters.

Now for the good news: Expert users have already scoured the Web for months and constructed a filter list that takes care of most ads you encounter. I recommend the AdBlock Filterset.G Updater extension, which automatically configures AdBlock to use such a list and keeps the list up-to-date as new ad networks are created.

How it works: After installing the AdBlock extension, install the AdBlock Filterset.G Updater extension and restart Firefox. You might see two scary-looking notices as soon as you restart. These are harmless; select the check box and click Close in each notice. Now you're ready to start surfing the ad-free Web! Because the purpose here is to reduce distraction caused by ads, AdBlock doesn't replace blocked ads with placeholder images or anything else; it just leaves the space empty. And don't worry about new advertisements: Your ad filter list is automatically updated each week.

AdBlock does the best it can to recognize and block advertisements, but some slip through anyway. Whenever you see an ad and sigh, just remember how things were *before* AdBlock!

A New Way to Surf with Mouse Gestures

Extension: Mouse Gestures

Categories: Message Reading, Navigation

I started this book by saying I want Firefox to make the Web fun again. That's a pretty hard thing to do when you consider that the basics of Web browsing haven't changed in the past decade. You click Back to go back. You click Forward to go forward. How can anyone improve on that?

Well, the other theme I harp on is making tasks simpler. And if you think about it, a step could be eliminated: moving the mouse all the way to the toolbar to click those buttons. (Hey, developers are lazy.) Sure, you could use the keyboard to go back and forward, but odds are that your hand is already on the mouse to scroll.

The answer to your troubles — which, until a minute ago, you didn't know you had — is the Mouse Gestures extension. As its name suggests, a *mouse gesture* is a way to execute commands by moving the mouse in certain ways. In a gesture world, you don't move the mouse pointer to the toolbar to click a button. You press and hold the right mouse button (to indicate that you're performing a gesture), jerk the mouse left a couple inches, and then release the button. To go forward, do the same thing but jerk the mouse to the right. Gestures work as long as the mouse pointer is over the Web site.

The backward and forward gestures are intuitive because you simply gesture to the left or right (respectively), but other commands — such as Close Page — are harder to model and have more arbitrary gestures. I list some of the more common ones in Table 22-1. After you get the hang of simple mouse gestures like these, there are plenty more to master, and you can discover more online at this address:

```
http://optimoz.mozdev.org/gestures/defaultmappings.html
```

You can even create your own gestures. First, open the Extension Manager (Tools⇨Extensions), select the Mouse Gestures extension in the list, and click the Options button at the bottom to open the Mouse Gestures options window. In this window, click the Edit Mappings button at the bottom of the General tab to open the Edit Gesture Mappings window (where gestures are mapped to the Firefox commands they perform). Next, click the New button to open the New Gesture Mappings window. Now, to define your gesture, you need to specify two things: the gesture itself, and the Firefox command it performs (e.g. minimize window). The easiest way to specify the gesture is to click the Recognize button next to Gesture Code and perform the desired gesture (using the right mouse button, as with all gestures) in the white screen that appears. Then choose the Firefox command to perform from the Functions list at the bottom of the window. When finished, click OK, and then click OK again to close the Edit Gesture Mappings window and the original options window. Your new gesture is ready to go!

You can share your gesture with the world at the Gesture Exchange (`http://optimoz.mozdev.org/gestures/redirect/gesture-exchange/`). You can also see what your fellow gesturers have come up with — and even install their gestures! When you find an intriguing gesture, simply click the link to it, and then click OK when the Import Gesture Mapping window appears. You can start using the new gesture immediately; no restart is required.

Table 22-1	Basic Mouse Gestures
Command	*Gesture (Press and Hold the Right Mouse Button as You Gesture)*
Bookmark Current Page	Down, then Right, then Down, then Left, then Up (which "draws" a lowercase B)
Go Back	Left
Go Forward	Right
Go Home	Down, then Up, then Right, then Down (which "draws" a lowercase H)
Open New Window	Down
Open New Tab	Up
Stop	Left, then Up
Close Page	Right, then Left, then Right

Release the right mouse button when you finish a gesture. If you continue to hold it, the gesture will be cancelled.

How it works: After installing the Mouse Gestures extension, you're ready to go. Navigate to a few Web sites so you have some browsing history and then try the Go Back gesture. A note appears in the Status Bar as soon as the gesture is recognized. You can configure mouse gestures from the extension's options window, which you access by selecting Mouse Gestures in the Extension Manager list (see Chapter 20) and clicking the Options button at the bottom. To create or change gestures, click the Edit Mappings button at the bottom of the options window, and note the key in the bottom left so you can follow the chart. You can also turn on a neat feature called *mouse trails* on the Visual Settings tab to have a line drawn on-screen each time you gesture. This feature is handy when you're getting acquainted with gestures because you can see exactly what the extension "sees" and discover how to perform the gestures it doesn't recognize more precisely. In Figure 22-3, I'm performing a Go Back gesture. (I didn't draw a very straight line, but the Mouse Gestures extension recognized it anyway.) Just be sure to read the note about this feature on the Visual Settings tab.

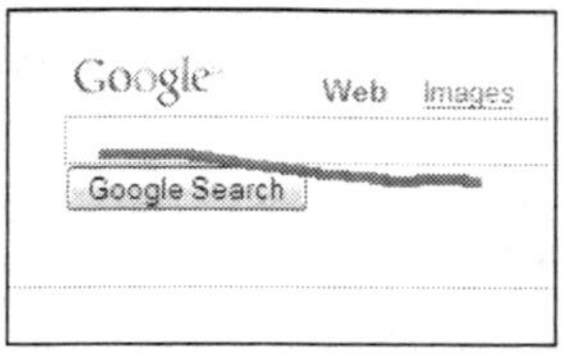

Figure 22-3: Turn on mouse *trails* to see the gesture on-screen as you perform it.

Additional help is available from `http://optimoz.mozdev.org/gestures/faqs.html`.

Playing Music without Leaving Firefox

Extension: FoxyTunes

Categories: Entertainment, Miscellaneous

Do you spend so much time using your Web browser these days that switching applications seems like a major distraction? Thankfully, some developers are creating extensions that bring the applications to you. One of my favorites is FoxyTunes, which integrates your favorite music player into Firefox by adding a slim toolbar that stays out of the way. The toolbar offers direct access to everything you need: Play, Stop, Rewind, Fast Forward, and Previous/Next song, which navigate through your current playlist. FoxyTunes works with all the popular music players, including WinAmp, iTunes, Windows Media Player, and RealPlayer. (See `http://foxytunes.org/firefox/features.html#supportedplayers` for a complete list of supported players.)

How it works: After installing FoxyTunes, you see a small toolbar in the bottom-right corner containing a few different sets of buttons (see Figure 22-4). You can hover over a button to see its purpose, so I mention only the important ones here. You can also see a handful of tiny black arrows. Click these arrows to expand the toolbar and see additional controls or information. For example, the first black arrow slides out a tray displaying the name of the current song.

Figure 22-4:
The slim, unobtrusive FoxyTunes toolbar is an audiophile's dream.

The FoxyTunes toolbar

The first button opens the FoxyTunes menu. Click it, choose Player⇨Select, and then choose your music player. The next set of buttons offers access to familiar commands like Previous/Next Track and Play and should be self-explanatory. Note that Previous/Next Track navigate through the playlist in your player if one exists.

Some players, such as iTunes, must be open to be controlled by FoxyTunes. The extension will automatically launch a player when necessary (such as when you click Play). If you don't want the player to clutter up your screen, you can tell FoxyTunes to hide (but not close) it with the Hide Player button.

If you don't like the FoxyTunes bar in the bottom-right corner of the screen, you can move it. Simply move the mouse pointer to the first black arrow on the toolbar and when it turns into a pointing hand, begin dragging the toolbar to the desired location on any of Firefox's toolbars.

Additional help is available from www.foxytunes.org.

The Web Your Way with Greasemonkey

Extension: Greasemonkey

Categories: Developer Tools, Web Annoyances, Website Integration

Since the birth of the Web, Internet surfing has been a very passive activity. You decide where to go, but when you get there, the site owner controls the experience. Greasemonkey allows you to customize Web sites to your liking. Think of it as your interior decorator for the Web: You can get inside other people's pages and move, redesign, or remove what's on them. You can even add to them. For example, some Greasemonkey users customize Google to show image previews of each search result, which helps you decide whether a result is any good before you waste time clicking through to it. Of course, none of your changes affect other visitors to the page.

Greasemonkey is the tool that makes this possible. Before you can start surfing the Web your way, you need to tell Greasemonkey what "your way" is. This is expressed in a set of programming instructions known as a *user script.* When a Web site finishes loading, Greasemonkey executes these instructions to customize it. However, you don't need to be a programmer to use Greasemonkey. Thousands of advanced users have already created user scripts that you can install with one click.

As with extensions in general, the Mozilla Foundation cannot guarantee the safety or function of user scripts.

Greasemonkey supports two kinds of user scripts:

- ✔ **Generic scripts** can affect any Web site you visit. For example, the Linkifier script changes text addresses (such as `http://www.google.com` or `john@smith.com`) on any page into actual links that you can click.

- ✔ **Site-specific scripts** are specifically designed for certain Web sites. For example, the Yahoo! Mail Keyboard Shortcuts script adds keyboard shortcuts to the Yahoo! mail interface so you can navigate it more quickly. This script is specially designed for Yahoo! and won't work elsewhere. Site-specific scripts are more fragile than generic scripts because they could stop working if the target Web site changes significantly.

Greasemonkey is one of the most complicated Firefox extensions available, but it's also one of the most powerful. Enjoy your Web!

How it works: After installing Greasemonkey, make your way to the user scripts collections:

Generic scripts:

```
http://dunck.us/collab/GreaseMonkeyUserScriptsGeneric
```

Site scripts:

```
http://dunck.us/collab/GreaseMonkeyUserScriptsSpecific
```

When you find a script you like, right-click the link to it (left-clicking shows you the script itself) and choose Install User Script. Greasemonkey asks you whether to exclude certain Web sites from the effects of the script, as shown in Figure 22-5. By default, generic and site-specific scripts behave as I explain earlier in this section. When the Install User Script window appears, click OK to continue with installation. And that's basically all there is to it. When you visit an applicable Web site, the script should automatically kick in after the page is done loading.

 You can turn Greasemonkey on and off by clicking the little monkey head in the bottom-right corner of the main Firefox window. You'll also notice some new Greasemonkey options on the Tools menu, but these are mostly technical features you can ignore.

 I recommend the scripts in Table 22-2 to first-time Greasemonkey users who want to get their feet wet.

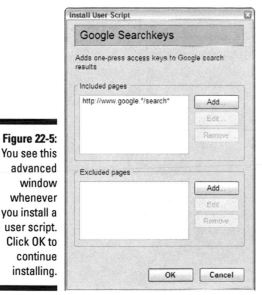

Figure 22-5: You see this advanced window whenever you install a user script. Click OK to continue installing.

Table 22-2		Greasemonkey Scripts to Try
Script Name	*Type*	*Description*
Linkifier	Generic	Automatically converts textual addresses (such as `http://www.google.com` or `john@smith.com`) into clickable links.
Expand TextArea	Generic	Lets you resize text entry boxes on a page so you don't need to scroll as much. (Works only with text boxes that accept more than one line of text to begin with.)
Zoom Image	Generic	Lets you zoom images by using a small toolbar that appears when you hover over them.
Google Search Keys	Site	Numbers the results of a Google search, as illustrated in Figure 22-6. Press a number on your keyboard to open the corresponding results. (For example, in Figure 22-6 you could press 6 to load the CNN Weather page.)

Figure 22-6:
The Google Search Keys script prefixes each Google search result with a number you can press to access it.

5 BBC - **Weather** Centre - UK and World **Weather**
Current conditions and forecasts for the UK and the world. Includes background material about **weather** including climate change, glossary, calculators, ...
www.bbc.co.uk/weather/ - 26k - Aug 28, 2005 - Cached - Similar pages

6 CNN.com - **Weather**
Features **weather** news and 5-day forecasts for cities or countries around the world.
www.cnn.com/WEATHER/ - 47k - Aug 28, 2005 - Cached - Similar pages

7 NOAA's National **Weather** Service
National **Weather** Service Home page. The starting point for official government **weather** forecasts, warnings, meteorological products for forecasting the ...
weather.gov/ - 63k - Cached - Similar pages

Additional help is available in Mark Pilgrim's free online book, *Dive into Greasemonkey,* at www.diveintogreasemonkey.org.

Managing Bookmarks More Efficiently

Extension: Flat Bookmark Editing

Category: Bookmarks

Firefox includes a powerful Bookmarks Manager for organizing your bookmark collection, but it has a quirk that might aggravate frequent filers: You have to edit a bookmark's properties through a separate window. Whenever you want to rename a bookmark, for example, you must right-click the bookmark, choose Properties, and work inside the Properties window.

The Flat Bookmark Editing extension streamlines this process by flattening the Properties window into the Bookmarks Manager, as illustrated in Figure 22-7. As you can see, the OK and Cancel buttons are gone. That's because changes to properties take effect as soon as you make them, with no need to save explicitly. The Flat Bookmark Editing extension saves you just a few seconds per bookmark, but over time that adds up to a big win.

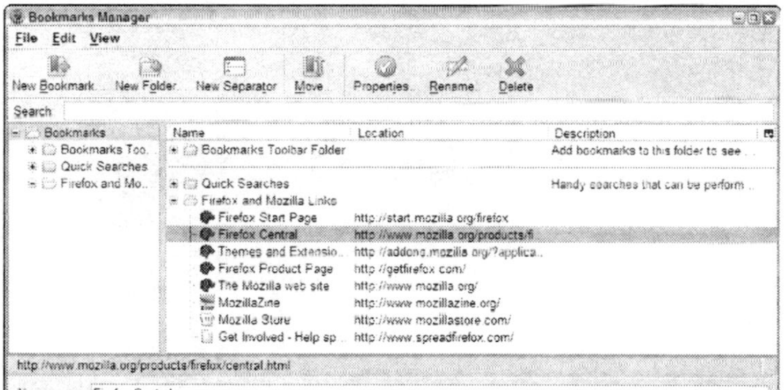

Figure 22-7:
The Flat Bookmark Editing extension flattens the Properties window into the Bookmarks Manager so you can organize faster.

How it works: After you install Flat Bookmark Editing, you see the property fields in a panel at the bottom of the Bookmarks Manager. You're ready to go!

Additional help is available at `http://bluweb.com/us/chouser/proj/mozhack`.

Keeping an Eye on Your Downloads

Extension: Download Statusbar

Category: Download Tools

Most browsers open one progress window per download, which can be pretty overwhelming if you're downloading multiple files. What's worse, closing a window cancels the download. Firefox improves the situation by integrating all download progress into a single Download Manager and will continue downloading even if you close the manager. But what if you could keep an eye on your downloads without needing a window at all?

The Download Statusbar extension adds an unobtrusive bar to the bottom of the Firefox window, as shown in Figure 22-8. This bar tracks the progress of all ongoing downloads. Each download is represented by a white button that is filled with color as the download progresses. You can pause, cancel, or launch downloads right from the download status bar.

Figure 22-8:
The Download Statusbar tracks the progress of ongoing downloads in a bar along the bottom of the Firefox window.

The Download Statusbar

How it works: After installing the Download Statusbar extension and restarting Firefox, you see a window with usage tips from the extension's creator, but the actual status bar doesn't appear until you start a download. While a download is in progress, the status bar displays three pieces of information: the progress, as indicated by the amount of color; the approximate time left, in the bottom-right corner; and the approximate download rate, in the top-right corner. The meaning of the download rate is unimportant, but higher is better. Left-click a download to pause it, and left-click again to resume. When a download finishes, double-click to launch it or single-click with the middle mouse button to remove it from the status bar. (If your mouse doesn't have a middle mouse button, right-click the download and choose Remove from the contextual menu.)

You can configure the download status bar in all sorts of ways from its options window. To access the window, choose Tools⇨Extensions to open the Extension Manager, select the Download Statusbar extension in the list, and then click the Options button at the bottom. (See Chapter 20 for more on the Extension Manager.)

Additional help is available from the user support forum at `http://dlstatusbar.proboards43.com/index.cgi?board=dlsb`.

Making the World's Largest Scrapbook

Extensions: Scrapbook

Categories: Download Tools

For all the benefits of the Web, paper documents have traditionally retained an edge. They don't magically disappear when your Internet connection does. And unlike Web sites, you can mark them, highlight them, and otherwise annotate them in any fashion you please. However, the Scrapbook extension — an innovative tool for archiving and annotating Web sites — puts the Web firmly in the lead.

A scrapbooked Web site is more than just a link. It is a complete copy of the page stored on your computer. So unlike a bookmark, you can still return to a scrapbooked page even if the original page is removed from the Internet or if your Internet connection is down. (The trade-off, of course, is that when the original page is updated, your copy is not.) And because Scrapbook has access to the full text of each page, searching for a scrapbooked page is much easier than searching for a bookmark; you aren't limited to searching titles.

Scrapbook also lets you capture copies of each Web site *linked* from a given page. Do you need some reading material for a long plane ride? Just go to CNN and capture the front page, links and all, for your Scrapbook. Now you have offline access to every article, including pictures, during the flight.

Sometimes, however, a Web page is more than you need — and this is where Scrapbook really shines. You can capture just a small portion of a page and Scrapbook remembers all the original formatting. Just as a real scrapbook is composed of ticket stubs and receipts, your online scrapbook can contain mere scraps of pages.

To top it off, Scrapbook offers powerful tools to annotate the items you archive. And because Scrapbook items are snapshots of their Web counterparts, you can actually edit them directly as if they were documents you created. Insert notes, highlight key sections, even remove elements you don't need — Scrapbook lets you do it all. No wonder *The New York Times* raved about it.

How it works: After you install Scrapbook, you're ready to begin scrapbooking. To capture a page, right-click it and choose Capture Page. This captures the entire page, including images, without presenting any options. Use the Capture Page As command for additional options, such as a destination folder for the captured page and the ability to capture linked pages.

To capture part of a page, select the part, right-click, and choose Capture Selection (or choose Capture Selection As if you need extended options).

You can view the Scrapbook Sidebar by choosing Tools⇨ScrapBook. Select an item in the sidebar to load it in the current tab or window. When an item is loaded, click the blue EDIT button in the bottom-right corner to open the editing toolbar, shown at the bottom of Figure 22-9. Use the buttons on the right to highlight, remove, or annotate text after selecting it on the page. You can hover over each button to see a description of its purpose. When you're done, click the disk button to save your edits.

When you install the Scrapbook extension, it adds a button to the Customize Toolbar window that opens and closes the Scrapbook Sidebar. As I describe in Chapter 18, you can drag this button to any of your Firefox toolbars for fast access to the sidebar.

To search items in your Scrapbook, enter a word or phrase into the text box at the top and press Enter. The Scrapbook Sidebar offers dozens of additional features you can experiment with as you grow more familiar with it.

Additional help is available from `http://amb.vis.ne.jp/mozilla/scrapbook`.

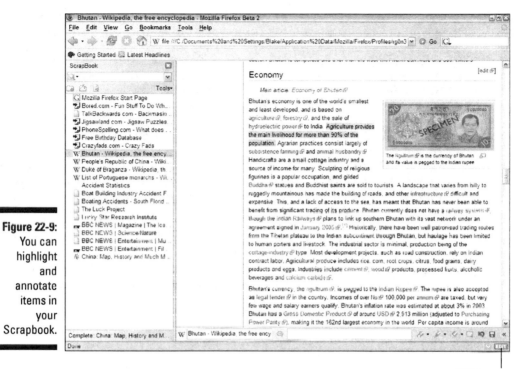

Figure 22-9:
You can highlight and annotate items in your Scrapbook.

EDIT button

Honey, I Shrunk the Link!

Extension: TinyUrl Creator

Categories: Miscellaneous, Navigation, Web Annoyances

Internet addresses are a pain. Apart from being complicated and hard to remember, they're often very long. For example, most MapQuest addresses, which are generated automatically, look like this:

```
http://www.mapquest.com/directions/main.adp?do=rev&mo=ma&2
si=navt&1gi=0&un=m&go=1&2gi=0&1a=1981%20Landings%20Dr&1c=M
ountain%20View&1g=3Q1zpeLc748QB0HJgOtqNw%3d%3d&2a=1350%20V
illa%20St&2tabval=address&1l=8qe7XqKPT90%3d&2c=Mountain%20
View&1da=%2d1%2e000000&1rc=L1AAA&1n=SANTA%20CLARA%20COUNTY
&cl=EN&2g=VoxgHLbzR2uOhZ6dpT36JA%3d%3d&1s=CA&2l=Sj1LyGkYzR
4%3d&ct=NA&1v=ADDRESS&2n=SANTA%20CLARA%20COUNTY&1y=US&1tab
val=address&1z=94043%2d0801&1si=navt&2s=CA&2da=%2d1%2e0000
00&2rc=L1AAA&2v=ADDRESS&did=1129956842&2y=US&2z=94041%2d11
26&rsres=1
```

Long addresses aren't just an eyesore; they're difficult to share with others. When you send an address like the previous example by e-mail or instant message, it often gets broken down into multiple lines. When your friend receives it, only the first line is linked, and because that isn't the full address, the link fails. He has to copy and paste the address into his browser — line, by line, by line. And when the link is for directions to your house and he's already 10 minutes late, that's a real problem.

The TinyUrl Creator extension for Firefox offers a brilliant solution. It allows you to automatically generate a very short address (such as `http://tinyurl.com/8f46`) that redirects to the original page. Think of it like a nickname or a shortcut; it's another way to get to the same place. Because this address is very short, it's easy to share with others. (*URL* is a technical term for an address, in case you're wondering.)

How it works: After installing TinyUrl Creator, you can generate a short address by visiting the offending page and choosing Tools⇨TinyUrl Creator⇨ From Current URL. The short address is automatically copied to your Clipboard (and it overwrites whatever's already there!) so it's easy to share with others by pasting it into an e-mail or instant message. The extension shows a notification window each time you create a short address, as shown in Figure 22-10, but you can turn this off in the extension's Options window (Tools⇨TinyUrl Creator⇨Options).

Figure 22-10:
Turn long
addresses
into very
short ones
with TinyUrl
Creator.

Additional help is available at the TinyUrl Creator user support forum (`http://forums.mozmonkey.com/index.php`). You can find additional information about how the TinyURL service works at `www.tinyurl.com`. Note that the TinyUrl Creator extension is not produced by the makers of the TinyURL.com service.

Appendix A

Firefox Menu Reference

In This Appendix

▶ Walking through the Firefox menu system

*T*rying a new program with dozens of new commands can be as overwhelming as meeting the in-laws. This appendix walks you through the
commands offered by the Firefox menu bar. I also list the command's keyboard shortcut under it (if it has one) and identify any scenarios that might
cause a command to be unavailable. If you want more information on a particular command or menu, I point you to the chapter where I discuss it.

The File Menu

The File menu (shown in Figure A-1) mostly contains commands that operate
on the currently displayed Web site, along with a few general Firefox commands (such as Import, for importing personal information from your previous browser, and Exit, for closing all Firefox windows).

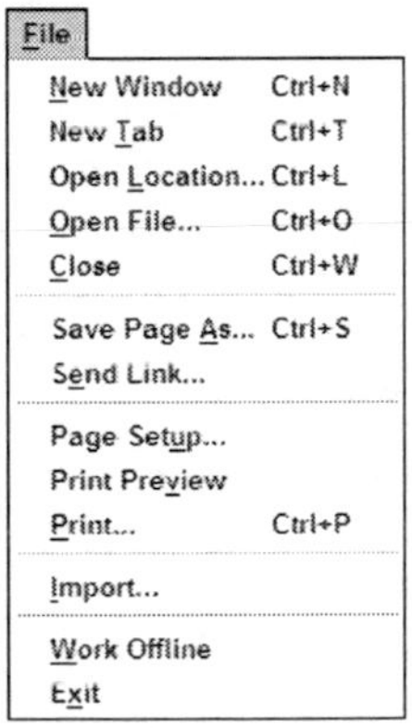

File	
New Window	Ctrl+N
New Tab	Ctrl+T
Open Location...	Ctrl+L
Open File...	Ctrl+O
Close	Ctrl+W
Save Page As...	Ctrl+S
Send Link...	
Page Setup...	
Print Preview	
Print...	Ctrl+P
Import...	
Work Offline	
Exit	

Figure A-1:
The File
menu.

New Window

Opens a new Firefox window.

Shortcut: Ctrl+N (⌘+N on a Mac)

New Tab

Opens a new Firefox tab.

Shortcut: Ctrl+T (⌘+T on a Mac)

See Chapter 7 for more information about tabbed browsing.

Open Location

If the Location Bar is on your toolbar, choosing this menu item selects it. If you remove the Location Bar by using toolbar customization, which I discuss in Chapter 18, this command opens the window shown in Figure A-2. Type the address of the page you want to load into the text box, or if you want to open a file that's on your computer, click the Choose File button and select the file in the window that appears. By default, Firefox opens the Web page or file in the current window. To open it in a new tab or window instead, choose the appropriate option from the dropdown list next to Open In. Finally, click the Open button to open the Web page or file.

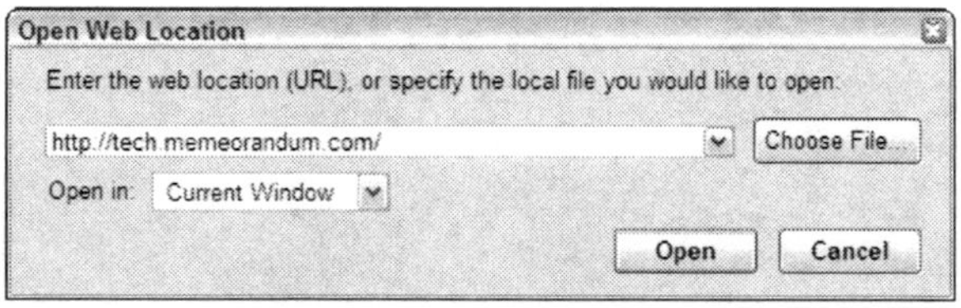

Figure A-2:
If you hide the Location Bar by using toolbar cus-tomization, the Open Location command shows this window.

Open Web Location

Enter the web location (URL), or specify the local file you would like to open.

http://tech.memeorandum.com/   [Choose File...]

Open in: Current Window

[Open]   [Cancel]

Shortcut: Ctrl+L (⌘+L on a Mac)

Open File

Allows you to display a file on your hard drive within Firefox. Only Web sites, text files, and images can be opened.

Shortcut: Ctrl+O (⌘+O on a Mac)

Close

Closes the current Firefox window. Firefox shows this command only if you have no tabs open in the current window. Otherwise, it displays Close Window and Close Tab commands.

Shortcut: Ctrl+W (⌘+W on a Mac)

Close Window

Closes the current Firefox window. Firefox shows this command in addition to the Close Tab command if you have multiple tabs open in the current window. If you don't, the Close command is shown. This is different from the Exit command, which closes *all* Firefox windows (and any tabs they contain).

Shortcut: Ctrl+Shift+W (⌘+Shift+W on a Mac)

See Chapter 7 for more information about tabbed browsing.

Close Tab

Closes the current tab. Firefox shows this command in addition to the Close Window command if you have multiple tabs open. If you don't, the Close command is shown.

Shortcut: Ctrl+W (⌘+W on a Mac)

See Chapter 7 for more information about tabbed browsing.

Save Page As

Saves the current Web page to your hard drive so you can view it even if the site or your Internet connection goes down.

Shortcut: Ctrl+S (⌘+S on a Mac)

See Chapter 11 for more information about saving Web sites.

Save Frame As

Saves the selected frame of the current Web site to your hard drive so you can view it even if the site or your Internet connection goes down. Firefox shows this command only if you're viewing a Web site that is partitioned into frames, where each frame is itself a page. To save a particular frame, click some *dead* space within it (that is, click somewhere other than on a link), and then choose this command. (Frames are rare on the Web these days.)

See Chapter 11 for more information about saving Web sites.

Send Link

Opens a new e-mail compose window that contains a link to the current page. Firefox offers this feature so you can send interesting links to friends and family easily. Simply address the e-mail, write a brief message, and then click Send.

This feature uses your computer's default e-mail program. To change the default e-mail program on Windows, click the Start button and choose Control Panel from the Start menu. In the Control Panel window, switch to Classic View and double-click on Internet Options, then click the Programs tab in the Internet Options window. Finally, select the program you want to set as default from the drop-down list next to E-Mail, and click OK. To change the default e-mail program on a Mac, you need to use a setting offered in the e-mail program itself, if it offers one.

Page Setup

Opens a window where you can configure the display of printed Web sites on paper.

See Chapter 12 for more information about printing.

Print Preview

Displays a preview of how the current Web site will look on paper if you print it. Use the Page Setup command to configure the print layout.

This command is unavailable on Macintosh.

See Chapter 12 for more information about printing.

Print

Displays a window that allows you to configure printing (for example, choosing a page range) and print the current document.

Shortcut: Ctrl+P (⌘+P on a Mac)

See Chapter 12 for more information about printing.

Import

Opens the Import Wizard, which walks you through the process of importing personal information (such as bookmarks and saved passwords) from your old browser.

See Chapter 3 for more information about importing.

Work Offline

Puts Firefox in a special Offline mode. In Offline mode, Firefox never actually connects to Web sites you visit; instead, it displays an archived version of the page from the last time you visited it. If you haven't visited the page before or if you cleared the Firefox cache (see Chapter 14), Firefox displays an error message. Offline mode is useful when you won't have an Internet connection for an extended period of time and you want Firefox to use its archive instead of failing to load each page. For example, if you're preparing to go on a plane, you could visit a few pages, board the plane, put Firefox in Offline mode, and navigate among them as if you were still online.

Putting Firefox in Offline mode doesn't actually turn off your Internet connection. It affects only the way Firefox displays Web sites.

If you shut down Firefox in Offline mode, it will be in Offline mode next time you open it. To return to Online mode, choose the Work Offline command again.

Exit

Closes all open Firefox windows and tabs. Firefox displays a warning if any downloads are in progress and if any open windows contain multiple tabs.

The Edit Menu

The Edit menu (shown in Figure A-3) lets you copy and paste text and images or find text in the current Web page.

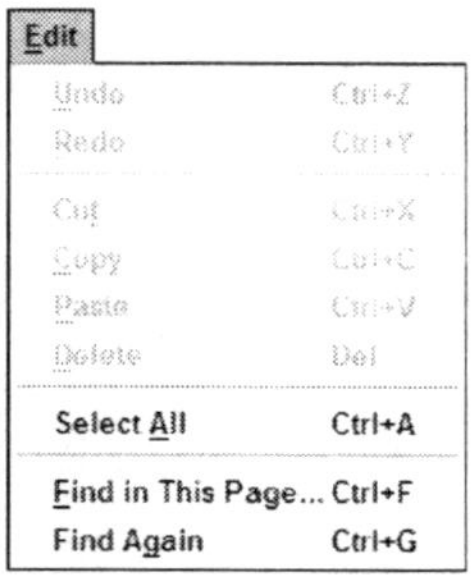

Edit	
Undo	Ctrl+Z
Redo	Ctrl+Y
Cut	Ctrl+X
Copy	Ctrl+C
Paste	Ctrl+V
Delete	Del
Select All	Ctrl+A
Find in This Page...	Ctrl+F
Find Again	Ctrl+G

Figure A-3: The Edit menu.

Undo

Reverses the last text edit you made in the current window (such as in the Location Bar or a text box on the page). Note that Undo *cannot* reopen a tab after you close it, return a bookmark after you delete it from the Bookmarks Toolbar, or otherwise undo any action besides text editing.

This command is unavailable (grayed out) when you haven't made any edits to undo.

Shortcut: Ctrl+Z (⌘+Z on a Mac)

Redo

Reverses the last Undo command. This is the opposite of Undo. If you type **Firefox** in the Location Bar and choose Undo, "Firefox" disappears. Choose Redo to restore it. As with Undo, Redo can only restore text edits.

This command is unavailable (grayed out) when you haven't undone an action.

Shortcuts: Ctrl+Y or Ctrl+Shift+Z (⌘+Shift+Z on a Mac)

Cut

Copies the current selection into the system Clipboard and deletes it from its original location. Use the Paste command to put the selection in a new location.

This command is unavailable (grayed out) when nothing is selected or when you have selected something that can't be cut out of its original location, such as text in a Web page.

Shortcut: Ctrl+X or Shift+Delete (⌘+X on a Mac)

Copy

Copies the current selection (which can contain both text and images) onto the system Clipboard, replacing whatever is currently on the Clipboard. You can then use the Paste command to put the selection in a new location. The difference between Copy and Cut is that Cut actually removes the text from a location, whereas Copy leaves the original and simply makes a copy of it. In both cases, the text that is cut or copied goes onto the Clipboard, and you can then paste it elsewhere. Although Cut doesn't work on text that is on a Web page, Copy usually does.

This command is unavailable (grayed out) when nothing is selected.

Shortcut: Ctrl+C (⌘+C on a Mac)

Paste

Puts the selection on the system Clipboard into the currently focused text box. The selection stays on the Clipboard until something else is cut or copied to replace it, so you can paste multiple instances of the selection if you want to.

This command is unavailable when the Clipboard is empty.

Shortcut: Ctrl+V (⌘+V on a Mac)

Delete

Deletes the current selection.

This command is unavailable when nothing is selected or when you have selected something that can't be deleted, such as text on a Web page.

Shortcut: Delete

Select All

Selects everything in the currently focused area. For example, if the Location Bar is focused, the Select All command selects the entire address. If the Content area is focused, the command selects the current Web site.

Shortcut: Ctrl+A (⌘+A on a Mac)

Find in This Page

Opens the Find Bar at the bottom of the window so you can find text within the current Web page.

Shortcuts: Ctrl+F or F3 (⌘+F on a Mac)

See Chapter 4 for more information about the Find Bar.

Find Again

If you previously searched a Web page in the current window, this command opens the Find Bar with the last search phrase and searches for the next instance. Otherwise, it just opens the Find Bar and waits for you to enter a phrase.

Shortcuts: Ctrl+G or F3 (⌘+G on a Mac)

The View Menu

The View menu (shown in Figure A-4) contains a mixture of commands for showing or hiding Firefox toolbars and sidebars, as well as changing the appearance of the current Web page.

View		
Toolbars	▶	
✔ Status Bar		
Sidebar	▶	
Stop	Esc	
Reload	Ctrl+R	
Text Size	▶	
Page Style	▶	
Character Encoding	▶	
Page Source	Ctrl+U	
Full Screen	F11	

Figure A-4:
The View
menu.

Toolbars

The Toolbars submenu allows you to show or hide the toolbars in the main Firefox window. It also offers access to toolbar customization, which I discuss further in Chapter 18.

Navigation Toolbar

Shows or hides the Navigation Toolbar, which contains commands you need while browsing (such as Back and Forward).

See Chapter 2 for more information about the Navigation Toolbar.

Bookmarks Toolbar

Shows or hides the Bookmarks Toolbar, where you can store your favorite bookmarks for fast access.

See Chapters 2 and 5 for more information about the Bookmarks Toolbar.

The list of created toolbars

If you have created additional toolbars, as I describe in Chapter 18, a menu item for each one will appear here. Click the menu item to show or hide the toolbar.

Customize

Opens the Customize Toolbar window, which allows you to add or remove items to and from your toolbars, change the toolbar display, and even create new toolbars.

See Chapter 18 for more information about toolbar customization.

Status Bar

Shows or hides the Status Bar at the bottom of the window. The Status Bar displays information about the current page.

See Chapter 2 for more information about the Status Bar.

Sidebar

The Sidebar submenu allows you to show or hide sidebars, which are vertical bars that open on the left side of the Firefox window. Firefox includes two sidebars by default: the Bookmarks Sidebar, which I discuss in Chapter 5, and the History Sidebar, which I discuss in Chapter 6. You can also set bookmarked Web pages to load in a sidebar, as I discuss in Chapter 5. Finally, certain extensions install their own sidebars; see Chapter 20 for more on extensions.

Bookmarks

Shows or hides the Bookmarks Sidebar, which contains your bookmarks list.

Shortcut: Ctrl+B or Ctrl+I (⌘+B on a Mac)

See Chapter 5 for more information about the Bookmarks Sidebar.

History

Shows or hides the History Sidebar, which contains a list of sites you've visited recently. This command is the same as choosing Go⇨History.

Shortcut: Ctrl+H (⌘+Shift+H on a Mac)

See Chapter 6 for more information about the History Sidebar.

The list of installed sidebars

If any extensions have installed new sidebars, a menu item for each appears here. For example, the Scrapbook extension I discuss in Chapter 22 installs its own sidebar. Click the menu item to show or hide the sidebar.

See Chapter 20 for more information about extensions.

Stop

Forces the current Web site to stop loading even though it hasn't finished. Only the part of the page that has finished loading will be available. This is the same as clicking the Stop button on the Navigation Toolbar.

This command is unavailable if the current Web site is already loaded.

Shortcut: Escape

Reload

Fetches the newest version of the current Web site. For example, you might want to leave the CNN Web site open and reload it occasionally to see the latest headlines. This is the same as clicking the Reload button on the Navigation Toolbar.

Shortcut: F5 or Ctrl+R (⌘+R on a Mac)

Text Size

The Text Size menu allows you to enlarge or shrink the text of Web pages you view in the current tab or window. See Chapter 19 for more information about changing text size.

Increase

Enlarges the text on the current page and all future pages visited in the current tab or window. Use this command repeatedly to enlarge the text further.

Shortcut: Ctrl++ (⌘++ on a Mac); in other words, press Ctrl (or ⌘ on a Mac) and the plus sign

Decrease

Shrinks the text on the current page and all future pages you visit in the current tab or window. Use this command repeatedly to shrink the text further.

Shortcut: Ctrl+- (⌘+- on a Mac); in other words, press Ctrl (or ⌘ on a Mac) and the minus sign

Normal

Returns the text size of pages you view in the current tab or window to normal, regardless of how much you increased or decreased it previously.

Shortcut: Ctrl+0 (⌘+0 on a Mac)

Page Style

From time to time, a Web site provides multiple themes that change the appearance of the page. This menu offers access to these different themes, and is intended for advanced users only.

No Style

Removes specialized fonts, colors, and other visual effects from the current page and all future pages visited in the current tab or window.

Basic Page Style

Displays the current page the way its author intended. This is the default, and the current page can change the name of this command if it wants.

The list of additional styles

If a Web site provides additional styles, a menu item for each appears here with the name specified by the page author. Click the menu item to choose the style.

Character Encoding

Allows you to manually specify the language of the Web site you're viewing. In most cases, Firefox can automatically detect the language and display text appropriately. However, if text isn't showing up properly, choose the language from this menu.

Page Source

Displays the code that created the current Web site. This command is useful only for Web site developers.

Shortcut: Ctrl+U (⌘+U on a Mac)

Full Screen

Hides Firefox toolbars and the system taskbar so you have more room to view the current Web site. Because the menu bar is hidden in Full Screen mode, you can't use this menu item to exit Full Screen mode. Instead, press F11 or click the Restore button (the button in the upper right corner to the left of the Close button).

This command is unavailable on the Mac.

Shortcut: F11

See Chapter 19 for more information about Full Screen mode.

The Go Menu

The Go menu (shown in Figure A-5) allows you to return to Web sites you visited recently.

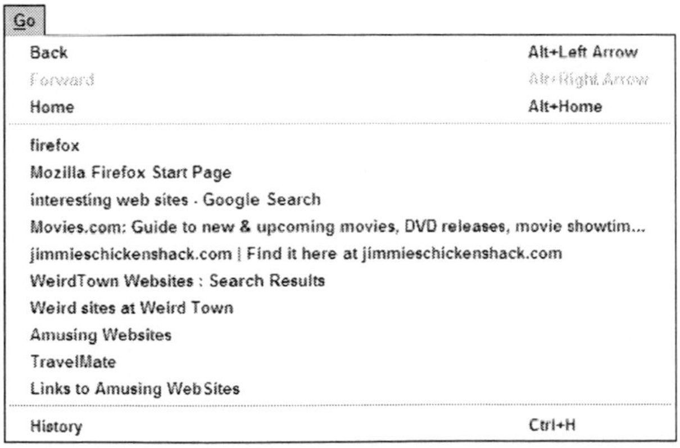

Go	
Back	Alt+Left Arrow
Forward	Alt+Right Arrow
Home	Alt+Home
firefox	
Mozilla Firefox Start Page	
interesting web sites - Google Search	
Movies.com: Guide to new & upcoming movies, DVD releases, movie showtim...	
jimmieschickenshack.com	Find it here at jimmieschickenshack.com	
WeirdTown Websites : Search Results	
Weird sites at Weird Town	
Amusing Websites	
TravelMate	
Links to Amusing Web Sites	
History	Ctrl+H

Figure A-5:
The Go menu.

Back

Takes you back to the last page you visited in the current tab or window. This is the same as clicking the Back button on the Navigation Toolbar.

This command is unavailable when you're viewing the first Web site you visited in the current tab or window.

Shortcuts: Alt+← or Backspace when the page is selected (⌘+← on a Mac)

Forward

Takes you forward one page in history. In other words, suppose you search Ask Jeeves (www.ask.com) for *improving short-term memory* and click the first search result. But by the time the new page finishes loading, you've forgotten what you're doing there, so you click Back to return to the search results page. A few seconds later, you remember again. Now you can click Forward to return to the page on improving your memory — and please, read it carefully. This command has the same effect as clicking the Forward button in the Navigation Toolbar.

This command is unavailable when you haven't used the Back command and there are no pages to go forward to.

Shortcut: Alt+→ or Shift+Backspace when the page is selected (⌘+→ on a Mac)

Home

Takes you to your Firefox home page. This is the same as clicking the Home button on the Navigation Toolbar.

Shortcut: Alt+Home (Option+Home on a Mac)

See Chapters 2 and 16 for more information about what a home page is and how to set it.

The list of Web sites

After the Home command, the Go menu contains a list of the last ten Web sites you visited in any Firefox tab or window at any time. Click on any Web site to load it in the current tab or window. In Windows, do any of the following: Shift+click to load it in a new window or Ctrl+click to load it in a new tab.

If your mouse has a middle button, you can also middle-click a site to load it in a new tab.

History

Shows or hides the History Sidebar, which contains a list of sites you've visited recently. This command is the same as choosing View⇨Sidebars⇨History.

Shortcut: Ctrl+H (⌘+Shift+H on a Mac)

See Chapter 6 for more information about the History Sidebar.

The Bookmarks Menu

The Bookmarks menu (shown in Figure A-6) contains your bookmarks list and allows you to bookmark the current Web page or all Web pages open in tabs in the current window. You can also open the Bookmarks Manager from the Bookmarks menu. See Chapter 5 for more information about working with bookmarks.

Figure A-6:
The
Bookmarks
menu.

Bookmark This Page

Adds the current page to your Bookmarks list. Firefox opens a window so you can choose a name and location for the bookmark.

Shortcut: Ctrl+D (⌘+D on a Mac)

Bookmark All Tabs

Adds all of the Web sites open in tabs in the current window to a new folder in your Bookmarks list. Firefox opens a window so you can select a name and location for the new folder.

Shortcut: Ctrl+Shift+D (⌘+Shift+D on a Mac)

See Chapter 7 for more information about tabbed browsing.

Manage Bookmarks

Opens the Bookmarks Manager, which helps you organize your bookmarks list.

The list of bookmarks

After the Manage Bookmarks menu item, the Bookmarks menu contains your bookmarks list. Click a bookmark to load it in the current tab or window. In Windows, do any of the following: Shift+click to load it in a new window or Ctrl+click to load it in a new tab. If your mouse has a middle button, you can also middle-click a bookmark to load it in a new tab. Finally, you can right click on a bookmark to delete it, change its properties, or sort your Bookmarks menu alphabetically.

The Tools Menu

The Tools menu (shown in Figure A-7) offers access to a variety of helpful Firefox utilities, such as the Download, Theme, and Extension Managers, and the (in Windows) Options window.

Tools	
Web Search	Ctrl+K
Read Mail (781 new)	
New Message...	Ctrl+M
Downloads	Ctrl+J
Extensions	
Themes	
JavaScript Console	
Page Info	
Clear Private Data...	Ctrl+Shift+Del
Options...	

Figure A-7:
The Tools
menu.

Web Search

Selects the Search Box at the right end of the Navigation Toolbar.

If you remove the Search Box using toolbar customization, which I discuss in Chapter 18, this command opens the window shown in Figure A-8. Type your search phrase into the Search For text box, and then choose the search engine you want to use from the drop-down list next to Search With. If you want the search results to open in a new tab, select the Open Search Results in a New Tab check box. Finally, click Search to close the window and load the search results page.

Shortcut: Ctrl+E or Ctrl+K (⌘+K on a Mac)

Figure A-8:
If you hide
the Search
Box by using
toolbar
customiza-
tion, the
Web Search
command
shows this
window.

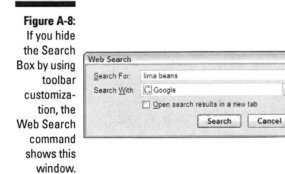

Read Mail

Opens your computer's default e-mail program. Depending on the e-mail program you use, Firefox might be able to detect whether you have new mail. If it can, it displays the number of new e-mails within the menu item. For example, the command might appear as Read Mail (4 new).

This command is only useful if you use an e-mail program, such as Thunderbird or Outlook, in which case it opens your default program. (See the "Send Link" section, earlier in this appendix, for instructions on changing your default e-mail program.) If you read your e-mail on a Web site, ignore this option.

New Message

Opens a new e-mail composition window. This is convenient if you need to send mail while browsing and don't want to open your e-mail program.

This command is only useful if you use an e-mail program, such as Thunderbird or Outlook. If you read your e-mail on a Web site, ignore this option.

This command uses your computer's default e-mail program. For instructions on changing the default e-mail program, see the "Send Link" section, earlier in this appendix.

Shortcut: Ctrl+M (⌘+M on a Mac)

Downloads

Opens the Download Manager, where you can monitor the progress of ongoing downloads and launch completed ones.

Shortcut: Ctrl+J (⌘+J on a Mac)

See Chapter 11 for more information about the Download Manager.

Extensions

Opens the Extension Manager, where you can configure, update, or uninstall your installed Firefox extensions.

See Chapter 20 for more information about the Extension Manager.

JavaScript Console

Opens the JavaScript Console, where you can see programming errors reported by Web sites. This window is useful only for Web developers.

Page Info

Opens the Page Info window, which contains a wealth of information about the current page. This window is intended for advanced users who need to closely analyze the contents of a Web page.

Clear Private Data

Allows you to clear the information Firefox stores about your surfing, such as browsing history and saved passwords. Firefox opens a window so you can choose which types of records to clear. If you clear your information frequently, you can bypass the window to minimize distractions, as I discuss in Chapter 21.

Shortcut: Ctrl+Shift+Delete (there is no Mac shortcut)

See Chapters 14 and 21 for more information about clearing your private data.

Options

Opens the Options window, where you can configure many aspects of Firefox. This command is only available in Windows. On the Mac, choose Firefox Preferences.

See Chapter 16 for more information about the Options window.

The Help Menu

From the Help menu (shown in Figure A-9), you can access the built-in Firefox help system, check for Firefox updates, view information about your version of Firefox, and report broken Web sites to the Firefox team.

Figure A-9:
The Help
menu.

Help Contents

Opens the Firefox built-in help system.

Shortcut: F1 (this shortcut works for Windows only)

See Chapter 13 for more on the Firefox help system.

For Internet Explorer Users

Opens a page designed to help Internet Explorer users transition to Firefox. Most people using Firefox have switched from Internet Explorer, which is the default browser on Windows. Chapter 3 includes everything on this page, plus plenty more.

See Chapter 13 for more on the Firefox help system.

Report Broken Website

Opens the Reporting Wizard, which you can use to inform the Firefox developers of Web sites that don't work properly in Firefox. These kinds of failures are typically the result of a programming error on the part of the Web site's developer. In this case, the Firefox team contacts the site developer and helps him fix the mistake. Sometimes, however, the errors are the result of a defect in Firefox itself, and these reports help us developers fix the problem.

The Firefox team respects your privacy, and no personal information is provided to us beyond what you offer if you use this feature. Read our Privacy Policy in the Reporting Wizard for more information.

See Chapter 3 for more information on the Reporting Wizard.

Check for Updates

Opens the Update Wizard and checks to see whether updates are available to Firefox as well as your installed themes, extensions, and Search Box engines. If they are, the Update Wizard walks you through the short update process.

See Chapter 15 for more information about staying up-to-date.

About Mozilla Firefox

Opens a window that contains information about your version of Firefox and a list of the people who made it.

Appendix B

Firefox Keyboard Reference

*A*nyone who uses the Web is painfully familiar with what I call the Surfer Shuffle: Reach for the keyboard and type an address. Reach for the mouse and scroll. Repeat hundreds of times a day.

Firefox provides a keyboard shortcut for nearly every action imaginable so you never have to reach for the mouse again. This appendix lists these shortcuts by category. Most work on all of Windows and Macintosh but a handful work only on certain systems. In these cases, I point out to you which shortcuts work on which system.

When an action has multiple shortcuts, I list them all.

Navigation

The shortcuts found in Table B-1 help you surf the Web more easily using the keyboard.

Table B-1	Navigation Keyboard Shortcuts	
Action	*Windows*	*Mac*
Back	Alt+← or (when the page is selected) Backspace	⌘+←
Forward	Alt+→ or (when the page is selected) Shift+Backspace	⌘+→

(continued)

Table B-1 *(continued)*

Action	Windows	Mac
Open the home page	Alt+Home	Option+Home
Focus the next element (for example, a text box or a link; see the end of this appendix for an explanation of focus)	Tab	Tab
Focus the previous element	Shift+Tab	Shift+Tab
Open the focused link (see the end of this appendix)	Enter	Return
Open the focused link in a new tab	Ctrl+Enter	⌘+Return
Open the focused link in New tab and select the new tab	Ctrl+Shift+Enter	⌘+Shift+Return
Open the focused link in new window	Shift+Enter	Shift+Return
Open the Web page contextual menu	Contextual menu key (if your keyboard has one)	None
Reload	Ctrl+R or F5	⌘+R
Reload the latest version and ignore Firefox's archived copy (see the section on caches in Chapter 14)	Ctrl+Shift+R or Ctrl+F5	⌘+Shift+R
Scroll down one line	↓	↓
Scroll up one line	↑	↑
Scroll down one page	Page Down	Page Down
Scroll up one page	Page Up	Page Up
Scroll to the bottom of the page	End	End
Scroll to the top of the page	Home	Home
Select the Location Bar	Ctrl+L or Alt+D	⌘+L

Action	Windows	Mac
Select the next frame on a page (advanced; works only on framed pages)	F6	F6
Select the previous frame on a page (advanced; works only on framed pages)	Shift+F6	Shift+F6
Stop	Esc	Esc

Tabbed Browsing

The shortcuts found in Table B-2 let you open, select, and close tabs from the keyboard.

Table B-2	Keyboard Shortcuts for Tabbed Browsing	
Action	*Windows*	*Mac*
Open the address in a new tab	Alt+Enter	Option+Enter
Open the focused link in new tab (see Figure B-1)	Ctrl+Enter	⌘+Enter
Open a new tab	Ctrl+T	⌘+T
Select the next tab	Ctrl+Tab or Ctrl+Page Down	⌘+Tab or ⌘+Page Down
Select the previous tab	Ctrl+Shift+Tab or Ctrl+Page Up	⌘+Shift+Tab or ⌘+Page Up
Select a specific tab (see Figure B-1)	Ctrl+[1 to 9] *	⌘+[1 to 9] *
Close the selected tab	Ctrl+W or Ctrl+F4	⌘+W or ⌘+F4

*The number corresponds to the tab you want to select. The leftmost tab is 1, its neighbor is 2, and so on. There is no keyboard shortcut for accessing the 10th tab or higher.

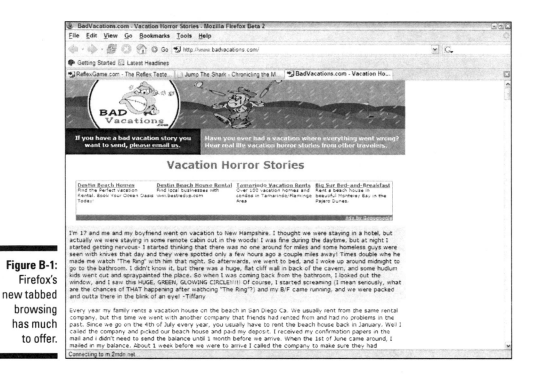

Figure B-1:
Firefox's
new tabbed
browsing
has much
to offer.

To select an open tab, hold Ctrl (or ⌘ on Macintosh) and then press the number corresponding to the tab you want to select. Tabs are numbered in order — the leftmost tab is 1, its neighbor is 2, and so forth.

Text Editing and Selection

The shortcuts found in Table B-3 allow you to edit and select text using the keyboard.

Table B-3	Keyboard Shortcuts for Text	
Action	*Windows*	*Mac*
Copy the selection	Ctrl+C	⌘+C
Cut the selection	Ctrl+X or Shift+Delete	⌘+X
Delete the selection	Delete	Delete

Action	Windows	Mac
Paste the selection	Ctrl+V or Shift+Insert	⌘+V
Undo the last edit	Ctrl+Z	⌘+Z
Redo the last edit	Ctrl+Y or Ctrl+Shift+Z	⌘+Shift+Z
Select all	Ctrl+A	⌘+A
Turn the flashing cursor on or off (see the section on the Advanced options category in Chapter 16)	F7	F7

Searching a Page

The shortcuts found in Table B-4 allow you to search for phrases in Web sites using the keyboard.

Table B-4	Keyboard Shortcuts for Page Searching	
Action	**Windows**	**Mac**
Open the Find Bar to search the current page	Ctrl+F	⌘+F
Find the next occurrence of the search phrase	Ctrl+G or F3	⌘+G
Find the previous occurrence of the search phrase	Ctrl+Shift+G or Shift+F3	⌘+Shift+G
Highlight all occurrences of the search phrase	Ctrl+Enter	⌘+Enter
Begin Fast Find mode for the text and links (advanced; see first section of Chapter 21)	/ while focus is in the Web site Content area	/ while focus is in the Web site Content area
Begin Fast Find mode for links only (advanced; see first section of Chapter 21)	' (apostrophe) while focus is in the Web site Content area	' (apostrophe) while focus site is in the Web Content area

Searching the Web

These shortcuts apply to the Search Box at the right end of the Navigation Toolbar as shown in Figure B-2.

The Search Box on the Navigation Toolbar is completely accessible from the keyboard. Press Ctrl+K (or ⌘+K on a Mac) to focus it, type your phrase, and then press Enter.

As I discuss in Chapter 4, the Search Box supports a wide selection of search engines. You can click the icon to open a drop-down list and switch between them, but you can also press Ctrl+↓ and Ctrl+↑ (or ⌘+↓ and ⌘+↑ on a Mac) to cycle through them downward or upward, one by one.

Table B-5 lists the shortcuts for searching the Web.

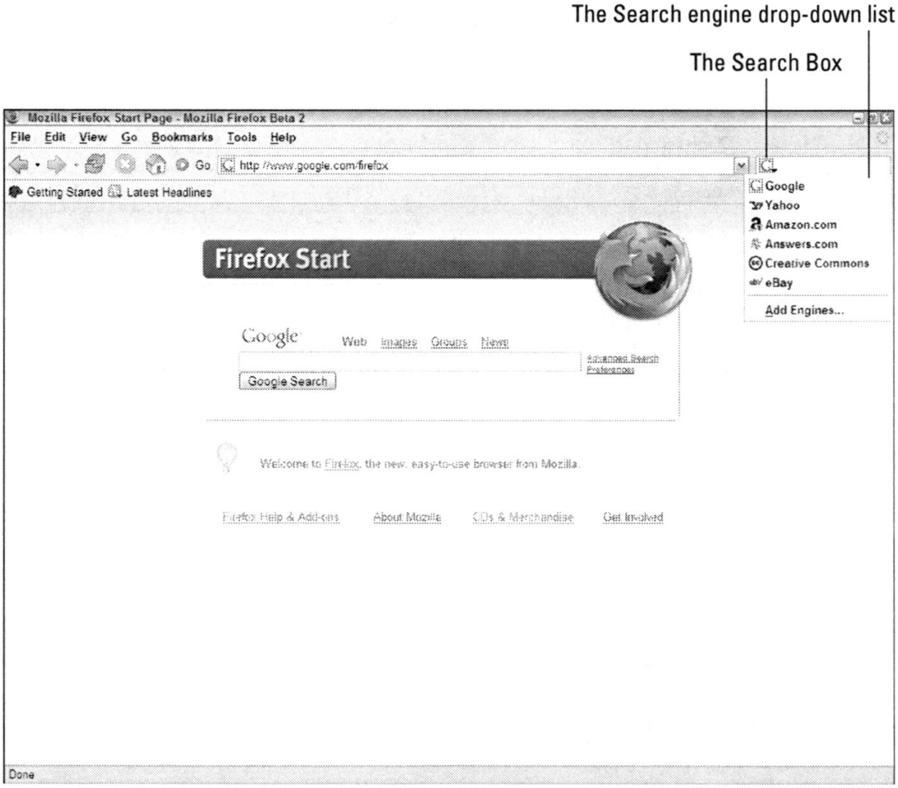

The Search engine drop-down list

The Search Box

Figure B-2:
The Search
Box offers
a handful
of search
engines
that you
can cycle
through by
using the
keyboard.

Table B-5	Keyboard Shortcuts for Web Searching	
Action	*Windows*	*Mac*
Select the Search Box	Ctrl+K or Ctrl+E	⌘+K or ⌘+E
Select the next search engine (see Figure B-2)	Ctrl+↓	⌘+↓
Select the previous search engine	Ctrl+↑	⌘+↑
Open a list of previous searches	↓ or ↑	↓ or ↑
Search for the phrase and load the results in the current tab or window	Enter	Return
Search for the phrase and load the results in a new tab	Alt+Enter	Option+Return

Loading Web Addresses

These shortcuts apply to the Location Bar (see Figure B-3).

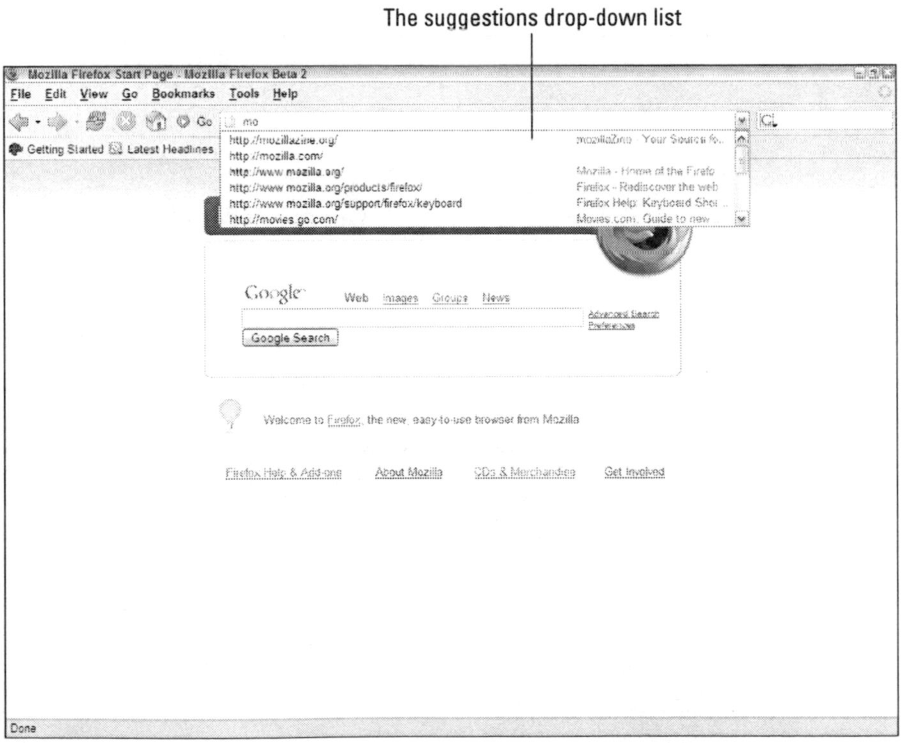

The suggestions drop-down list

Figure B-3:
As you type into the Location Bar, Firefox suggests Web sites from your browsing history.

As you type in the Location Bar, Firefox suggests similar Web sites you've visited in the past. To choose a suggestion, press the ↓ key until it is highlighted in the list, and then press Enter.

Table B-6 lists keyboard shortcuts you can use in conjunction with the Location Bar.

Table B-6	Keyboard Shortcuts for Using the Location Bar	
Action	*Windows*	*Mac*
Focus/Select Location Bar	Ctrl+L or Alt+D	⌘+L
Open the address	Enter	Return
Open the address in new tab	Alt+Enter	Option+Return
Add www and .com to the given address	Ctrl+Enter	
Add www and .net to the given address	Shift+Enter	Shift+Return
Add www and .org to the given address	Ctrl+Shift+Enter	None
Select the next autocomplete entry (see Figure B-3)	↓	↓
Select the previous autocomplete entry	↑	↑
Delete the selected autocomplete entry	Shift+Delete	Shift+Delete

Opening and Closing Windows and Sidebars

The shortcuts found in Table B-7 let you open or (if they're already open) close various Firefox windows and sidebars.

Table B-7	Keyboard Shortcuts for Opening and Closing	
Action	*Windows*	*Mac*
Open a new browser window	Ctrl+N	⌘+N
Open a new tab	Ctrl+T	⌘+T
Open/Close the Bookmarks Sidebar	Ctrl+B or Ctrl+I	⌘+B

Action	Windows	Mac
Open/Close the History Sidebar	Ctrl+H	⌘+Shift+H
Open the Download Manager	Ctrl+J	⌘+J
Open the Help window	F1	None
Open the Page Info window (advanced)	None	⌘+I
Open the Page Source window (advanced)	Ctrl+U	⌘+U
Close the selected tab	Ctrl+W	⌘+W
Close the window	Ctrl+W (if one tab is open)	⌘+W (if one tab is open)
	Ctrl+Shift+W (if two or more tabs are open)	⌘+Shift+W (if two or more tabs are open)
	Alt+F4 (always)	Option+F4 (always)

Miscellaneous

The shortcuts found in Table B-8 run the gamut and let you do everything from bookmark the current page to enter Full Screen mode — all, of course, from your beloved keyboard.

Table B-8	Yes, Even More Keyboard Shortcuts	
Action	Windows	Mac
Bookmark the current page	Ctrl+D	⌘+D
Compose a new e-mail message	Ctrl+M	⌘+M
Full Screen mode	F11	
Enlarge the text size on the page	Ctrl++ (Ctrl and the plus sign)	⌘++ (⌘ and the plus sign)
Reduce the text size on the page	Ctrl+− (Ctrl and the minus sign)	⌘+− (⌘ and the minus sign)
Return the text size to normal	Ctrl+0	⌘+0

(continued)

Table B-8 *(continued)*

Action	Windows	Mac
Print	Ctrl+P	⌘+P
Save the current page	Ctrl+S	⌘+S
Save the focused link (see the end of this appendix)	Alt+Enter	Option+Return

Accessing Web Site Elements with the Keyboard

Firefox is completely keyboard-accessible, which means anything you can do with your mouse, you can also do with your keyboard. That's a pretty remarkable achievement when you consider all the things you can do with your mouse in a Web page alone: Select text on the page, click buttons and links, and select items from drop-down lists, among other things. All this is easy with a mouse because you can target the element you want to interact with using the mouse pointer.

Because you don't have this luxury when you're using the keyboard, you must first *focus* the element you want to interact with. Throughout this appendix, you can find a number of references to *focusing* and you might have wondered whether I've lost my mind. In fact, even though you might not have heard the term, the concept of focus is common to all software programs, and you use it all the time. When you focus an element (such as a text box or a Web page link), you are simply indicating that you want to work with that particular element by using the keyboard. For example, when you focus a text box, a flashing cursor appears in the box, and now you can begin typing. This example points out the three main questions that pertain to focusing:

✔ How do you focus an element with the keyboard?

✔ How does an element indicate when it has focus?

✔ What can you do with a focused element?

To answer the first question, you must be familiar with the concept of *Tab order.* When you target an element on a Web page with the mouse, you probably don't give much thought to how the page is oriented. You don't need to: The mouse pointer allows you to reach any element easily. However, the keyboard offers much less freedom, and so reaching an element takes much longer. You must focus element by element until you reach the one you want. You do this by pressing Tab repeatedly. Elements are focused in a left-to-right, top-to-bottom fashion (approximately), as I demonstrate in Figure B-4, and this is called the Tab order. To navigate elements in reverse Tab order (in a right-to-left, bottom-to-top fashion, approximately), you press Shift+Tab. The reason I say these orders are approximate is because unfortunately, Web designers have the final say over the Tab order of elements on their pages. Don't be surprised if the ordering seems erratic sometimes.

Only one element can have focus at a time. The concept of focus is not limited to Web page elements; it extends throughout the Firefox interface. For example, clicking within the Location Bar focuses the bar so you can enter an address, and whichever element currently has focus (even if it's part of the Web page) loses focus.

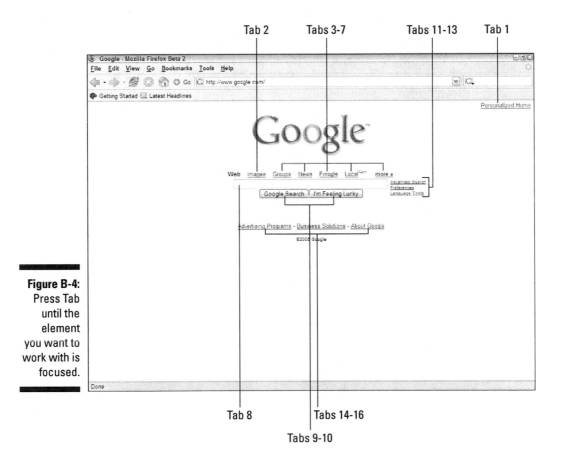

Figure B-4:
Press Tab
until the
element
you want to
work with is
focused.

To know when the element you want to work with is focused, you need to know how that particular type of element indicates focus. Of course, you'll also want to know what you can do with the focused element. Because each of these things varies among elements, I include a list of focusable elements in this section.

As if the topic of focus weren't complicated enough, the situation gets worse. Unfortunately, the Web designer ultimately has the final say over how a particular element on his or her page looks when it's focused. By default, elements have the appearances I describe in the following list, but the designer can override the appearance. For example, some designers indicate a focused link by bolding the text of the link instead of using a dotted rectangle. Because hundreds of possible styles are available for a designer to use, I can't cover them all; it's just something to watch out for. Fortunately, most designers stick to the tried-and-true defaults in the following list:

- **Web pages themselves:** As strange as it sounds, the Web page itself (the Content area) can have focus. You can scroll the focused page by using the arrow keys, or select text by holding Shift+← or Shift+→ (depending on the direction in which you wish to select). When text is selected, you can use the keyboard shortcuts listed in Table B-3, earlier in this appendix.

When the Web page has focus, a particular portion of the page actually has the focus. Which portion is focused controls where selection begins when you use the text selection method I describe. To see which part of the page has focus, you can turn on a flashing cursor, just like the flashing cursor you see in focused text boxes. This is called *Caret Browsing,* and you can activate it by pressing F7, or by setting an option in the Advanced category of the Options window, as I discuss at the end of Chapter 16.

Firefox focuses a page automatically when it finishes loading. If you then focus the Search Box or the Location Bar (by clicking within either), you can restore focus to the page by pressing the Tab key once or twice, or by clicking an empty spot within the page. Unfortunately, the Web page is the only element that doesn't indicate when it has focus (a bug we developers hope to fix soon). Try ↑ and ↓; if the page scrolls, it has focus.

When the page has focus, pressing Tab focuses the first element within the page. Pressing Shift+Tab focuses the Search Box in keeping with the reverse Tab order of right to left, bottom to top.

- **Links:** When a link has focus, its text is surrounded by a dotted, rectangular border, as shown in Figure B-5. You can load the Web page pointed to by the focused link by pressing Enter. To load the page in a new window, press Shift+Enter. To load the page in a new tab, press Ctrl+Enter (Windows) or ⌘+Return (Mac). (Just as when you open a link in a new tab using the mouse, the new tab is not automatically selected.) To save the linked page to your computer instead of following the link, press Alt+Enter (Windows) or Option+Return (Mac), and then select a destination and filename in the window that appears.

✔ **Buttons:** When a button has focus, its text is surrounded by a dotted, rectangular border, as shown in Figure B-5. You can click the focused button with the keyboard (execute whatever command the button executes when clicked) by pressing the spacebar.

✔ **Drop-down lists:** When a drop-down list has focus, its text is surrounded by a dotted, rectangular border, as shown in Figure B-5. You can cycle through the other items in the focused list one-by-one, upward or downward, by pressing the up- or down-arrow keys. You can cycle through the list in intervals of 20 by pressing Page Up or Page Down. If the list has fewer than 20 items, Page Up selects the first item in the list, and Page Down selects the last. You can also press Home to select the first item or End to select the last, which works even in lists of more than 20 items.

✔ **Regular lists:** When a regular list has focus, the selected item in the list is surrounded by a dotted, rectangular border, as shown in Figure B-5. Because the selection color tends to be dark, this border can be hard to see, but it's there if you look closely. You can select another item in the focused list by pressing the up or down arrow until you reach it. To navigate the list more quickly, press Page Up or Page Down. You can also press Home to select the first item in the list or End to select the last.

✔ **Text box:** When a text box has focus, it contains a flashing cursor, as shown in Figure B-5. You can type text into a focused text box, and it is inserted at the location indicated by the cursor. To select text on either side of the cursor, hold down Shift+← or Shift+→ (depending on the direction of the selection) until the desired text is selected. Then you can use the keyboard shortcuts that I list in Table B-3, earlier.

✔ **Check box:** When a check box has focused, its box is surrounded by a dotted, rectangular border, as shown in Figure B-5. You can select or (if it's currently selected) deselect a check box by pressing the spacebar.

✔ **Radio button:** A radio button is similar to a check box, but it is part of a group in which only one option can be selected. Thus, radio buttons are used for mutually exclusive options. For example, many online forms use two radio buttons to allow visitors to specify their gender. (The name *radio buttons* is a throwback to old car radios, from which large buttons protruded. Pressing one button popped the other buttons out.)

When a radio button has focus, its circle is surrounded by a dotted border, as shown in Figure B-5. You can select an adjacent radio button in the group by pressing any of the four arrow keys depending on the direction in which the other button lies. To select a button in the group that's further away, just continue pressing the arrow key until you reach it.

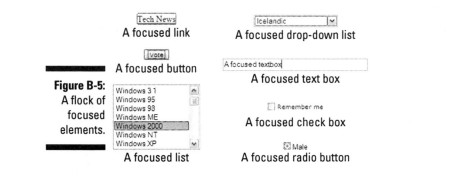

Figure B-5:
A flock of focused elements.

A focused link

A focused button

A focused list

A focused drop-down list

A focused text box

A focused check box

A focused radio button

Appendix C

Firefox Drag-and-Drop Reference

Computer features are rarely intuitive, but drag-and-drop is one of those features that just feels right. It mimics the real-world experience of moving an item from one spot to another: Simply pick it up by pressing the mouse button, move it by moving the mouse, and put it down by releasing the mouse button over the new location. The Firefox philosophy is that anywhere drag-and-drop *could* work, it *should* work. This appendix outlines the possibilities, and I keep it short and sweet — just like drag-and-drop.

Getting to Know Drag-and-Drop

Most people are familiar with drag-and-drop from other programs, but in case you aren't, I walk through the process with a brief example. In the following steps, you load a Web page by dragging a link:

1. **Navigate to a Web site normally.**

   Google (www.google.com) or Wikipedia (http://en.wikipedia.org) would be good for practice.

2. **Drag a link by moving the mouse pointer over it and holding down the left mouse button.**

Do not release the button.

3. **Move the mouse pointer to the Go button that sits to the right of the Location Bar.**

   Notice that as you move the mouse pointer over the page, the arrow turns into a "no" sign (the circle with a line through it). This sign means that you can't drop the link at that spot. When the pointer reaches the Go button, it returns to being an arrow and shows a tiny box to indicate that you can drop on the Go button.

4. **Release the mouse button.**

   Firefox loads the page that the link led to. Of course, this is a rather silly example, because you could simply have *clicked* the link to load the page. However, I want to start with something that has no side effects so you can get the hang of it.

Getting to the Good Stuff

I use the term *link* in this section to refer to both normal Web page links *and* other items that point to Web sites. For example, bookmarks, history items, files, and even text that happens to be an address (for example, `http://www.google.com`) are all considered links here.

Furthermore, the tiny picture to the left of an address in the Location Bar (see Figure C-1) is a link to the current page, and you can drag it.

The draggable link image

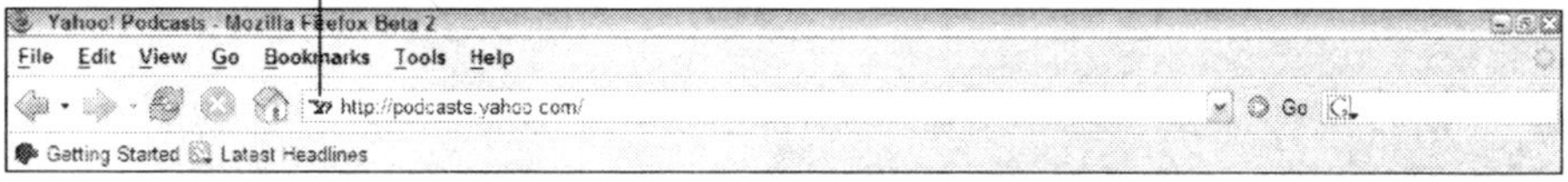

Figure C-1:
The Yahoo!
draggable
link image.

| Yahoo! Podcasts - Mozilla Firefox Beta 2 |
| File Edit View Go Bookmarks Tools Help |
| ⬅ ▾ ➡ ▾ 🔄 ❌ 🏠 Y! http://podcasts.yahoo.com/   ▾ ⊙ Go 🔍 |
| 🔴 Getting Started 📰 Latest Headlines |

For example, the red Y! here is the Yahoo! logo. If Firefox can't find a picture to represent the current site, it uses a generic one, that also acts as a link, as shown here.

Loading a link in a tab or window

To load a link in a tab or window, drag and drop it onto the Location Bar, the Go button, or (if you're using tabs) the tab.

Loading a link in a new tab

To load a link in a new tab, drag and drop it onto an empty part of the tab bar. To load it in an existing tab, drag and drop it onto the tab. See Chapter 7 for more information about tabbed browsing.

Adding a link to your bookmarks

You can add a link to your bookmarks in a few different ways. If the Bookmarks Sidebar is open, you can drag and drop a link onto it. As you move the mouse pointer over it, a solid line indicates the drop location, as shown in Figure C-2.

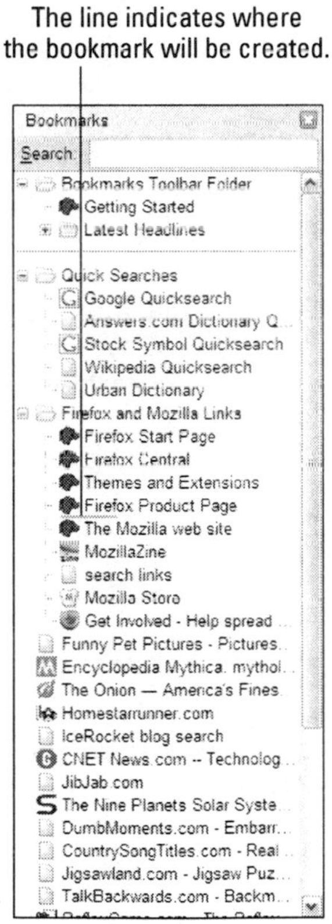

The line indicates where
the bookmark will be created.

Figure C-2:
As you
move the
mouse
pointer over
a link in the
Bookmarks
Sidebar,
a line
indicates
where the
bookmark
will be
created.

If you're using Windows, you can also drag and drop a link right into the Bookmarks menu. Simply begin to drag, move the mouse pointer to the Bookmarks menu, and pause for a second. The menu opens, and then you can drop the link in the desired spot. To add a bookmark to your Bookmarks Toolbar, drag and drop it onto the desired spot.

Downloading a file

To download a file with drag-and-drop, the Download Manager (Tools⇨ Downloads) must be open and positioned alongside the Firefox window. Simply drop a link to the file into the manager to begin the download.

Searching for text

Select and then drag text out of a Web site and drop it onto the Search Box at the right end of the Navigation Toolbar to begin a search. Firefox uses whatever search engine is currently selected.

Setting your home page

To change your Firefox home page, drag and drop a link to the page you want to use onto the Home button on the Navigation Toolbar. When Firefox asks you to confirm the change, click Yes. For more information about home pages, see Chapter 2.

Creating a desktop shortcut

Your computer desktop contains shortcuts to applications that you double-click every day. In the same way, you can add shortcuts to Web sites, and double-click them to load the Web site in Firefox. To create a shortcut, ensure that the desktop is visible, and then drag and drop a link to the desktop. For example, to create a shortcut to the page you're viewing, drag the little icon at the left end of the Location Bar out of the Firefox window, and drop it onto the desktop.

Because you must be able to see both the Firefox window and the desktop to complete the drag-and-drop, your Firefox window cannot be maximized. Click the little Restore Down button in the top-right corner to un-maximize it.

Customizing your toolbars

Firefox provides powerful tools to reshape your toolbars. First, open the Customize Toolbar window (View⇨Toolbars⇨Customize). To add buttons to your toolbars, drag and drop them from the Customize window to the desired spot. To remove buttons from your toolbars, drag and drop them from the toolbar to the Customize Toolbar window. For more information about toolbar customization, see Chapter 18.

Rearranging your tabs

When you open a new tab, Firefox positions the tab to the right of all your existing tabs. However, you might often find that you want to group related tabs together to switch between them quickly. To move a tab to a new position on the tab bar, simply drag and drop it to the desired position. As you drag the tab along the bar, a purple arrow indicates the new position of the tab should you decide to drop it there, as shown in Figure C-3.

Figure C-3:
You can drag a tab to a new spot on the tab bar.

The insertion arrow

Extending Drag-and-Drop Further

If you're an advanced drag-and-dropper, the Firefox Super Drag and Go extension offers even more drag-and-drop fun. For example, it allows you to drag-and-drop a link on a page half an inch in any direction to open it in a new tab. Likewise, you can drag and drop text half an inch in any direction to search for it on the Web. The extension is available in the Navigation and Tabbed Browsing categories of the official Mozilla Update page. After you install it, be sure to check out its options window for all the things you can do.

One other neat extension deserves a mention, even though it isn't strictly a drag-and-drop extension — more just drag. It's called Grab and Drag, and it's a novel approach to scrolling Web pages. The simple act of scrolling has seen a number of innovations over the past decade. Where you once had to reach for the scroll bar along the window edge, you can now scroll without moving the mouse, thanks to scroll wheels (or buttons) featured by most modern mice. But scrolling itself remains somewhat jerky and can be distracting when you're intently reading a long document line by line.

With Grab and Drag, you scroll a page simply by grabbing it (beginning a drag in an empty part of the page) and dragging it up, down, left, or right depending on the direction you want to scroll. The farther you move the mouse from the place where you began the drag, the farther the page scrolls. As confusing as this might sound, it's very intuitive when you try it out because it mimics the tactile experience of sliding a long scroll up or down along a table. It's a great way to scroll long documents because you control how much of the document to scroll, and the experience is as smooth as your drag. All the traditional scrolling mechanisms, such as the scroll bar and mouse wheel, continue to work as usual.

When Grab and Drag is enabled, you can't select text on a Web page (because selection requires the same kind of grabbing action). To temporarily disable Grab and Drag so you can select text, choose Tools➪Toggle Grab and Drag, or press Alt+Shift+Delete (Option+Shift+Delete on a Mac). To turn Grab and Drag back on, do the same thing.

See Chapter 20 for more information about installing and configuring extensions.

Index

Notes

SPORTS, FITNESS, PARENTING, RELIGION & SPIRITUALITY

0-7645-5146-9   0-7645-5418-2

Also available:
- Adoption For Dummies
  0-7645-5488-3
- Basketball For Dummies
  0-7645-5248-1
- The Bible For Dummies
  0-7645-5296-1
- Buddhism For Dummies
  0-7645-5359-3
- Catholicism For Dummies
  0-7645-5391-7
- Hockey For Dummies
  0-7645-5228-7

- Judaism For Dummies
  0-7645-5299-6
- Martial Arts For Dummies
  0-7645-5358-5
- Pilates For Dummies
  0-7645-5397-6
- Religion For Dummies
  0-7645-5264-3
- Teaching Kids to Read For Dummies
  0-7645-4043-2
- Weight Training For Dummies
  0-7645-5168-X
- Yoga For Dummies
  0-7645-5117-5

TRAVEL

0-7645-5438-7   0-7645-5453-0

Also available:
- Alaska For Dummies
  0-7645-1761-9
- Arizona For Dummies
  0-7645-6938-4
- Cancún and the Yucatán For Dummies
  0-7645-2437-2
- Cruise Vacations For Dummies
  0-7645-6941-4
- Europe For Dummies
  0-7645-5456-5
- Ireland For Dummies
  0-7645-5455-7

- Las Vegas For Dummies
  0-7645-5448-4
- London For Dummies
  0-7645-4277-X
- New York City For Dummies
  0-7645-6945-7
- Paris For Dummies
  0-7645-5494-8
- RV Vacations For Dummies
  0-7645-5443-3
- Walt Disney World & Orlando For Dummies
  0-7645-6943-0

GRAPHICS, DESIGN & WEB DEVELOPMENT

0-7645-4345-8   0-7645-5589-8

Also available:
- Adobe Acrobat 6 PDF For Dummies
  0-7645-3760-1
- Building a Web Site For Dummies
  0-7645-7144-3
- Dreamweaver MX 2004 For Dummies
  0-7645-4342-3
- FrontPage 2003 For Dummies
  0-7645-3882-9
- HTML 4 For Dummies
  0-7645-1995-6
- Illustrator CS For Dummies
  0-7645-4084-X

- Macromedia Flash MX 2004 For Dummies
  0-7645-4358-X
- Photoshop 7 All-in-One Desk
  Reference For Dummies
  0-7645-1667-1
- Photoshop CS Timesaving Techniques
  For Dummies
  0-7645-6782-9
- PHP 5 For Dummies
  0-7645-4166-8
- PowerPoint 2003 For Dummies
  0-7645-3908-6
- QuarkXPress 6 For Dummies
  0-7645-2593-X

NETWORKING, SECURITY, PROGRAMMING & DATABASES

0-7645-6852-3   0-7645-5784-X

Also available:
- A+ Certification For Dummies
  0-7645-4187-0
- Access 2003 All-in-One Desk
  Reference For Dummies
  0-7645-3988-4
- Beginning Programming For Dummies
  0-7645-4997-9
- C For Dummies
  0-7645-7068-4
- Firewalls For Dummies
  0-7645-4048-3
- Home Networking For Dummies
  0-7645-42796

- Network Security For Dummies
  0-7645-1679-5
- Networking For Dummies
  0-7645-1677-9
- TCP/IP For Dummies
  0-7645-1760-0
- VBA For Dummies
  0-7645-3989-2
- Wireless All In-One Desk Reference
  For Dummies
  0-7645-7496-5
- Wireless Home Networking For Dummies
  0-7645-3910-8